Banned in the U.S.A.

BANNED
IN THE U.S.A.

A Reference Guide to Book Censorship in Schools and Public Libraries

Herbert N. Foerstel

GREENWOOD PRESS
Westport, Connecticut · London

Library of Congress Cataloging-in-Publication Data

Foerstel, Herbert N.
    Banned in the U.S.A. : a reference guide to book censorship in
schools and public libraries / Herbert N. Foerstel.
        p.   cm.
    Includes bibliographical references and index.
    ISBN 0–313–28517–9 (alk. paper)
    1. Censorship—United States.   2. Textbooks—Censorship—United
States.   3. Public libraries—Censorship—United States.   4. Public
schools—Censorship—United States.   5. Book selection—United
States.   I. Title.   II. Title: Banned in the USA.
Z658.U5F64   1994
025.2′13—dc20   93–29095

British Library Cataloguing in Publication Data is available.

Library of Congress Catalog Card Number: 93–29095
ISBN: 0-313-28517-9

First published in 1994

Greenwood Press, 88 Post Road West, Westport, CT 06881
An imprint of Greenwood Publishing Group, Inc.

Printed in the United States of America

∞™

The paper used in this book complies with the
Permanent Paper Standard issued by the National
Information Standards Organization (Z39.48-1984).

10 9 8 7 6 5 4 3 2 1

Contents

Acknowledgments and Dedication

For much of the documentation in this book, I have relied on the important and continuing work of People for the American Way and the American Library Association's Office for Intellectual Freedom. By monitoring the disturbing tide of censorship and organizing social and political action against it, they lead the way for librarians, educators, and First Amendment advocates.

This book is dedicated to my grandchildren, Herbert and Lauren, who are encouraged to read whatever appeals to their minds and imaginations.

Introduction

Arthur Schlesinger, Jr., reminds us that throughout most of human history, authority, "fortified by the highest religious and philosophical texts, has righteously invoked censorship to stifle expression." He cites the Old Testament proscription "Tell it not in Gath, publish it not in the streets of Askelon; lest the daughters of the Philistines rejoice, lest the daughters of the uncircumcised triumph." Schlesinger also offers the injunction of Plato: "The poet shall compose nothing contrary to the ideas of the lawful, or just, or beautiful, or good, which are allowed in the state; nor shall he be permitted to show his compositions to any private individual until he shall have shown them to the appointed censors and the guardians of the law, and they are satisfied with them."[1]

The issue of banned books has been escalating since Johannes Gutenberg introduced the printing press in 1455. Once speech could be printed, it became a commodity, to be controlled and manipulated on the basis of religion, politics, or profit. After Pope Leo X condemned Martin Luther's *Ninety Five Theses* in 1517, both Catholics and Protestants began censoring materials that they considered dangerous or subversive. Religious censorship quickly led to political censorship when Luther defied the Pope, bringing an immediate response from Emperor Charles V. On May 26, 1521, the emperor issued the Edict of Worms, containing a "Law of Printing," which prohibited the printing, sale, possession, reading, or copying of Luther's works.

In 1564 the papacy promulgated its *Index librorum prohibitorum*, defining those books and authors that Catholics were prohibited from printing or reading. In addition to banning individual titles, the *Index* listed authors whose entire works were prohibited. It also provided guidelines for expurgating books that were otherwise acceptable and established broad rules for the regulation of the book trade. As papal decrees banned new books, the *Index* was revised to keep it up to date.

Protestant censorship followed the same pattern as Catholic censorship, with one important exception: Because most Protestant religious leaders accepted substantial state authority over the church, the *state* became the source of most censorship. For example, in England the crown defined heresy, issued censorship regulations, and authorized civil agencies to enforce them. Nonetheless, despite the joint efforts of church and state to impose censorship throughout Europe, printed works were surprisingly protected from effective control owing to a clandestine network of distribution. In addition, throughout the sixteenth and seventeenth centuries, Europe's heterogeneity and lack of political cooperation allowed authors to avoid local censorship by having their books printed in other countries.

In the eighteenth century, the breakdown of political power in France made censorship virtually unenforceable. By 1762, when Jean-Jacques Rousseau published the controversial *Émile,* there was a flood of European novels depicting the decadence and debauchery of the aristocracy and monarchy. The police did their best to suppress these books, but without success. In fact, despite the frequent use of police informers to identify the novels and punish their readers, a censored book in Europe was almost always commercially successful.

However, in the United States and England a social consensus on censorship was emerging that would be far more repressive than overt state or church power. By the 1830s, this new ideology was proclaiming the necessity for propriety, prudence, and sexual restraint. During the remainder of the nineteenth century, private virtue became public virtue, and American and British editors, publishers, writers, and librarians felt obliged to examine every book for crude language or unduly explicit or realistic portrayals of life. In her introduction to the 1984 New York Public Library exhibition on censorship, Ann Ilan Alter said that there may have been more censorship, self-imposed or otherwise, during the ninteenth century in England and the United States than during all the preceding centuries of printed literature.[2] The twentieth century in America has seen the emergence of pressure groups that maintain an uneasy balance in the struggle to interpret our First Amendment rights. The federal government tips that balance in whatever direction the winds blow, and since 1980, those winds have been chilling. Arthur Schlesinger notes: "[T]he struggle between expression and authority is unending. The instinct to suppress discomforting ideas is rooted deep in human nature. It is rooted above all in profound human propensities to faith and fear."[3]

Indeed, as we approach the twenty-first century, faith and fear are still prominent in determining our right to free expression. The most spectacular international act of bookbanning in this century has surely been Iran's death sentence on the British author Salmon Rushdie, and America's response to it has not been encouraging. Rushdie has been in hiding since 1989, when his novel *The Satanic Verses* offended Iran's Ayatollah Khomeini, who called for his execution and placed a $1 million bounty on his head. The Tehran underground publisher of *The Satanic Verses* has already been killed. "The real book is struggling to get out from under all the rhetoric," says Rushdie. "But I've always said that the best defense of the book is the book itself, when people read it openly and realize that some terrible injustice has been done not only to me, but to the book." Rushdie warns:

> I have tried repeatedly to remind people that what we are witnessing is a war against independence of mind, a war for power. The case of *The Satanic Verses* is, however—and I hope this can be conceded without argument—at present the most public battle in that war. It is a battle that can only be won, because the consequences of losing it are horrendous.[4]

In the spring of 1992, Rushdie made a five-day trip to Washington—his longest time "out of the box," as he put it—to plead for help. The State Department and the White House refused to speak to Rushdie. Margaret Tutwiler, the State Department spokesperson, said there had been no meeting with Rushdie "because at this time we felt that such a thing could and possibly might be misinterpreted." Marlin Fitzwater, speaking for the White House, said: "There's no reason for any special relationship with Rushdie. I mean, he's an author, he's here, he's doing interviews and book tours and things that authors do. But there's no reason for us to have any special interest in him. . . . He doesn't write about government policies."[5]

Art Buchwald reported a fanciful conversation about the incident with his imaginary White House contact Charlie, who explained the president's snub of Rushdie: "If we let him in to see the President, we risk losing the Hezbollah vote this year. . . . The White House never takes sides between a writer and those who pass a death sentence on him." When Buchwald asked Charlie how we could ignore Rushdie's plight at the hands of the nation that took more American hostages than any other country, he was told:

> That doesn't compare with someone who writes a satire containing blasphemous statements about a religion. The White House disapproves of

people being sentenced for what they write. At the same time, you don't rub a book in a nation's face. . . . Americans don't understand other people's cultures. In some countries they kill you for reading a book and in others they kill you for writing one.[6]

In September 1990, the Thomas Jefferson Center for the Protection of Free Expression announced the results of the most comprehensive opinion survey ever conducted on free expression and declared the First Amendment to be "in perilous condition across the nation." The survey revealed that nearly a third of all Americans believe that constitutional protection of free speech does not extend to the media and arts. Robert O'Neil, the center's founding director, cited evidence of an "alarming double standard—a sense that the First Amendment protects what the speaker wants to say, but not equally the expressions of others." Forty-eight percent of those surveyed mentioned some nonnational security aspect of the media or the arts in which they felt government should have the power of censorship. Only one quarter of those questioned would support use of their tax dollars to fund art they found offensive. "Obviously," said O'Neil, "Congress is not required to fund any form of art, or to fund art at all. . . . But it is one thing for government simply not to be a patron of the arts; it is quite another for government to say it will support only individual works or artists it does not deem objectionable."[7]

The American compulsion to censor government-subsidized expression can be seen in the trials and tribulations of the National Endowment for the Arts (NEA), whose director, John Frohnmayer, was forced to resign in 1992 after he complained of pressure from the Bush administration to function as a "decency czar." Acting chairman Anne-Imelda Radice, appointed by President George Bush, quickly rejected two grants for exhibits containing sexual themes, overruling the NEA review panels and advisory council that had traditionally judged whether works were appropriate for funding. The next day, Stephen Sondheim, the Tony Award–winning lyricist and composer, turned down the 1992 National Medal of the Arts administered by the NEA. To accept the award, he said, "would be an act of the utmost hypocrisy." He charged that the NEA "is rapidly being transformed into a conduit and a symbol of censorship and repression rather than encouragement and support."[8]

Under overt political pressure from the White House and conservative members of Congress, Radice dutifully testified on Capitol Hill that she would avoid funding sexually explicit or "difficult" work. In an unprecedented protest, the entire NEA peer review panel for visual arts resigned, complaining that the process of peer review had been "severely compromised and placed in great jeopardy." Panel member

Susan Krane said, "We have no desire to participate in a puppet process." In another 1992 protest, Artist Trust of Seattle turned down an NEA award, declaring, "Radice's actions are so reprehensible that artists whose work has been approved by the NEA are forfeiting their grants in a show of solidarity for censored artists."[9]

The issue of government funding is increasingly invoked to cloud the First Amendment aspects of book censorship. Just as Jesse Helms can glibly claim that Congress has the right, indeed the obligation, to censor state-funded art in the name of the people, so do various pressure groups insist that the public funding of most schools and libraries makes them subject to "community censorship." This view does not conform to America's cultural or legal history. It may be true that federal and state legislators have the right to arbitrarily withhold funds to the NEA or to public schools and libraries. But once that money is allocated, whether it be for NEA exhibitions or public library books, we enter First Amendment territory. There is no more constitutional authority to censor public-funded expression than private expression.

At the 1991 annual meeting of the National Society of Newspaper Editors, John Seigenthaler, publisher of the *Nashville Tennessean*, outlined the disturbing results of a national survey on free expression that confirmed the previous year's report by the Jefferson Center. In a 281-page report analyzing the survey, Robert Wyatt, a journalism professor at Tennessee State University, and David Neft, research chief for Gannett, Inc., stated, "After nearly a year of surveying, it is apparent that free expression is in very deep trouble." The report noted that the respondents displayed an inability to distinguish between what the law protects and what they dislike personally. It concluded that Americans display "an alarming willingness to remove legal protection from forms of free expression they disagree with or find offensive. . . . That is, they only believe that they believe in free expression."[10]

This popular willingness to suppress whatever we find personally objectionable often takes the form of ill-advised legislation. A badly crafted 1988 Child Pornography Act was struck down as unconstitutional in 1989 by the U.S. District Court but was resurrected in the closing days of the 1990 Congress. In May 1992, after heavy opposition from the American Library Association and the National Association of Artists' Organizations, that bill was also declared unconstitutional by U.S. District Judge Stanley Sborkin, who said it would chill the exercise of constitutionally protected First Amendment rights to free expression.

Even more disturbing is the recent Pornography Victims Compensation Act (S. 1521), which would impose civil liability on commercial producers of "obscene material" if a plaintiff demonstrates that the material "inspired" or "incited" a crime. Thus, while a criminal who has never been charged with a crime may still be at large, a victim of an assault may file suit against a publisher, claiming that expressive material incited the crime. Because of the court's "community standard" definition of obscenity, publishers would have no way to predict what materials a given jurisdiction would consider "obscene" and subject to such a lawsuit. The result would be a kind of prior restraint by uncertainty, with publishers avoiding the possibility of costly litigation by electing not to publish important works.

In a *New York Times* article, Teller (of Penn and Teller fame) wrote:

> Producers, writers, directors and actors who depict rape are not rapists. They are makers of fiction. To punish them is insane. We might as well punish Agatha Christie for murder and John Le Carre for espionage. . . . It's a death knell for creativity, too. Start punishing make-believe, and those gifted with imagination will stop sharing it. A writer's first thought will be, "If I write anything original or bold, a reader could get me sued." We will enter an intellectual era, even more insipid than the one we live in.[11]

Even conservative columnist James J. Kilpatrick wrote:

> In the matter of the "Pornography Victims Compensation Act of 1992," Sens. Kennedy, Metzenbaum, Biden, Simon, et al. are right. The bill is a bummer. . . . I never expected to agree with these gentlemen on anything, and the experience is painful. . . . The measure is stamped from a familiar pattern: good intentions, bad law. It ought to be quietly shelved, but in an election year the thing may pass.[12]

Indeed, it came very close to passage and may yet come back to haunt us. It was favorably (though narrowly) reported by the Senate Judiciary Committee and actually adopted by the Republican party into its platform. Only the rush to adjourn prevented congressional action.

Sex remains a major issue in bookbanning, and Madonna's best-seller *Sex* will surely be among the most-banned books in the mid-1990s. Because it was published in late 1992, *Sex* does not appear in our survey of most-banned books (see Chapter 4), but *Library Journal* has reported that the question of whether to purchase the book has "set off a number of small explosions at libraries around the country." Some library directors have avoided the book on the claim that it was "ephemeral," and review journals have made excuses for not reviewing it. Even *Library Journal* admitted, "[W]e decided, like many libraries, to abstain from *Sex.*"[13]

When the director of the Mesa Public Library in Arizona ordered one copy of *Sex,* the library and the mayor's office were deluged with complaints. As a result, the mayor directed the library to cancel its order for *Sex*, and the library's director reluctantly acceded. A Colorado Springs public library had a similar experience, receiving several hundred "anti-*Sex*" phone calls, many of them from the conservative religious organization Focus on the Family. Christian radio stations told their listeners to call the library and threaten to vote against a pending library bond issue. The library decided not to purchase *Sex*. In Connecticut, the Whiton Branch of the Manchester Public Library held a public meeting to discuss *Sex*. Some in the audience characterized the book as pornographic. Others claimed that putting the book on the library shelves would attract undesirable people. There were statements like: "There is too much freedom in this country," "This book will make my child immoral," and "The book should be burned and then buried." Another member of the audience asked, "If we burn *Sex*, what will be burnt next?" Peter Chase, the Connecticut Library Association president, told the gathering that the library's book selection policy authorized the purchase of both popular and controversial materials, and he urged each town resident to decide for himself or herself which books to read. The board then voted to retain *Sex* but to restrict access to library users eighteen years or older. The board added ominously that they intended to scrutinize the library's liberal book selection policy.[14]

The 1991–1992 report *Attacks on the Freedom to Learn,* prepared by People for the American Way (PAW), revealed that censorship attempts in classrooms and school libraries had increased to the largest single-year total in the ten-year history of their report. Some 376 attacks on the freedom to learn, including 348 demands that curricular or library materials be removed, were reported in forty-four states. Nearly one fifth of all challenges to school and library materials came from conservative political groups, some of which have successfully run candidates for school boards. One leading censorship group, Citizens for Excellence in Education (CEE), has published a handbook entitled *How to Elect Christians to Public Office.* Some of the fundamentalist groups, including televangelists, have used the media to spread a message of general hostility toward public schools, using rhetoric that has appeared in challenges to books in schools and libraries around the country. Other conservative organizations have been involved nationally in challenges to elementary school reading programs, state-approved health curricula, and self-esteem programs.

In the 1990s, these political and religious organizations have increasingly gone to court in their attempt to control school curricula. Among the religious organizations frequently bringing suit are the CEE, the Rutherford Institute, the Blackstone Society, Christian Advocates Serving Evangelism, and the Western Center for Law and Religious Freedom. Don Wildmon's organization, the American Family Association

(AFA), has formed a legal arm, which has filed suit against the *Impressions* reading series in Ohio and California, charging that the series promoted "the religion of witchcraft" or "neo-Paganism." In both Ohio and California, suit was brought against small, financially troubled school systems, where the AFA might assume the schools would be unable to defend against litigation. Both lawsuits appeared to derive from the same draft complaint, which the AFA has circulated to other states as well.

Although the count of challenges to materials each year is disturbingly high, it is certainly underestimated, since the majority of challenges go unreported. School systems have often sought to avoid controversy by quietly acceding to the censors' demands. PAW notes that, in the past, educators often had to defend their curricular choices against media and lobbying campaigns, including letter-writing drives, petitions, and even paid advertising. Today, most schools have developed an orderly process for addressing challenges, ensuring that materials selected on the basis of educational merit will not be removed for ideological or sectarian considerations.

The PAW study found that the three most common reasons for challenging schools' materials in 1991–1992 were:

1. The materials were "anti-Christian," "Satanic," "New Age," or generally contrary to the challengers' religious views. Of the 376 documented censorship attempts in 1991–1992, 140 of them were based on this sectarian point of view. Typical challenges were to books like *Of Mice and Men* and *Catcher in the Rye.*

2. The materials contained profane or otherwise objectionable language. Almost one third of the challenges were on this basis, including books like *The Chocolate War* and *Blubber.*

3. The materials' treatment of sexuality was considered offensive. Over one fifth of the challenges were on this basis, including books like *Grapes of Wrath* and *Slaughterhouse Five.*

PAW found that the success rate of the censors in the 1991–1992 school year was disturbingly high, with fully 41 percent (144 instances) of all requests to remove materials succeeding in some measure. During the previous year, only 34 percent of the challenges were successful. "The unfortunate conclusion," states the PAW report, "is that while school systems have grown better equipped to deal with censorship attempts, challengers have more than kept pace in terms of their ability to apply political pressure to achieve their ends." Ominously, the report observed:

The last several years have witnessed an apparent diminution of Americans' appreciation and willingness to defend freedom of speech and expression. . . . The result has been a series of compromises on freedom of expression, each of which has sent the message to Americans that speech and expression are free, but only within certain parameters. That message, badly at odds with the First Amendment, has fed the wave of curricular attacks in our public schools.[15]

The school censorship movement often defends their activities as reasonable exercises of parental authority, but, all too often, book challenges seek to dictate not just what one parent's children may read but what all children may read. Indeed, PAW's report did not bother to cover instances in which parents requested that their children be permitted to "opt out" of a particular text or reading assignment. Most school districts have such policies in place, allowing teachers to provide alternative reading to students whose parents request it. Forty-nine percent of the documented challenges during 1991–1992 were to books that no child was required to read—books in libraries and on optional reading lists. The number of these censorship incidents more than doubled over the previous year.

The PAW report concludes:

In the community, the single best preparation for challenges is vigilance. In instances where teachers or school administrators are left to battle would-be censors on their own, the chances for censorship increase dramatically. But where schools enjoy the support of their communities, the censors are hard-pressed to prevail. This simple and most democratic of strategies is far and away the best safeguard against attacks on the freedom to learn.[16]

Kurt Vonnegut, a frequently banned author, says, "I hate it that Americans are taught to fear some books and some ideas as though they were diseases. . . . Well, my books have been thrown out of many libraries. . . . My publisher and I have two agreements on this. One is that we will not seek publicity about the banning of the book. . . . And the other is to see if the individual librarian or teacher is in a jam and whether we can help."[17] Yet Vonnegut admitted that when parents of the students he was teaching in Cape Cod complained of his assignment of *Catcher in the Rye*, he agreed to change the assignment to *Tale of Two Cities*. "My job was to teach," he explained, "not to defend the First Amendment."[18] Though most authors and teachers may not be so blunt, a surprising number of the authors I interviewed for this book (see Chapter 3) expressed emotional exhaustion and growing anger at having to divert so much of their time from writing to defending their works, or those of others, against the censors.

In modern society, the censorship of books can be initiated by the federal or state government, by local bureaucrats, or by community pressure. It may occur at any stage of publication, distribution, or institutional control. America's federal government has been inclined to cast its national security veil over massive amounts of scientific, diplomatic, and historical documents, invoking the classification system and export controls to withhold information, the espionage and sedition laws to punish communication, and even prior restraint to prevent publication. Today, there is some indication that the end of the cold war may diminish such forms of national security censorship, but there is a simultaneous escalation of community censorship, particularly in schools and libraries. These local attempts at information control have targeted books, periodicals, newspapers, films, videos, and even the performance of school plays.

In this book, we will focus on the most common form of "institutional" censorship, bookbanning in public schools and libraries, a practice that prohibits or restricts access to books already published, distributed, and even approved by school or library boards. Such materials may already be on library shelves or part of the teaching curriculum, and the pressure to remove them usually comes from groups outside the institution in question. All too often, the strident demands of a well-organized minority are accommodated by politically sensitive school and library boards or harried teachers. As we have seen, the major grounds for such censorship are sex, profanity, and religion, but they are often intertwined to cover a broad range of "unacceptable" attitudes or ideas.

Chapter 1 analyzes several major bookbanning incidents in American schools and libraries from 1976 through 1992. Some of these disputes were extended and quite violent, leaving the community torn and exhausted, with the conflict essentially unresolved. Others revealed the ability of school or library officials to establish an uneasy truce with the bookbanners through compromise and consensus. Some of these conflicts entered the courts to challenge existing law or community standards, whereas others generated new, often ill-conceived legislation. Some focused on a single book, while others attacked a broad range of authors and subjects. All of the incidents described in Chapter 1 were difficult and instructive for the communities involved. Most of them occurred in schools and their libraries, rather than in public libraries, a pattern seen consistently throughout this book. Although the number of preliminary challenges to books in public libraries is comparable with the number of challenges in school libraries and curricula, the sensitivity of the school environment produces more severe and emotional censorship conflicts and much more litigation.

Chapter 2 analyzes the modern court cases that compose the body of precedent concerning First Amendment rights in schools and libraries, revealing the evolving status of constitutional protection afforded to textbooks and library materials in public institutions. What are the limits on bureaucratic and administrative authority to determine what may be read in public schools and public libraries? The case law in this area is unsettled, but librarians and educators should be aware of the legal context within which the bookbanning conflict proceeds. As indicated earlier, virtually all important case law addresses schools and school libraries, revealing public library protections by implication only.

Chapter 3 presents the voices of some frequently banned authors and the basis for their controversy. Although many of their books have won national awards, these authors find their works suppressed in schools and libraries around the country. Who are these dangerous writers whose work must be kept from our impressionable youth? How actively do these authors enter the fray to defend their books against the censors? What pressure is brought to bear on them by their editors and publishers? Are they tempted to adjust their writing to avoid the continuing controversy?

Chapter 4 surveys the fifty most-banned books in the 1990s, summarizing the challenges to these books and the basis for their controversy. The ranking of these books was calculated from the incidents reported by the American Library Association's Office for Intellectual Freedom and the PAW from January 1990 through December 1992.

Among the book's appendixes are: "PAW's Most Frequently Challenged Books, 1991–1992"; "PAW's Most Frequently Challenged Books, 1982–1992"; "PAW's Most Frequently Challenged Materials, 1982–1992"; "PAW's Most Frequently Challenged Authors, 1982–1992"; and "PAW's States with the Most Challenges, 1982–1992."

NOTES

1. Arthur Schlesinger, Jr., Preface to *Censorship: 500 Years of Conflict*, by New York Public Library (New York: Oxford University Press, 1984), p. 7.

2. New York Public Library, *Censorship: 500 Years of Conflict*, p. 19.

3. Schlesinger, in ibid., p. 7.

4. "Rushdie Comes to Seek U.S. Support," *New York Times*, March 25, 1992, p. A8.

5. Al Kamen, "Senators Back Rushdie at Hill Lunch," *Washington Post*, March 26, 1992, p. A6.

6. Art Buchwald, "The White House's Rushdie Brushoff," *Washington Post*, April 2, 1992, p. D1.

7. Office for Intellectual Freedom, *American Library Association Memorandum*, September 1990, Attachment I.

8. "New NEA Chair Comes Out Shooting," *Newsletter on Intellectual Freedom,* July 1992, p. 114.

9. "NEA Storm Grows as Panel Quits in Protest," *Washington Post,* May 16, 1992, pp. B1, B8.

10. "Survey Finds Weak Support for Free Expression," *Newsletter on Intellectual Freedom,* July 1991, p. 122.

11. Teller, "Movies Don't Cause Crime," *New York Times,* January 17, 1992, p. A29.

12. James J. Kilpatrick, "Huff-and-Puff Porn Bill," *Washington Post,* August 29, 1992, p. A19.

13. Francine Fialkoff, "Inside Track: Sex in the Library," *Library Journal,* November 15, 1992, p. 63.

14. Janet Vaill-Day, "Sex in the Land of Steady Habits," *Connecticut Libraries,* January 1993, pp. 1, 6.

15. People for the American Way, *Attacks on the Freedom to Learn: 1991–1992 Report* (Washington, D.C.: PAW, 1992), pp. 9, 21.

16. People for the American Way, *Attacks on the Freedom to Learn: 1990–1991 Report* (Washington, D.C.: PAW, 1991), p. 15.

17. *Censorship or Selection: Choosing Books for Public Schools,* transcript of a videotape produced by Media and Society Seminars, Columbia University, 1982, pp. 27, 41.

18. "Vintage Vonnegut," *Johns Hopkins Magazine,* February 1992, p. 8.

1

A Survey of Major
Bookbanning Incidents

KANAWHA COUNTY: WEST—BY GOD—VIRGINIA

Charleston, West Virginia, is the state capital and the urban center of
Kanawha County, which contains some of the most depressed rural
society in America. The entire county forms a single school district,
within which was waged the mother of all school censorship battles. In
December 1973, a West Virginia Board of Education resolution directed all school districts to select school materials that accurately portray minority and ethnic group contributions to American culture and
that illustrate the intercultural character of our society. In Kanawha
County the English Language Arts Textbook Committee, composed of
four teachers and one principal, was authorized to make recommendations for textbook purchase. On March 12, 1974, the Textbook Committee recommended 325 titles for adoption by the board, and neither
the local citizenry nor the media took notice. Among the basic texts
ratified by the board were the Heath Company's *Communicating* and
Dynamics of Language, Scott Foresman's *America Reads* and *Galaxy,* and
Silver Burdett's *Contemporary English.* Among the supplemental texts
adopted were McDougal-Littell's *Language of Man* and Houghton
Mifflin's *Interaction.*

School board member Alice Moore, wife of a fundamentalist minister, took some of the books home for examination. She then telephoned Mel and Norma Gabler, self-appointed textbook evaluators operating a corporation called Educational Research Analysts out of
Longview, Texas. Many of the Kanawha texts were under consider-

ation within the Texas school system, and the Gablers, famous since the 1960s for their well-financed textbook protests, airmailed their "reviews" of the Kanawha titles to Alice Moore. Mrs. Moore passed her concerns, and the Gablers' evaluations, to other board members and to a local newspaper reporter. Community grumbling and rumor soon reached the point where the school board decided to schedule a meeting to "explain" the textbook selections. At the heated May 23 meeting, Mrs. Moore charged that the textbooks were filthy, disgusting trash, unpatriotic and unduly favoring blacks. Some parents and a fellow board member at the meeting supported her, and a June 27 meeting was scheduled to continue discussion and finalize the actual purchase of the already-approved books.

Alice Moore chose to take her cause to the public, appearing on television and reading passages from the challenged texts in churches and community centers. As a result, the local Parent-Teacher Association (PTA) was moved to oppose several of the textbook series, claiming: "Many of the books are literally full of anti-Americanism, anti-religion, and discrimination. Too, these books are woefully lacking in morally uplifting ideas. Many of the statements flout law and order and respect for authority. Several passages are extremely sexually explicit." The Magic Valley Mother's Club joined the fray by circulating a petition to ban from the schools any materials that "demean, encourage skepticism or foster disbelief in the institutions of the United States of America and in western civilization."[1]

A coalition of ministers from the West Virginia Council of Churches and from Catholic, Jewish, and Protestant clergy soon issued a statement in support of the textbooks:

> Any treatment, especially in the schools, of questions like war and peace, racism—black and white—religion and patriotism, is bound to raise disagreements and stir emotional response. . . . We know of no way to stimulate the growth of our youth if we insulate them from the real issues. We feel this program will help our students to think intelligently about their lives and our society.[2]

The June 27 board meeting was held before an audience of more than 1,000 people, with crowds overflowing into hallways and outdoors into the rain. After hours of stormy debate, the board voted to purchase all of the disputed books, except for eight titles from the *Interaction* series. But the conflict was far from over. A new organization, Christian-American Parents, sponsored letter-writing campaigns, newspaper advertising, rallies, picketing, and demonstrations in opposition to all of the books. Still another new antibook group, Concerned Citizens, picketed the board of education and sponsored a Labor Day protest rally where the Reverend Marvin Horan exhorted a crowd of 8,000 to boycott the schools when they opened the next day.

New fliers containing purported excerpts from the books were being circulated throughout the community, some containing blatantly sexual material that had no connection with the textbooks adopted by the Kanawha County schools. The fliers contained excerpts from books like Kate Millet's *Sexual Politics* and a book titled *Facts about Sex for Today's Youth*. Such fliers inflamed the controversy tremendously. During the first week of school, when parents examined the textbooks brought home by the students, they were, of course, unable to find the passages they had seen in the fliers. Ironically, they accused the administration of hiding the books containing the advertised excerpts.

Boycotts, strikes, and pickets became the primary tactic to force the offending books out of the schools. During the first week of school, 9,000 of the county's 45,000 students were kept home by their parents. Miners from all the mines in the county also stayed home rather than cross picket lines set up by parents. Sympathy strikes closed down mines in adjoining counties. Picketing spread to mines, schools, school bus garages, industry, and trucking companies. City bus drivers soon honored the picket lines, closing down service to about 11,000 people.

As a result of these tactics, as well as illegal demonstrations outside the Department of Education building, the board announced on September 11, 1974, that they were withdrawing the offending textbooks from the schools to allow a thirty-day review by a committee of citizens selected by board members. But at a large ballpark rally, the Reverend Marvin Horan repudiated any such compromise, demanding a continuation of the boycotts and picketing until all the challenged books had been permanently removed and the school superintendent and board members who voted "the wrong way" were dismissed.

In the weeks that followed, the antibook campaign reached the boiling point. Reverend Horan, who was later sentenced to three years in prison for conspiracy to blow up two elementary schools, was soon joined by other fundamentalist ministers. Reverend Ezra Graley and Reverend Avis Hill were soon sentenced to thirty days in jail for defying a court injunction, and Graley received an additional sixty days for contempt of court. The Reverend Charles Quigley shocked the county by asking Christians to pray that God would kill the three board members who voted to keep the books.

Many of the students in whose name the fundamentalists terrorized the county found the furor ironic. One pointed out, "They're shooting people because they don't want people to see violence in books." Violence escalated further in September during the second week of school. As the number of wildcat mine strikers reached almost 10,000, two men were wounded by gunfire at a picket line. A CBS TV crew was attacked, and car windows were smashed. Threats of violence were leveled at the school superintendent, board members, and parents who tried to send their children to school. Kanawha's sheriff joined other county officials in asking West Virginia Governor Arch Moore to send in state troopers, but the governor said he would not interfere in local political disputes. By September 13, 1974, Superintendent Kenneth Underwood ordered all 121 public schools closed for a four-day weekend, during which time all extracurricular activities were banned. Underwood and several board members, including Alice Moore, quietly slipped out of town. Moore said, "I never dreamed it would come to this."[3]

A *Charleston Gazette* article revealed: "A few extremists among the churchmen who wanted 'godless' textbooks removed from the schools became so fanatical they discussed bombing carloads of children whose parents were driving them to school in defiance of a boycott called by book protesters." Assistant District Attorney Wayne Rich stated that one of the convicted bombers testified that he and others had discussed ways to stop "people that was sending their kids to school, letting them learn out of books when they knew they was wrong." One method discussed was to place a blasting cap in the gas tank of a car, hooking the wire to the brake or signal light. When the brake was applied or the signals used, it would blow up the car.[4]

The protesters' hysterical attacks on "the books" quickly extended beyond particular titles or passages, to all 325 books approved for the curriculum and then to many of the world's most respected literary works, including Plato's *Republic,* Herman Melville's *Moby Dick,* John Milton's *Paradise Lost* and *Paradise Regained,* and even *The Good Earth,* the Pulitzer Prize novel by Pearl Buck, West Virginia's most renowned author! By now the dispute had attracted the national media. From magazines like *The New Yorker* and *U.S. News & World Report* to scholarly journals and the national press and television, the significance of this controversy over school books was dramatically acknowledged.

The controversy forced the resignations of the president of the school board and Superintendent Underwood, and when the new Textbook Review Committee began its deliberations on September 24, it came under heavy pressure from community organizations, some of which now had national support. The Business and Professional People's Alliance for Better Textbooks, led by businessman Elmer Fike, published antibook ads and pamphlets with the support of the Washington-based Heritage Foundation. On the other side, the Kanawha County Association of Classroom Teachers passed a resolution denouncing the removal of the textbooks and censuring the school board for abdicating its legal responsibilities under public pressure. The association voted to oppose any recommendation of the Textbook Review Committee that would revoke the original approval of the texts.

During the Review Committee's deliberations, one local elementary school was dynamited and another fire-bombed. Other schools were vandalized and attacked with gunfire. School buses were stoned, as were the homes of parents whose children attended school. Two school buses were hit by shotgun blasts, and eventually the county's fleet of buses was virtually inoperable. Even Alice Moore was threatened by phone, and after shots were fired outside her house, she was accompanied by guards at all times.

On November 8, 1974, amid fears of violence, the school board met to make a final decision on the recommendations of the Textbook Review Committee. The board heard testimony from the majority and minority factions of the committee, one recommending return of virtually all of the books and the other rejecting them all. The board then unanimously passed resolutions to protect students from the imposition of any books that their parents found objectionable. It was agreed that a form would be sent to parents, on which they could indicate any books they did not want their children to read. With only Mrs. Moore dissenting, the board voted to authorize the return of all the basic and supplemental books to the classroom except the elementary school series *Communicating* and the senior high school portion of the series, *Interaction*, which was confined to the library only. The board's vote actually imposed more severe restrictions than the majority recommendation of the Textbook Review Committee, which would have approved *Communicating* for classroom use.

The long-awaited board decision did little to defuse the conflict. Protesters intensified their boycotts, bomb threats increased, and one Kanawha town had Superintendent Underwood and two board members arrested for contributing to the delinquency of minors. Only after two police cars were fired upon as they escorted a school bus did the West Virginia State Police commit itself to enforcing the law against the protesters.

On November 21, 1974, the board passed a resolution setting guidelines for future textbook selection. Those guidelines closely followed the requirements that the Gablers' Texas organization had sent to Mrs. Moore. The National Education Association asserted that these guidelines, "if given the interpretation obviously meant by their proponent, would not only bar the disputed books from Kanawha County classrooms, but would proscribe the use of any language arts textbooks."[5]

On January 30, 1975, the U.S. District Court in Charleston considered a lawsuit brought by a group of Kanawha County citizens who complained that their religion required them to place their children in private schools to avoid the use of the controversial textbooks. The plaintiffs claimed that the texts not only were offensive to Christian morals but defamed the nation and attacked civic virtue. Alleging that they and their children would suffer irreparable harm unless the court enjoined the school board from violating their constitutional rights, the plaintiffs sought an injunction restraining the schools from using the challenged textbooks. District Judge K. K. Hall dismissed the plaintiffs' action, ending the legal phase of the Kanawha battle.

On February 10, 1975, operating under new West Virginia procedures for textbook selection, a Kanawha County screening committee of fifteen lay members and five teachers rejected parts of all four textbook series under consideration. After the West Virginia Department of Education ruled that the Textbook Selection Committee was not bound by the screening committee, the board approved one of the series by a vote of 4 to 1, Mrs. Moore dissenting. Technically, the dispute over the books had been resolved, but demonstrations and boycotts continued until April 1975, when the Reverend Marvin Horan was tried and sentenced to three years in prison for conspiracy to bomb schools. Finally, shortly after school began in the fall of 1975, the board restored to Kanawha classrooms the *Communicating* series that had been dropped in November 1974. Ironically, this textbook series had been the most violently opposed of all the challenged books, yet it was now approved without objection.

The war was over, but in its wake remained an atmosphere of caution. Though technically reinstated, the controversial textbooks were never reordered, and the original copies were gingerly sidestepped, even by most teachers who supported them. The new books that eventually replaced the offending texts came from intimidated publishers who provided only the most sanitized subjects and bland authors. The retrenchment led some of Kanawha's schools to reintroduce the textbook series they had used in the 1940s.

Looking back, education professor George Hillocks, Jr., called the Kanawha County dispute "the most prolonged, intense, and violent textbook protest this country has ever witnessed." A few years after the conflict had been subdued, Hillocks visited the Kanawha County school system and observed:

> Children whose parents granted permission must use the controversial books only in the library, not in the classroom where other children might overhear discussions of them. Or teachers must make special provisions for use of the books. The result is that many do not use them at all. Many of the texts sit in the board of education warehouse. One elementary principal told me that she will not order the books. . . . She does not want to disrupt the school again. . . . Some teachers are looking for ways out of education, many others are angry at the vilification to which they feel they have been subjected, and many say they will never feel the same about teaching again.[6]

James Moffet, author/editor of Houghton Mifflin's *Interaction* series, one of the most vilified of the texts in Kanawha County, concludes:

The fact that nothing like it has occurred since gives a good indication of how effective it was: no publisher has dared offer to schools any textbooks of a comparable range of subjects and ideas and points of view to those the protesters vilified and crippled on the market. Theoretically returned to the Kanawha County schools, they may as well not have been. In many other ways the bitter controversy closed up its own school system as much as it did textbook editorial offices.[7]

GODLESS TEXTBOOKS IN WASHINGTON COUNTY, VIRGINIA

In February 1974, a customer came to Bobby's Market, a small grocery store in the rural community of Benhams, Virginia, and told the proprietor, Bobby Sproles, about the profanity he had discovered in his son's high school English textbook series. When the customer showed him one of the volumes in Ginn and Company's *Responding* series, Sproles was outraged. Upon returning home, Sproles examined his daughter's English text, also from the *Responding* series, and he found it equally objectionable. Soon the word had spread from Bobby's Market that "dirty" books were being used in the local schools.

Sproles was never very clear on the "dirty" language in the stories presented in the *Responding* series. He complained of words like *damn* and *hell*, but these are not normally considered dirty words. He identified particular stories like Erskine Caldwell's "Indian Summer," which describes a mud bath given to an adolescent girl by two young boys. But there was no profane or vulgar language of any kind in that story. Sproles did cite a particular passage in John Updike's "A & P" in which a character refers to a girl's "sweet soft broad-looking can." This was apparently representative of the "filth" that made the *Responding* series unacceptable.

Sproles advised his customers to contact Dr. R. G. Raines, acting superintendent of schools for Washington County, and the complaints began to mount. When Raines failed to take action against the books, several angry parents decided to take their grievance to the school board. On March 2, 1974, Sproles spoke at the school board meeting, presenting his group's objections to the *Responding* series as well as other books in the school libraries. Sproles passed out copies of the books for the board members to examine, and the board agreed to look into the matter. This satisfied Sproles, who told his supporters that he was confident that the board would not tolerate dirty books in the school system.

At the next board meeting in April, D. M. Cooke, the director of instruction, described the school's procedure for adopting textbooks and the justification for continuing to use the *Responding* series. He stressed that the primary aim of each teacher in the language arts program was to get the students to love to read. To accomplish this, the schools would need to accept occasional profanity, because "the students like these books and they read them because they reflect the student's world and his language of the present." Cooke did, however, promise that an alternative to the *Responding* text would be sought, though this would involve a lengthy process. Sproles was shocked at the board's decision. He asked all children to leave the board room, then proceeded to read from the offending books. The Reverend Tommy Tester, pastor of the Gospel Baptist church, led a prayer asking that the devil be defeated. "The demons of Hell have entered into the bodies of our educators," he said.[8]

Sproles soon organized the first of many public meetings to oppose the books. The 200 people who attended the meeting at the Baptist church in Benhams later came to call themselves the Concerned Citizens for Better Government, and Sproles became their spokesperson and leader. At that first meeting, Sproles demanded the resignation of Acting Superintendent Raines, Director of Instruction Cooke, the school board, and the Textbook Adoption Committee. His demands were communicated to Virginia's governor, attorney general, and various other state and county officials.

Though Sproles had complained of the profane language in *Responding*, he now seemed more concerned that the books were unpatriotic and irreligious, "communist inspired" and un-American, undermining love of country and parental authority. But attacking the books on the basis of profane language was an easier public task than analyzing their political implications. In an interview, Sproles admitted: "I think there's things in the books that to me, personally, is more damaging psychologically than the words is. Now I've played on the profanity, I've fought the issue on the profanity, simply because I guess I didn't know any other way to do it."[9]

On April 17, 1974, Sproles and the Concerned Citizens took their case before the board of supervisors, where they requested that the school budget be reduced as a tactic to effectively remove the books. The board then considered a motion to oppose the use of *Responding* in Washington County schools, but after heated debate, the motion failed by a vote of 3 to 2.

The following day, a disappointed Sproles chose to begin a petition drive, circulating copies in churches and schools throughout the county. On May 4, 1974, the school board met again to hear the Concerned Citizens' complaints and receive the petition. On May 10, Sproles received the board's reply to his complaint. The letter from Acting School Superintendent R. G. Raines reiterated the board's policy that whenever parents object to a book, their children may be assigned alternative reading materials. In particular, parents objecting to

Responding could have their children placed in classes that used a different text. When Sproles notified the board that the Concerned Citizens could not accept such an arrangement, Raines requested that the case be put on the docket of the Washington County Circuit Court.

When the matter came to trial, Sproles himself acted for the plaintiffs. He argued that the school board had denied the citizens of Washington County their freedom of religion by teaching doctrines contrary to their beliefs. Sproles also said the board had acted corruptly in failing to warn parents of the books' offensive contents. But Judge Aubrey Matthews decided in favor of the board, concluding that its actions were neither corrupt nor beyond its jurisdiction. After court was adjourned, Sproles accosted the newly appointed superintendent of schools, W. Grant Tubbs, saying that the Concerned Citizens would back candidates for the Board of Supervisors who were more sympathetic to their aims. The following day, Sproles began distributing 10,000 copies of a list of alleged profane words that he had culled from *Responding*. The list was immediately printed in the *Bristol Herald-Courier*, along with a sympathetic editorial and instructions on how to contact Sproles and receive his materials. On July 26, 1974, Acting Superintendent Raines announced that two books would be offered as possible alternatives to *Responding*. Those books were made available for public inspection at the local library, after which a public hearing was held on their acceptability. At that hearing, Sproles and his supporters dominated the audience and opposed both of the proposed series, claiming that they also contained profanity such as "by God." More important, Sproles said *any* alternative books would be unacceptable as long as *Responding* was used by *any* child in the school system.

The August 10 school board meeting was attended by about 500 persons, assembled not in the usual boardroom but in the large high school auditorium. Eight of the speakers, including one minister, defended the books. Twelve speakers, eight of them ministers, were opposed to the books. Reverend Tom Williams, an emerging fundamentalist leader within the Concerned Citizens, described the *Responding* series as a symptom of, and a contributing factor to, a collapse of morals and traditional values that endangered America's survival. As a result of his speech, Williams was soon receiving as much media attention and publicity as was Sproles. Interviewed at his home, Reverend Williams said the disputed books were wrong religiously, wrong morally, and wrong constitutionally. He warned: "There will be no peace in the school system as long as the present Board sits and as long as these books remain and as long as our libraries are not cleaned up. We're determined to clean up the libraries too. All these filthy books have been brought into the library. They're going out."[10]

Not to be outdone, Sproles promised:

We're still going to try to get the books out, but at the same time we're going to try to get some of the people out of the school system too. . . . Some of these teachers that approved these books, they need to go. I think really that we're going to have to get rid of the Superintendent, the Assistant Superintendent and the School Board and some of these teachers before we can get rid of the books.[11]

After the August 10 school board meeting, Sproles and Reverend Williams met with board members and Superintendent Tubbs. Tubbs attempted to negotiate a compromise, but Sproles would accept nothing short of removing the books entirely from the schools. Another board meeting was arranged for the following week, at which the protesters were told that the board was willing to have offending portions of the *Responding* texts "blocked out." Sproles again rejected the board's offer, claiming that the children might find some way to circumvent the excisions. The board then offered to restrict the texts to classroom use only, under the supervision of a teacher. Reverend Williams agreed to present that proposal to the Concerned Citizens.

Feeling his leadership challenged, Sproles soon decided to move toward more extreme tactics, including a school boycott. Through the local newspapers, Sproles announced an August 20 meeting of the Concerned Citizens to develop plans for the boycott. Before the meeting, Washington County Sheriff Robert Clendenen visited Sproles to warn him of the grave consequences of a boycott, including the growing possibility of violence, and Sproles agreed to allow Clendenen to speak at the meeting. Clendenen told the Concerned Citizens that any parents participating in the boycott would be arrested. As a result, the Concerned Citizens concluded that rather than organizing a formal boycott, parents should decide independently whether to enroll their children in school.

On September 5, the school board announced a compromise proposal. Teachers would select inoffensive portions from both *Responding* and *Adventure*, a proposed alternative text, using the established criteria for book selection. Parental input would be sought in choosing the excerpts, and even these sanitized selections could be used only in the classroom under teacher supervision, unless a parental consent form was signed. Sproles was suspicious of the compromise and continued to threaten boycotts.

At the first board meeting of 1975, Sproles read from a Virginia statute that called for "moral education" in the public schools, and Reverend Williams demanded the resignation of Tubbs and Raines. The board said it would respond at an appropriate time, but after the protesters had left the meeting room, the board gave a unanimous vote of confidence to Tubbs and Raines. At the next board meeting, a motion was made to remove one of the books in the *Responding* series and to appoint a committee to review the entire series. Superintendent Tubbs objected, saying this would result in denying these books not only to the protesters' children but to all children. He said school officials, board members, and teachers had been threatened by protesters, and he asked, "What will be next? Where will the witchhunt end?" Nonetheless, he expressed grudging support for the motion to remove one of the *Responding* volumes and to establish a committee to review the series. When Tubbs finished speaking, the board unanimously approved the motion.[12]

The Textbook Advisory Committee, appointed to evaluate the *Responding* series and recommend a resolution to the conflict, filed its final report on March 13, 1976. The official report vaguely declared that the books may be inappropriate for use in public schools but that the dispute was a complex issue with no simple answer that would be acceptable to all. The committee report offered two possible courses of action: Remove the *Responding* series entirely from the school system, or cease its use as the basic text while retaining it as supplemental reading. In addition to its "official" report, the Textbook Review Committee provided the board with an "unofficial" report, which made no pretense of objectivity. That report criticized *Responding* for encouraging disobedience, disrespect for authority, disrespect for God, and contempt for American institutions and the free enterprise system.

Perhaps on the basis of the committee's "unofficial" report, the school board, at its next meeting, voted 5 to 2 to remove the *Responding* series entirely from the Washington County School System. A school bureaucracy had thus consummated a bookbanning, and a fundamentalist group had established permanent influence over the process of textbook selection in Washington County, Virginia.

ISLAND TREES V. *PICO*: A FIRST AMENDMENT VICTORY

In September 1975, in Long Island, New York, the seven members of the Island Trees School Board, including the board president, Richard Ahrens, attended a conference sponsored by a conservative organization called Parents of New York United (PONYU). The Island Trees board members heard a speech on the subject of controlling textbooks and library books in the public schools, and they obtained a list of books that PONYU opposed. At the top of the list was the heading "Objectionable Books," followed by thirty-three titles, along with excerpts from those books and editorial comments. Most of the excerpts concerned sex, but some of the editorial comments were political in nature. For example, one book was described as objectionable because it "equates Malcolm X, considered by many to be a traitor to this country, with the founding fathers of our country."[13]

After the conference, when the board members returned to Island Trees, they decided to examine their own library's collections. On a night when the school was closed and the building empty, the board members entered the library. Steven Pico, the student who later led the opposition to the Island Trees censorship, recalls the episode:

> Now please don't ask me why book banners feel more comfortable working during the night. . . . I guess they decided that is how censors should act. So, they had the janitor unlock the library, proceeded to go through the card catalog, and found that our district had eleven of the books on that list.[14]

Several weeks later, at its February 1976 meeting, the board ordered the principals of the junior and senior high schools to immediately remove all copies of the eleven books: *The Fixer*, by Bernard Malamud; *Slaughterhouse Five*, by Kurt Vonnegut; *The Naked Ape*, by Desmond Morris; *Down These Mean Streets*, by Piri Thomas; *Best Short Stories by Negro Writers*, edited by Langston Hughes; *Go Ask Alice*, anonymous; *A Hero Ain't Nothin' but a Sandwich*, by Alice Childress; *Black Boy*, by Richard Wright; *Laughing Boy*, by Oliver LaFarge; *Soul on Ice*, by Eldridge Cleaver; and *A Reader for Writers*, edited by Jerome Archer. At that time, Malamud's *The Fixer* not only was in the library but was assigned reading in a senior literature course in the Island Trees district.

When Superintendent of Schools Richard Morrow discovered what had been done, he publicly objected and wrote a memo to the board stating his opposition to banning the books on the basis of a list from an unknown source and with no criteria specified. "[W]e already have a policy," said Morrow, "designed expressly to handle such problems. It calls for the superintendent, upon receiving an objection to a book or books, to appoint a committee to study them and make recommendations. I feel it is a good policy—and it is board policy—and that it should be followed in this instance." The board responded to the superintendent's memo by repeating its directive that "*all copies* of the library books in question be removed from the libraries to the Board's office."[15]

In March 1976, the board agreed to form a Book Review Committee consisting of four Island Trees parents and four school staff members, to be appointed jointly by the superintendent and the board. The committee was to read the books in question and make recommendations to the board concerning their educational suitability, good taste, appropriateness, and relevance. The board then held a public meeting on the book dispute, at which it distributed copies of excerpts from the offending books. Superintendent Morrow once again expressed his concern in writing, saying it was wrong for the board or any other group to remove books without following established procedure and without considering the views of the parents whose children read the books and the teachers who use them. He also said it was wrong to judge any book on the basis of brief excerpts taken out of context and from a list prepared by someone outside the Island Trees community. Morrow recommended that, pending review by a committee, the challenged books should be returned to the shelves.

In July, the Book Review Committee made its final report to the board, recommending that five of the listed books be retained and that two others be removed from the school libraries. As for the remaining four books, the committee could not agree on two, took no position on one, and recommended that the last book be made available to students only with parental approval. The board overruled the committee's report, deciding that only one book *(Laughing Boy)* should be returned to the high school library without restriction; that another *(Black Boy)* should be made available, subject to parental approval; but that the remaining nine books should be removed from elementary and secondary libraries and from use in the curriculum. The board gave no reasons for rejecting the recommendations of the committee that it had appointed, nor did it justify its disregard for the concerns of School Superintendent Morrow.

Within a year, Morrow had left the school district, replaced by an administrator from California with ties to former Governor Ronald Reagan's administration. The head librarian in the Island Trees schools, who like the superintendent had opposed the book removals, was demoted and transferred to a small elementary school.

The Island Trees book dispute attracted considerable news coverage. The fact that two of the school board members were running for reelection further heightened tensions. So began a seven-year First Amendment struggle, during which the books remained banned from the library shelves. When the controversy reached the media and the community at large, the board issued a press release explaining that while at the PONYU conference they had learned of books in schools throughout the country that were "anti-American, anti-Christian, anti-Sem[i]tic, and just plain filthy." The board said that after finding some of those books in their own libraries, they verified that they contained "obscenities, blasphemies, brutality, and perversion beyond description." The press release concluded: "[I]t is our duty, our moral obligation, to protect the children in our schools from this moral danger as surely as from physical and medical dangers."[16]

Students at the high school and junior high school, led by seventeen-year-old Steven Pico, sued the board in U.S. District Court, claiming a denial of their First Amendment rights. The plaintiff in *Island Trees v. Pico* (see Chapter 2) was an Island Trees student who recently recalled this epic legal conflict in a speech before the Missouri Association of School Librarians. Pico said he remembered quite clearly his first reaction to the bookbanning:

> I could not believe the hypocrisy of the censorship of books in the United States. In school, year after year, I had been told how books were banned in communist countries and burned in Nazi Germany. I could not believe that it was happening in the United States in the 1970s. . . . I found it hard to believe that students didn't care and that every single teacher remained silent. For the first time in my life I felt that I understood what happened during the McCarthy era. After twelve years of schooling, my education had in many ways finally begun.[17]

Steven Pico told the assembled librarians that the events in Island Trees were not unusual but in fact represented the norm in schools around the nation. He noted that in this case, as in many other censorship incidents, the books had not been read by the censors and were praised by educators and reviewers. In the Island Trees case, two of the books were Pulitzer Prize winners, yet the opinions of professionals were ignored, the attitudes of students were never sought, and those who defended the books were ostracized.

Before initiating his suit, Pico conferred with representatives of the American Library Association, but realizing that he needed the support of a group with the resources to sustain protracted litigation, he turned to the American Civil Liberties Union (ACLU). Pico's attorneys began by taking depositions from the school board members to establish a record of their objections to each book. The board members said *The Fixer* was anti-Semitic because derogatory terms were used to describe Jews. Yet the book was written by a Jewish author who was simply describing the persecution of Jews. The board gave two reasons for banning *A Hero Ain't Nothin' but a Sandwich:* first, because *ain't* appears in the title, and second, because George Washington was identified as a slaveholder. *A Reader for Writers* was banned because, among selections like the Declaration of Independence and President John Kennedy's inaugural address, the editors included a satirical essay by Jonathan Swift. The bookbanners said *Go Ask Alice* glorified sex and drugs, though it was simply a moving account of the horrors of drug addiction.

The district court found in favor of the school board, but the students appealed to the U.S. Court of Appeals, which reversed the decision and remanded the case back to the district court for trial. The school board then appealed to the U.S. Supreme Court, which granted a review in 1982. Pico and his fellow students asked the Court for a declaration that the board's actions were unconstitutional and that it should return the nine books to the school libraries and refrain from interfering with their use in the schools' curricula.

By the time the case was argued before the Supreme Court, the school board was no longer claiming that they had banned the books because they were anti-American and antireligious. Now they simply said the books were "vulgar." But one of these books, *A Reader for Writers*, contained no vulgarity at all. When the school board attorney appeared before the Supreme Court, Justice John Paul Stevens asked him why *A Reader for Writers* was banned, since it contained no vulgarity. The attorney answered that the board considered the book to be in bad taste. An incredulous Justice Stevens then asked whether "bad taste" was really an appropriate basis on which to ban books in the United States.

The Supreme Court ruled 5 to 4 in favor of Pico and his fellow students, but Pico says they won by the skin of their teeth. The case came to the most conservative Court in sixty years at a time when the Reagan administration and groups like the Moral Majority were fueling anti-intellectualism. Asking that Court to recognize a First Amendment "right to know," which had no firm history in constitutional law, was risky business. (For an in-depth discussion of the legal implications of this case, see Chapter 2.)

The Supreme Court decided that the case should have been tried to determine the board's *motivation* in banning the books, and so the case was remanded for trial. The Island Trees School Board considered their options, and then, rather than going to a trial that they might lose, they voted to return *all* of the disputed books to the library shelves to be used without restriction.

Stephen Pico believes that since that decision school officials have not been eager to have their motives examined at trial and scrutinized in the press. They may also be less willing or able to justify to taxpayers the hundreds of thousands of dollars in legal fees that would be necessary to ban a library book. But to this day, Pico remains disappointed at the passive community response to the bookbanning:

> Not one parent in Island Trees ever complained about these eleven books. Not one teacher, not one student, ever objected to these books. A group of activists from around the country . . . succeeded in keeping these books off the shelves for seven years. . . . I do look back now and then and recall how it felt to be called a "communist" in public because I was defending the right to read a book. That's sad and ironic, but I can easily brush it off. What I shall never forget is the silence of my teachers during the book banning. Only one of my teachers ever commented to

me about the book banning. . . . One day after class she whispered to me, "Steve, you're doing the right thing." I will never be able to forget that she felt the need to whisper.[18]

CONFLICT AND COMPROMISE IN PRINCE GEORGES COUNTY

Public libraries have been subject to much the same kinds of censorship controversies as have school libraries, yet perhaps because public libraries serve all ages and have no link to an obligatory curriculum, they have been better able to find compromise and consensus in dealing with bookbanning.

In September 1977, the rumbling of an approaching censorship storm could be heard in Maryland's Prince Georges County when County Executive Winfield Kelly received a letter complaining about a book, *Our Bodies, Ourselves,* that was owned by the local public library. The letter was signed by C. Paul, a member of the Coalition for Children, a local religious group headed by Beth Trotto. Ms. Paul claimed that the book described and illustrated sexual acts that were illegal in the state of Maryland. She said that exposure to books like *Our Bodies, Ourselves* made it difficult to raise Christian children with the hope of eternal life with their Creator. She opposed the use of her tax dollars for the purchase of "pornography" produced by "feminist degenerates," and she warned the county executive that if even one more cent of her taxes was spent on such "smut," she would be forced to read aloud from *Our Bodies, Ourselves* at the county executive's next town meeting.

County Executive Kelly wrote to Ms. Paul, informing her that the Prince Georges County Memorial Library System was an autonomous body and that the county government had no control over a library's internal policy, including material selection. He advised her of the library's procedure for handling complaints, and enclosed a blank complaint form. Ms. Paul filled out the form, stating that the book encouraged sexual activity among adolescents, including lesbianism, birth control, and abortion, all of which were against her religious convictions. A member of the library staff responded to the complaint, explaining why the book was in the library's collection.

Perhaps disappointed with the library's response, Ms. Paul sent a letter to the editor of the *Prince Georges Journal,* attacking sex education in the schools and taking particular aim at *Our Bodies, Ourselves.* The letter stated:

> *The Wanderer,* in its February 23, 1978 edition, called this literary effort "a veritable litany of the most disgusting and outrageous sexual immoral-

ity available today." . . . . Currently 184 copies of the book reside in the 18 branches of the County library system—enough for everyone to have at least one peek. Additionally, the paperback may find its way into the classroom (remember, it is not approved for school use) as a resource material used by teachers. It also is used as a major reference work in many sex and psychology texts. . . .

It advocates abortion, lesbianism, and masturbation. . . . With such volumes as this available and in use by our youngsters, are our children really discouraged from becoming sexually active at an early age or are we merely piquing their curiosity to experiment with that which they ordinarily would not if alternatives were not provided at taxpayer expense?[19]

Just what was it in this book that was arousing such emotional controversy? *Our Bodies, Ourselves,* written by the Boston Women's Health Collective, was first published in 1973 by Simon & Schuster. A female correspondent for the *Washington Post* recently reviewed *Our Bodies, Ourselves* and recalled her early affection for the book: "It filled in the gaps of high-school-hallway and pajama-party discussions. . . . And its tone assured us that this wasn't privileged information. There was nothing wrong with knowing the difference between the pituitary and the pelvis, and we weren't too dense to understand." Indeed, when the 1992 edition of the book was published, it was greeted with a lengthy congratulatory essay on the front page of the *Washington Post* "Style" section, with nary a word about immorality nor any suggestion that it might be bookbanning fodder. Jacqueline Trescott wrote:

The women who read it were reassured. Is that what a fallopian tube looks like? How could it be causing all these problems? Should you worry about birth control pills and blood clots? . . . Perhaps most importantly, the book gave me and others material for a short list of questions that would make doctors stop the merry-go-round and actually respond to us. Often it became a second opinion.[20]

But in 1978, *Our Bodies, Ourselves* was a hot item in Prince Georges County libraries. In response to the complaints, County Executive Kelly asked the State Attorney's Office to review the book's original and revised editions. The review, expressed in an internal memo from Stephen Orenstein to State's Attorney Arthur Marshall, said:

The text is occasionally explicit but is done so to develop the thought espoused. The explicit language is minimal. Vulgar words and phrases are also minimal. . . . The text does deal with some controversial subjects such as abortion and homosexuality and one could conclude that the authors espouse or condone certain unpopular views regarding these subjects. In my view it is clear that these books are not obscene under the law of Maryland. The dominant theme of the material taken as a whole does not appeal to a prurient interest in sex. . . . There is much contained in each volume that has significant social value. . . . Since the books are not obscene in my view, the distribution is not a crime. Another issue presented is whether a public library should offer these books for loan and to whom. This is both a political question and a first amendment censorship question not for the State's Attorney for Prince George's to decide.[21]

Based on Mr. Orenstein's review, State's Attorney Marshall wrote to Beth Trotto, nominal leader of the Coalition for Children, assuring her that the distribution of *Our Bodies, Ourselves* did not violate the obscenity laws and that decisions on its use in the public library system were up to the county executive.

By now, William Gordon, director of the Prince Georges County Memorial Library System, had been informed of the growing controversy, and on November 21, 1977, he sent a memo to the library board members, warning,

Mr. Kelly is understandably concerned about C. Paul's threat to read portions of the book at the Town Meeting scheduled for September 28. We will work with Mr. Kelly's office to attempt to avoid a public confrontation. . . . In any event, I am sending selected staff members to the Town Meeting. They will be prepared to defend the selection of the book, and advise those who wish to submit complaints that a routing for such complaints has been established.[22]

Gordon recently looked back on the origins of this bookbanning struggle:

The main challenge was directed toward *Our Bodies, Ourselves,* but growing from that were complaints about *all* the Norma Klein books and *all* the Judy Blume books. The controversy grew through the activities of an organization headed by a woman named Beth Trotto. It was called Coalition for Children, the sort of name that would make people feel cozy and good. The organization was formed to see to it that *Our Bodies, Ourselves* and other "objectionable" material was removed from the library.[23]

On October 13, 1977, two county councilmen wrote to the president of the board of library trustees to protest *Our Bodies, Ourselves,* expressing their strong objection to making the book available to county youngsters. The councilmen claimed that most adults would consider the book objectionable and would indeed find portions of it thoroughly disgusting. They declined to quote any particular passages from the book in order to spare their secretary the indignity of typing the material. The councilmen then urged the board to investigate the appropriateness of placing the book in county libraries.

A prompt response from the board of library trustees described the library's selection policy and its reevaluation procedure, already under way as the result of Ms. Paul's written complaint. Further problems or inquiries were to be referred to William Gordon, director of the library system. But the threatened town meeting confrontation occurred nonetheless. At two consecutive town meetings, complaints were voiced about a number of books in the county libraries, and Gordon discussed the matter face-to-face with Beth Trotto. An agreement was reached to continue those discussions in a subsequent meeting with Gordon, Mrs. Trotto, and other members of her organization.

In the meantime, the widely circulated *Newsletter* of the Coalition for Children had printed isolated quotes from *Our Bodies, Ourselves,* which, taken out of context, caused more members of the community to complain to William Gordon. In his written response to these people, Gordon explained the exhaustive research done by his staff to verify the book's objectivity and medical authority. He urged parents to continue to exercise responsibility over their own children but said the library must provide information for a multiplicity of interests.

On December 2, County Executive Kelly wrote to William Gordon, asking him to "personally review" *Our Bodies, Ourselves* for appropriateness in the libraries. Gordon formed an Ad Hoc Reconsideration Committee to examine the book, asking its members to be "as objective as possible and approach your review as though you were considering it for the first time." The committee subsequently delivered a positive evaluation of the book to Gordon, who then wrote County Executive Kelly to express his official judgment. In his letter to Kelly, Gordon said that he had carefully reviewed and approved *Our Bodies, Ourselves* several years earlier when working at another library. He noted that *Our Bodies, Ourselves* had been available and in use in the Prince Georges County libraries for over four years, with no complaints until now. Gordon concluded:

> Now that I have re-examined the book word-for-word, I can only say that my attitudes toward it are unwavering, and that I support its being available in the young adult and adult sections of the library. *Our Bodies, Ourselves* is not sensational; it does not appeal to one's prurient interest. It is a straightforward presentation which deals with the physical and sexual realities of the female body. Any information about human sexuality is going to offend someone. For too long, the tendency has been to withdraw from making sexual information available, particularly to young people who, during their developmental years, are most desperately in need of such information. . . . But it is in opposition to our

philosophy that freedom of access to information is basic to public library service.[24]

Gordon enclosed a letter from Dr. Murray M. Kappelman of the University of Maryland School of Medicine, attesting to the medical accuracy of the book. He also attached the American Library Association's 1976 list of best books for young adults, on which *Our Bodies, Ourselves* appeared.

But the dispute was not yet resolved. On January 11, 1978, Councilman Frank Casula wrote to Mrs. Lucille Zugay, president of the board of library trustees, asking that *Our Bodies, Ourselves* and other "adult" materials in the library's collections be physically sequestered so that younger persons could not browse through them. Mrs. Zugay wrote Councilman Casula that it would be awkward logistically to restrict physical movement from one section of the library to another. She said it would be difficult for her to accept any suggestion that the library "lock up" certain materials to restrict their use, since such restrictions would stand in the way of general access and freedom of information. Zugay emphasized the parental responsibility to guide a child's reading, noting that if the library refused information to a child whose parents had approved access to the information, the library would have failed that child. She said the reverse was also true, confirming the importance of the parent in guiding a child's reading, whether it is done at home or in a library. Zugay concluded that it was impossible to expect library personnel to police the reading that people do in the library.

By January 1978, the strategy of Beth Trotto's Coalition for Children took a new turn. There were already county council members sympathetic to her attacks on *Our Bodies, Ourselves,* but she now began to recruit political support for a campaign against local bookstores. At one of the town meetings, Mrs. Trotto spoke with County Executive Kelly, expressing concern over materials in the library system *and* in commercial bookstores throughout the county. Kelly subsequently wrote to Mrs. Trotto, describing William Gordon's positive decision on *Our Bodies, Ourselves* while acknowledging the concern of county council members over the availability of "pornographic" materials in bookstores. Kelly said Councilmen Casula and Hartlove were considering amendments to the zoning regulations applying to such bookstores, and he assured Trotto of his support for such amendments.

Ms. Trotto's organization was soon able to persuade the county council to introduce legislation concerning "obscene reading matter" in bookstores and libraries, and that initiative received considerable media attention. County Bill No. CB–42–1978, entitled "An Act concerning Obscene Matter," would have made it unlawful for any person knowingly to sell or loan to a juvenile, or to display in a manner whereby juveniles can or may examine, peruse or otherwise view any picture, photograph, drawing or other graphic . . . image of a person or portion of the human body which depicts nudity, sexual conduct, sexual excitement or sadomasochistic abuse and which is predominantly harmful or potentially harmful to juveniles.

The bill defined *harmful* to mean anything that "appeals to the prurient, shameful or morbid interest of juveniles." Violations of the bill's provisions could result in fines of up to $1,000 or a jail term of six months, or both. Each *day* that a violation continued would be considered a separate offense.[25]

William Gordon told me, "We understood that the penalties would apply to the Head of the library personally, or that it could apply to the library's public service staff individually."

When the bill was initially proposed, William Gordon warned that the law, if strictly interpreted, would ban from public display any art books that depict nudes, as well as some health books, encyclopedia volumes, magazines like the *National Geographic,* or even the *Smithsonian* or *Sports Illustrated.* He told the *Prince Georges Journal,* "We're concerned about how this law could be interpreted. It makes no distinction as to the type of book."[26]

The original bill would have exempted public libraries and schools, but an amended version covered both, implying the need to remove a wide variety of books and magazines from library shelves. At the time the bill was introduced, Gordon was quoted as saying, "We are very seriously concerned about this. It would be extremely difficult for us to operate effectively [with this bill]. . . . The law is so broad in definition it would restrict access to a substantial part of our collection to people under 18." Gordon said the law could also affect the thirty-five students, called "pages," employed by the public libraries. "If the bill were to pass in its present form," said Gordon, "the library board would have to meet to decide what to do about the pages, and about parts of our collection."[27] Other libraries in the area were equally concerned. At the University of Maryland in College Park, officials were worried that the law would force them to sequester major portions of their collections from the eyes of the hundreds of freshmen under eighteen years of age.

The proposed bill was aimed at a very broad swath of materials, and of course, *Playboy* was prominent among the magazines that might be banned. In a newspaper interview, William Gordon tried to explain his library's choice of periodicals: "We attempt to have all magazines that are indexed in the *Reader's Guide to Periodical Literature,*" he said.

Playboy is indexed. Setting aside its pictorial content, it has long been regarded for its critical coverage of current issues, fine fiction and the best interviews. The only things we keep [hidden] behind a desk now are materials that are frequently stolen, such as auto repair manuals and the Sunday *Times*. These may soon be joined by health books, including *Our Bodies, Ourselves,* which aroused controversy earlier this year when a parent group protested that it was pornographic.

Gordon predicted that even the less controversial books purchased for the county libraries would fall prey to the new law, noting that "nearly every publication selected, even with the elaborate set of criteria, is going to offend someone, whether it's on the basis of religion, philosophy or sex. We attempt to fulfil the needs and wishes of over 600,000 people." Gordon warned that if a child checked out a book on home medicine and his mother discovered that it had a drawing of the female reproductive system, the proposed bill would leave the library open to a lawsuit.[28]

County council member Francis Francois insisted that the concerns raised by librarians and teachers were "simply not valid issues." He acknowledged, however, that the bill was "confused" and would probably be further amended. As written, the bill would have prevented doctors and nurses from handing out to juveniles anything classified as obscene, but François said the council would discuss exempting the doctors and nurses, as well as schools and libraries. He was confident that people could "tell what is bad and what is good. This is the kind of bill that requires a lot of common sense to administer."[29]

The bill came under attack by county librarians and teachers. Toby Rich, president of the Prince Georges.County Educators Association, said it amounted to bookburning. He explained that the county schools already had procedures by which to decide the books to be used by students, and the teachers objected to allowing the council to decree what materials may be used by the public.

Gordon recalls:

The first thing we were able to accomplish was a change to the bill, adding a clause excluding from the penalties any person operating or employed by any public or research library. We succeeded in adding that exclusion, but even then we opposed the bill. The legislation was eventually defeated, but it was not an easy process. We sent out information to some of the library's customers in an attempt to rally them around the issue and to write their legislators. Ms. Trotto's organization charged that we had used public money to oppose the county legislation. We had not, but we had failed to indicate on our fliers and informational materials that the items were being paid for with private money, not tax money. That created a great furor.

Gordon attended a hearing on the bill in the county council chambers, but he told me:

I did not testify against the bill at that hearing. Our interests were so vested, we believed at that point that testimony from me, or from a library board member for that matter, would not be as effective as testimony from residents of the community. We had solicited testimony from people who were informal friends of the library, people whom we knew were library users. Only four of them were allowed to testify, but when the chairman of the County Council asked for a show of hands from the audience, many people raised their hands against the bill. On the other side, all who spoke in support of the bill were from Beth Trotto's group, and they probably did as much to damage their case as anything. They proclaimed that God had spoken to them and told them to testify. One woman had seen a vision while she was eating her oatmeal, telling her that she should testify. But Beth Trotto was very articulate and effective. She was absolutely superb, and frankly that gave us some concern.

Fortunately, the anti-pornography bill was defeated in its entirety, amendments and all. The struggle had gone on for about a year and a half, and eventually the bookbanners simply wore out. The defeat of the legislation was really the benchmark of when their activity dramatically began to decline. Mrs. Trotto did not go away. She took up other campaigns dealing with censorship. She hassled the board of education over similar censorship issues for a very long time afterwards, and appeared regularly at the board's media center, complaining about school materials. But after the legislation was defeated, even she pulled back from the harassment of public libraries. She regarded me as a problem and knew that I was in some respects vulnerable, because I had only been Director here since April 1977. I had not really developed the kind of base that one needs to respond quickly and effectively to censorship pressure. During that period, Winfield Kelly was the County Executive, and he held regular Town Meetings throughout Prince Georges County. Mrs. Trotto's group would appear at every one of those meetings for more than a year, and they would lay on each seat copies of excerpts from *Our Bodies, Ourselves.* The excerpts were chosen, as you can imagine, such that the audience would become very upset.

I asked Gordon if he had changed any of the library's policies as the result of this extended bookbanning incident. "No, we didn't," he said.

We already had in place, and still do, a policy that some libraries may not agree with. That is, we have a parental consent clause on our library card, authorizing children to have access to all of our collections. The parent has to be proactive in the process of acquiring a child's library card. The child's card is valid anywhere in the library, unless the parent takes action to restrict it. We believe that parents want some supervision over what their children view or read. Of course, we also have a book selection policy. That's critical for institutional buying. We feel censorship should not play a role in selection, but there is a fine line between censorship and selection in the minds of many, because choices must be made. Choosing between book A and book B can be terribly difficult, particularly on a tight budget. But we believe when we choose not to buy a book, it's because it does not meet the standards established in our selection policy.

I asked Gordon what kind of bureaucratic pressure a public library director feels from within the system when community pressure groups attempt to impose censorship. "I report to a library board," said Gordon.

Whatever actions we take have to be justified to the board, which can function as a voice for the community. We didn't have any trouble with the library board during the controversy with Mrs. Trotto. They were very supportive, and that was very important to us. The kind of people who apply to be members of the library board tend to have an understanding of the issue of censorship. I never felt caught in the middle, never felt pressure there. The next level above is the County Council and the County Executive, the legislative and executive branches of the county government. They made no demands on the library to remove the challenged materials. What they really wanted was for this problem to simply *go away*. It was an election year and people were running for office, and they did not want a library book that talks about female masturbation to be the pivotal point on which their success as candidates would rest. So I was expected to make this thing go away, however that might be accomplished. If that meant taking the book off the shelf, so be it. Of course, none of them came out in favor of censorship.

But what are the appropriate limits of community control over the collections in public libraries? To what degree are public librarians simply agents of the community, responsive to the most strident, often censorial, voices in the community? Gordon said:

Libraries, particularly of this size, do not bend very easily to these strident demands. We are more likely to fight the necessary battle. I've been in smaller settings where we have dealt with vaguely similar situations, but none where the group was so well organized. I don't believe that public libraries give in to the demands of the censors, but the director becomes involved in a kind of political whirlwind that has to be played out very carefully. You've got to try to see that no elected official gets hurt or blamed. You've got to be sure that your board of trustees doesn't get hurt or blamed, and that your staff comes out feeling that, without bending, you have been supportive of them and at the same time you have somehow generally met the grievances of the community. Public librarians must still exercise professional discretion in these matters. I believe in a very strong exercise of professional judgment, but you certainly don't ignore the politics or demographics of the community. The demographics are important in collection development, but that does not mean that censorship is appropriate to collection development.

A decade and a half after the furor over *Our Bodies, Ourselves,* Bill Gordon assessed today's pressures for censorship in the Prince Georges County Public Library:

We continue to receive regular requests to review library materials, but the volume of such requests ebbs and flows. I have a very fat file of such requests that have come in during the past year, but we have not had an organized effort since the episode more than a decade ago. We have a regular trickle of complaints or challenges. Not a stream, but a trickle. So far we have been able to resolve them. The complaints that we are having a little more difficulty resolving are the ones concerning videos. People can get terribly excited about videos. With respect to books, the kind about which we now receive the greatest number of complaints are the books about witches and goblins and the like . . ., and we have lots of them. It seems the devil is lurking behind every bush and under every stone.

HAWKINS COUNTY, TENNESSEE: MY WAY OR THE HIGHWAY

The 1983 edition of the *Basic Reading* series, published by Holt, Rinehart and Winston for use in grades K through 8, differed very little in content from the previous editions, but it used a new approach, teaching reading, writing, spelling, and language as a unified language arts program. In late 1982, Tennessee's State Textbook Committee, consisting of five elementary school teachers and five middle school teachers, had formally recommended the 1983 edition of the Holt series to the Hawkins County School Board for adoption at the beginning of the following year. The new Holt readers replaced eleven-year-old readers.

In late August 1983, Vicki Frost's oldest daughter asked for her mother's help in answering questions at the end of a story in the Holt series. Mrs. Frost noticed mention of mental telepathy, which she considered contrary to her religious beliefs. To Frost, a devout fundamentalist, such mental powers belong to God alone, and attempting to share them suggests that man is aspiring to rule the world apart from God. Indeed, Frost regarded any use of fantasy or imagination as a temptation that could lead a Christian away from biblical truths. Frost was also concerned that any communication without language barriers could contaminate Americans with foreign ideas or, even worse, lead to global unity, one-world government, and the end of the free enterprise system and America's prosperity.

Frost examined the other textbooks used by her children in the first, second, and seventh grades and concluded that none of these Holt readers fostered American Christian values like patriotism and the American family. She was disturbed that the books spoke of minorities, foreigners, environmentalism, and women in nontraditional roles.

Soon afterward, she contacted Bill Snodgrass, the county school supervisor, who suggested that perhaps the offending stories could be excised, but Frost did not consider that an acceptable solution. She called Jay Salley, principal at the Church Hill Middle School, and requested a meeting with interested parents, teachers, and school officials to air her concerns. That meeting, held on September 1, 1983, was the first public discussion of the dispute, at which Frost and others warned of an educational conspiracy, beginning with John Dewey, that was destroying the parents' role in raising their children. In particular, Frost charged that the Holt readers were promoting idolatry, demon worship, gun control, evolution, and feminism while opposing free enterprise, the military, lawful authority, and Christianity.

About a week later, Frost called Mel Gabler, the famous textbook protest leader based in Longview, Texas. Soon the Hawkins County parents were receiving literature from the Gablers indicating that the Holt series had not been approved by the Gablers' organization. The Gablers' *Parental Guide to Combat the Religion of Secular Humanism in the Schools* warned: "As long as the schools continue to teach ABNORMAL ATTITUDES and ALIEN THOUGHTS, we caution parents NOT to urge their children to pursue high grades or class discussion, because the harder students work, the greater their chance of brain washing."[30] These organizational materials were subsequently shared with school officials and others in Hawkins County, giving the impression that the local protest was in fact under the influence and direction of the Gablers.

Early in the textbook dispute, Vicki Frost was the chief spokesperson for the complaining parents. She identified herself as "born-again" and a "fundamentalist Christian," explaining that her faith extended beyond her home and church into the school. Frost and other protesting parents officially presented their objections at the September 8, 1983, meeting of the school board, which had unanimously adopted the Holt series four months earlier. Now the board heard claims that the texts taught telepathy, witchcraft, black magic, sorcery, astrology, Hinduism, and Shintoism. The charge was also made that the Holt series taught children to use mind control over their parents. Mrs. Frost asked that the books be removed and replaced with texts that do not teach these concepts and religions. The discussion was concluded when board chairman Harold Silvers stated that since the Holt series had been selected by a committee of teachers and unanimously approved by the board, it would be taught in Hawkins County schools until either the State Department of Education or the courts prohibited it.

After failing to convince the school board to ban the Holt readers, Frost went to see Jay Salley, principal of Church Hill Middle School, where two of her children were students. As the result of that meeting, Frost and several other parents were allowed to use alternate readers acceptable to them. These alternative reading arrangements may have seemed like a reasonable compromise, but they conflicted with the state's obligation to teach reading effectively. For one thing, the alternative readers were twenty-five years old, providing a very narrow and dated glimpse of American culture. In addition, the children using these readers were from different grades and had their reading classes at different times. They spent their time in isolation, reading stories and answering assigned questions. These children were supervised by any adult who happened to be in the area, including cafeteria workers. But their parents were satisfied as long as their children did not read the Holt books.

On September 22, 1983, the *Rogersville Review* printed a large advertisement stating the religious and social beliefs of an organization identified as Citizens Organized for Better Schools (COBS). Local citizen Bob Mozert was soon revealed to be the director of COBS, and under that title, Mozert began submitting "Letters to the Editor" each week. In these letters, he "reviewed" various volumes from the Holt series, claiming that his reviews would better inform the taxpayers and parents in the area about the corruption of public education. In the October 6 issue, a letter appeared as part of Mozert's review series, complaining about *The Three Little Pigs* and *Goldilocks,* as presented in the Holt readers. In that letter, Mozert complained that punishment was meted out in *The Three Little Pigs* without a crime being committed. Even worse, in *Goldilocks* the little girl commits the crime of trespassing on the private property of the three bears, yet she is not punished. This, claimed Mozert, was a deliberate attempt to preach "secular humanism" to impressionable minds.

As the result of the Goldilocks letter, the fundamentalist parents became the target of considerable public ridicule. In a letter to the *Kingsport Times-News*, the principal of the Valley Elementary School mocked the parents' objections to "Satan-oriented" stories such as *The Three Little Pigs* and *Goldilocks.*

By now the national media had discovered the Hawkins County dispute. A *USA Today* editorial began, "Goldilocks is on trial in Greenville, Tennessee. So are the three little pigs, Jack and Jill, and a little boy who cooks. . . . What have they got against Goldilocks? Well, she didn't go to the slammer for breaking and entering. What's wrong with *The Three Little Pigs?* Well, dancing around a kettle promotes witchcraft. And the jollity of Jack and Jill suggests satanism, and the lad who cooks advances feminism. That's so ridiculous it's hard to take seriously."[31]

County School Superintendent Bill Snodgrass complained that "narrow thinking" was tearing up a good school system. "I think they are too far right of center for Hawkins County people," he said. "Most of the people here are moderate conservatives. I don't think you're going to turn Hawkins County folks against the three pigs and the three bears."[32]

In a letter to a local newspaper, Mozert defined *secular humanism* as a "lethal religion" that denies God and morality by endorsing evolution, self-authority, situation ethics, distorted realism, sexual permissiveness, antibiblical bias, anti–free enterprise, one-world government, and death education. Mozert presented new demands at the October 13 school board meeting, including a mandatory moment of silence in the schools, a mandatory Pledge of Allegiance, and a dress code. The board took the demands under advisement and formed a committee to look into them. At the November 10 school board meeting, the board declared that teachers must use only textbooks approved by the board of education, ruling out any future assignment of alternative reading materials. Board members expressed the belief that anything other than a uniform textbook would place an undue burden on the schools, their teachers, and students. Jay Salley, principal of the local middle school, then met with the protesting parents and made clear that no student would be allowed to use any reader other than the Holt series. The next day, several students were suspended from school for three days when they refused to attend reading class or read the Holt books. Upon their return to school, the students still refused to use the Holt readers, and Salley suspended them for another ten days.

Vicki Frost had planned to take over her daughter Sarah's elementary school reading instruction by removing her child from class each day and taking her to another part of the school building. Principal Jean Price told Frost that she was not allowed to teach reading on school property, but Frost nonetheless went to Sarah's reading class, removed her, and took her to the school cafeteria. When Price once more told Frost that she would have to leave the premises, the mother and daughter simply relocated outside the building but still on school property. When Frost returned the next day, she was ordered to leave the school grounds. When she refused, a police officer read her the trespassing law and took her into custody. Frost was subsequently released on her own recognizance but was told to stay away from the school until this matter came up for trial.

Around this same time, conservative religious groups nationwide were complaining that Supreme Court decisions had introduced secularism and humanism into the schools, threatening the social values associated with religious faith. Moral Majority cofounder Tim LaHaye charged that the public schools had exposed American youth to atheism, evolution, amorality, human autonomy, and a socialist one-world concept. LaHaye's wife Beverly, who headed Concerned Women for America (CWA), not only played a significant role in the Hawkins County textbook controversy but simultaneously initiated a federal lawsuit—*Grove v. Mead School District No. 354* (1985)—over a similar textbook controversy in Washington State (see Chapter 2). The district court dismissed the case, and the dismissal was upheld on appeal, largely because the child had not been compelled to read the disputed book. Because the Hawkins County schools *were* requiring students to use the Holt readers, CWA had high hopes for victory in *Mozert v. Hawkins County Board of Education* (1987).

In her book *Who But a Woman,* Beverly LaHaye warned: "The days are evil, but you and I can stand for righteousness against the oncoming darkness. . . . [W]e have no other alternative but to wage warfare against those who would destroy our children, our families, our religious liberties." LaHaye claimed that the humanists in public schools were "going to do everything they can to preserve the grim stranglehold they have on our children. They are the priests of religious humanism and are evangelizing our children for Satan."[33]

Hawkins County resident David Wilson was a typical spokesperson for the local opponents of the Holt books.

> [T]he textbooks promote equal rights for women. . . . They promote peaceful coexistence between nations. . . . They are pro-gun control. . . . [T]hose are some of the social values that are promoted in the textbooks. And those values are not values that are held by Hawkins Countians. . . . Religious values involved in the textbooks promote a[n] understanding of other people involved in other religious beliefs from other cultures. . . . But when it comes to Baptists accepting the religious beliefs of Islamic people or Buddhists, that is beyond the value system of rural East Tennessee.[34]

But a large majority of Hawkins County residents supported the school board and its choice of the textbook series. Hawkins County is overwhelmingly white, native Tennessean, conservative Republican, and strongly Baptist. The teachers, school administrators, and members of the school board were seen as trustees of the local culture. One mother wrote to the *Kingsport Times-News,* saying she had read the Holt books and found nothing that was humanistic, feminist, or self-authoritative. Branding COBS as a bunch of fanatical troublemakers, she told them that if they didn't like the local public schools, they should take their children out and go elsewhere. She concluded by warning COBS to keep their fanatical beliefs within their own group and stay out of her children's education.

School board member Conley Bailey had a similar view: "I think that COBS is trying to dictate education regardless of textbooks or anything else. If textbooks were not the issue, they'd bring up something else." He claimed, "Every tactic they've used so far has come out of Longview, Texas."[35]

On December 2, Jean Price sent a letter to the parents of all children at her school, asking them to attend a meeting to counter the COBS demands. In her letter, Price said: "As principal of your school and a mother, I now feel that we must stand for your child's rights. It is not appropriate for a few local people controlled by outside sources to try to impose their beliefs on all, and be allowed to disrupt the education of our boys and girls in Church Hill."[36] Price also announced the formation of a support organization, Citizens Advocating the Right to Education (CARE), which was to become the voice for the anticensors against COBS. CARE distributed a written declaration opposing the disruptive tactics of COBS and the censorship attempts of a fanatical minority.

Almost 1,000 people met at the December 1983 CARE rally. Speakers included Jean Price, School Board Chairman Harold Silvers, and School Superintendent Bill Snodgrass, who gave a fiery speech characterizing the protesters as extremists, outsiders, and a threat to local institutions. Snodgrass said:

> My message to extremists groups is to become a carpenter and help us build a great school system. If you cannot do this and insist on being a wrecking crew, take your unsound ideas to Washington, D.C. . . . or Longview, Texas. The right to have challenging and interesting material must not be taken away by outside agitators with their fat wallets and attorneys from Washington, D.C.[37]

On December 2, 1983, Robert and Alice Mozert, represented by the national conservative organization CWA, filed suit in federal district court seeking injunctive relief and money damages for the alleged violation of their First Amendment right to free exercise of religion. Mozert, Frost, and the others claimed that the Holt series violated their religious beliefs, promoted the breakdown of the family and the denial of the primacy of Christ, and advocated a one-world government.

Mozert v. Hawkins County Board of Education (1987) was assigned to Federal District Judge Thomas G. Hull and was heard without a jury. Although the protesters had originally attempted to remove the Holt books totally from the public schools, the plaintiffs now chose to focus on the need for alternative readers for their children. In February and March of 1984, Judge Hull dismissed eight of the plaintiffs' nine complaints, including allegations that the Holt readers promoted disrespect for parents, the Bible, and Jesus Christ, and that it advocated witchcraft, situational ethics, idol worship, humanistic values, and evolution. The one complaint that Hull said should be examined in court was the claim that the Holt books teach that any faith in the supernatural is an acceptable means to salvation.

In their replies to Judge Hull's ruling, the plaintiffs insisted that mere exposure to the ideas in the Holt books was a violation of their First Amendment rights, whereas the school authorities argued that leaving children ignorant of and hostile to any ideas outside of a single religious group was not proper education. After reading the briefs submitted by CWA and PAW, Judge Hull dismissed the case without trial, saying the Holt books presented religion in a "neutral" manner and were well calculated to equip today's children to face our diverse society with sophistication and tolerance. The plaintiffs immediately appealed, and in July 1985, the Sixth Circuit Court of Appeals ordered Judge Hull to try the case. The appeals court instructed Hull to determine whether the mandatory use of the Holt books violated the plaintiffs' religious rights and, if so, whether there was any compelling state interest to justify that burden. Accordingly, the plaintiffs tried to convince Judge Hull that the Holt readers promoted the religion of secular humanism and that reading the books violated their own religion.

In their pretrial depositions the plaintiffs presented more than 400 objections to the Holt readers, many of them relating to the books' inadequate patriotism. Any criticism of America's founders, its policies, or its history would allegedly offend God and promote a communist invasion by discouraging young boys from fighting for their country. According to the plaintiffs, war was God's way of vindicating the righteous and punishing the wicked. The protesters regarded kindness to animals as another form of support for diversity, which could lead to religious tolerance, world unity, the reign of the anti-Christ, and the destruction of the world. An empathy toward animals could also soften children, discouraging hunting, war, and violence in general.

The plaintiffs attacked everything in the Holt readers that could conceivably relate to world unity, nontraditional gender roles, family democracy, moral relativity, the brotherhood of man, nonreligious views of death, imagination, reason, neutral descriptions of religion, socialism, social protest, magic, environmentalism, kindness toward animals, vegetarianism, fear of nuclear war, disarmament, or gun control. They did not want Hispanics to be mentioned in schoolbooks because most Hispanics are Catholic and Catholics are not real Christians. They opposed stories that discussed poverty or social justice, claiming that the poor and unemployed were simply lazy. They challenged *The Wizard of Oz* because it promoted self-reliance and personal responsibility. The Lion wanted courage, the Tin Man wanted a heart, and the Scarecrow wanted brains, but none of them prayed to God. *The Wizard of Oz* thus promoted secular humanism by suggesting that goodness and salvation can be acquired through human effort. It also promoted Satanism by showing the good witch Glenda.

The school board rebutted such arguments and noted that the state had a compelling interest to teach children to read, to uphold the authority of school officials, and to avoid the expense of alternative reading programs. The school authorities noted that the Supreme Court had repeatedly ruled that public education cannot function in a pluralistic society if it must avoid all information and ideas that might be offensive to any religion.

On October 24, 1986, to the surprise of all who followed the case, Judge Hull ruled in favor of the plaintiffs, focusing on their demand that they not be forced to choose between their religious beliefs and a free public education. He ruled that the state's obligation to teach children to read did not require that all children read the same books. He therefore ruled that the plaintiffs could teach reading to their children at home, while their children would continue to participate in the rest of the school curriculum. Hull did caution that his ruling did not require the school system to make alternative reading arrangements to any other persons or to these plaintiffs for any other subject. By this time the children who were involved in the suit had transferred to private schools, where they intended to remain, and Hull ruled that the plaintiffs were entitled to reimbursement for that expense and for lost wages during the trial.

The school board promptly appealed Hull's decision, claiming that home schooling would encourage religious divisiveness. They also questioned whether Hull's ruling could be restricted to one school subject and one group of parents. On August 24, 1987, the Sixth Circuit Court of Appeals overturned Hull's ruling by a 3-to-0 vote, with each judge addressing a different aspect of the case. Writing for the court, Judge Pierce Lively stated:

> The only conduct compelled by the defendants was reading and discussing the material in the Holt series, and hearing other students' interpretations of those materials. This is the exposure to which the plaintiffs objected. What is absent from this case is the critical element of compulsion to affirm or deny a religious belief or to engage or refrain from engaging in a practice forbidden or required in the exercise of a plaintiff's religion.

Lively rejected the claim that certain ideas were being inculcated rather than simply being mentioned in the books. He stated: "The plaintiffs did not produce a single student or teacher to testify that any student was ever required to affirm his or her belief or disbelief in any idea or practice mentioned in the various stories and passages contained in the Holt series."[38] Lively concluded that the plaintiffs' definition of religion was too broad to be accommodated within the public schools.

Judge Cornelia Kennedy agreed with Lively that reading the Holt books did not violate the plaintiffs' religious rights, but she said, in any case, there was an overriding state interest in teaching children to draw conclusions, express opinions, and deal with complex and controversial social and moral issues. Kennedy also said the state had a compelling interest in promoting cohesion among a heterogeneous democratic people, something that could not be accomplished through religious segregation. The third member of the appeals court panel, Judge Danny Boggs, accepted the board's overriding authority to forbid the use of alternative readers, basing his ruling entirely on a school board's right to control the curriculum.

The appeals court's reversal of Judge Hull's ruling dismissed the plaintiffs' complaint, leaving the Hawkins County School Board free to forbid alternative reading instruction and removing any obligation to compensate the protesters. On December 5, 1988, the U.S. Supreme Court denied certiorari on the last of Mozert's two appeals, effectively ending the attempt to ban the Holt readers. The plaintiffs petitioned the Supreme Court to hear the case, but their petition was denied.

On the surface, *Mozert* represented a defeat for fundamentalist attempts to censor textbooks, but on closer view, the repercussions of the case are disturbing. Keith Waldman in the *Rutgers Law Journal* compared the 1983 and 1986 editions of the Holt books and found that passages opposed by the *Mozert* plaintiffs had been removed from the 1986 edition. For example, a reference to the humanistic ideals of the Declaration of Independence was no longer in the 1986 edition. In her book *What Johnny Shouldn't Read*, Joan DelFattore observed:

> If the *Mozert* plaintiffs' children attend public school, they now have to read the books school officials select. School officials, however, have to choose from what is on the market; . . . Since the textbooks produced by America's largest publishers were more in keeping with the Gablers' beliefs in 1986 than they were in 1980, it is not at all clear that the *Mozert* plaintiffs were on the losing side.[39]

GRAVES COUNTY: KENTUCKY-FRIED FAULKNER

Graves County, Kentucky, four hours from Louisville, has a population of about 30,000 people. A third of them live in Mayfield, the county seat, where the county school board administers a single school, the Graves County High School. In late August 1986, sixteen-year-old Chris Hill returned from school and told his mother that he was being asked to read a book on reincarnation. The boy's mother, LaDone Hill, read the book, William Faulkner's *As I Lay Dying,* and concluded that it was an example of "secular humanism." At first, Mrs. Hill accepted the school's offer to assign a different book, *Moby Dick,* to her son, but after deciding that the other students required protection from Faulkner's dangerous novel, she complained to school board member Johnny Shelton.

In early September 1986, as the Graves County School Board was concluding its regular monthly meeting, Chairman Jeff Howard asked if there was any other business. Board member Johnny Shelton held up a paperback copy of *As I Lay Dying* and demanded to know why it was being taught at Graves County High School. In addition to the five board members, the boardroom contained Superintendent of Schools Billy Watkins, school board attorney Dan Sharp, high school principal Jerald Ellington, several local media representatives, and a few spectators. They watched as Shelton waved a copy of William Faulkner's *As I Lay Dying,* pointing to passages that he had highlighted with a yellow marker.

"This is the kind of book you'd pick up in a backways place and read," said Shelton. He held the book in front of Jerald Ellington, the principal of Graves County High School, and demanded that he read some of the underlined passages out loud. Principal Ellington tried to decline, but Shelton insisted. Finally Ellington took the book, and turned to one of the highlighted passages. He read aloud from the words of one of Faulkner's characters, the son of a dying woman: "If there is a God, what the hell is he for?" Ellington continued to leaf through the book, reading aloud any passage marked in yellow. Some of the passages referred to God, or to abortion, and some used curse words like *bastard, goddamn,* or *son of a bitch.* Ellington found nothing wrong in Faulkner's words when he read them aloud. He told the board that his teachers did not necessarily condone some of the language in the book but that it had to be seen in the context of the character's personality. Ellington also explained to the board how the high school selected its books, following the recommendations of the American Library Association. But the board was disdainful of such niceties.[40]

The meeting room was suddenly alive with tension. Principal Ellington realized that by reading the passages aloud he had ignited the emotions of the board members. He tried to defuse the situation by explaining that a review procedure existed that allowed administrators and parents to express their opinions and, if necessary, appeal to the superintendent and the board of education. And parents always had the right to request that a different book be assigned to their children. Ellington warned that none of this procedure had been followed in this case and the board was therefore encroaching on First Amendment rights. The board was unimpressed. Bob Spaulding declared that it was wrong to ban the sale of "pornography" while teaching it in the schools. Another board member, ignoring Ellington's caution, stood up, pointed his finger at the principal, and demanded that the book be removed from the shelves by the next day. A motion was made that William Faulkner's *As I Lay Dying* be banned from the Graves County High School. The board voted unanimously in favor of the motion, the meeting was adjourned, and Ellington subsequently had the book removed from the school and its library.

None of the board members had read the book, though a few said they had thumbed through it. Dan Sharp, the school board attorney, estimates that the school board's discussion of Faulkner's book lasted about five minutes.

> The board member who brought this up very definitely caught everyone by surprise. He said, "I want it banned, I want it out of this school, trash and filth, let's have a vote on it." Without much discussion at all, the motion was passed unanimously, and I was kind of scratching my head about it. It happened so fast I'm not sure everyone realized the significance.[41]

Lonnie Harp, a reporter for the local *Mayfield Messenger,* was also present at the board meeting, and he recalls that there was no discussion of the merits of the book or why it was used in the high school. The board's vote was taken so fast that the reporters present were not sure what had occurred. Harp examined John Shelton's copy of the book and wrote down the seven or eight passages highlighted in yellow ink, all of them dialogue. Harp recalls, "At that point we—the radio reporters and I—said to ourselves, *They've just banned a book!* We knew it would be big news."[42]

On the morning after the board's vote, the Mayfield radio station, whose reporters had attended the board meeting, opened its seven o'clock news show with a description of the bookbanning. The story was repeated on the local news each hour thereafter, and it soon was carried nationally on the Associated Press (AP) wire.

Mike Turley, editor of the *Mayfield Messenger,* said the school board's action caught him by surprise. He ran the story on the bookbanning the next day, no larger than a normal school board story would be, but he led with the headline "County Bans Faulkner Book." When reporter Lonnie Harp began work on his story of the bookbanning, he telephoned Principal Ellington, who told him he was very disappointed that the board didn't follow "appropriate channels" in removing the book. Ellington pointed out, "A sentence or paragraph out of about every book in print can be taken out of context." Harp then called Delora English, the teacher in whose class *As I Lay Dying* had been assigned. English had been forced to retrieve all thirty-three copies of the book from her sophomore students. She defended the book, saying it was a fine example of "stream of consciousness" literature and something that her students should read. She concluded firmly that discussions on the book would begin in her class the following week.[43]

The bookbanning had a devastating effect on the teachers involved. The English Department consisted of twelve people, most of them Sunday school teachers and one of them a minister. Delora English, the teacher most directly involved in the book dispute, took it personally when the chairman of the school board criticized her judgment in using *As I Lay Dying*. The entire department felt abandoned by the school board. Ellington said he felt caught in the middle as he tried to hold his faculty together. He met with them and told them that he supported them 100 percent and that he was not going to side with the board. School Superintendent Billy Watkins called Dan Sharp, the board's attorney, to express his concern and ask for advice. Sharp told him that there were First Amendment questions involved, matters of free speech and censorship that could become embarrassing.

Johnny Shelton, the board member who had proposed the book ban, held to his position. "The book may be literature, but there's some literature you use on the street about midnight," said Shelton. "We don't allow students to use that language in school and then we give them that stuff to read."[44] A reporter from the *Paducah Sun* called school board chairman Jeff Howard, who admitted that he had read "only portions" of the book and didn't know if other board members had read it. Still, he didn't think the book should be required reading. "God's name is used in vain in several places," he said. "In there, a young girl goes to a so-called doctor to get an abortion. . . . We had hoped the teacher would select a book more appropriate for the sophomore class." The *Paducah Sun* newsroom then called Bob Spaulding, who had seconded the motion to ban Faulkner's book. "There's a lot better literature for students to read than to learn how to curse," Spaulding said. He admitted he had not read *As I Lay Dying* but said his own daughter had been assigned the book the year before. "It just didn't make sense to her why she should have to study it," he said, describing his daughter's discomfort with both the language and content of the book. He added that none of his five children were allowed to read the book.[45]

When Suzanne Post, director of the Kentucky branch of the ACLU, heard of the Mayfield bookbanning, she commented, "This one is pretty extreme. We rarely get a Nobel prize winner thrown out of a public school."[46] Ironically, her major area of study in graduate school had been the work of William Faulkner. She told the *Paducah Sun* that the board's action was "certainly an infringement on academic freedom and probably is unconstitutional." Claiming that the board was "on some thin ice," she added, "I would hope that a school board would have more respect for issues that involve academic freedom."[47]

Elwin Abrams of the Kentucky Council of Teachers of English complained that the school board's decision allowed one parent to impose her tastes on all parents. He said the board had acted contrary to "what a free society should be doing. We should be exchanging ideas freely, not banning books."[48]

Two days after the school board vote, LaDone Hills wrote a letter to the *Mayfield Messenger*, identifying herself as the parent who had complained to John Shelton about *As I Lay Dying*. She wrote that her son did not want to read the book because of some of the words in it, and she said she was shocked by its contents. Principal Jerald Ellington had explained to her that her son would be allowed to read an alternative book, but she wanted to protect every child from this blasphemy. She said she wanted to remove *As I Lay Dying* because of her "concern for other students and to make other parents aware of the content of the material in this book and perhaps other books." LaDone Hills placed her full faith and confidence in the board members, characterizing their action as "the hand of God working in a few people." She asked, "Can we not stand without compromise not only regarding this, but also against other things which lower morals, weaken character and usher in secular humanism?"[49]

Simultaneously, more than 200 miles away, Suzanne Post of the ACLU was writing her letter to the Graves County School Board. Post's letter called the board's action unconstitutional, a violation of the First Amendment's guarantees of free expression. She said the board had followed improper procedures in removing the Faulkner book from the Graves County schools. After formally requesting that the school board rescind its action, she told the *Paducah Sun:*

> We are asking that they rescind their action, which we consider unconstitutional. We have had an outpouring of offers of free legal assistance from a number of well-established attorneys. People are angry about this. Our fear is that if one school district gets away with this, it will have a ripple effect—it will send a message to other thoughtless people.

She said she had sent a copy of the ACLU letter to school board attorney Dan Sharp, who admitted that the school board was "off base."[50]

As the battle escalated in the media, the executive committee of the Graves County Baptist Association held its regular monthly meeting and agreed to set forth in writing its support for the school board's action. Reverend Al Cobb was chosen to write the letter for the association. He had read *As I Lay Dying* and said it was dull, uninteresting, and unworthy of a Nobel Prize. The letter, addressed to the Graves County School Board, commended the board for removing *As I Lay Dying* from the libraries and concluded: "We urge you to continue to take measures which will safeguard our children from being forced to read and study filthy literature in the classroom."[51]

The editorial in the September 11 *Paducah Sun* began:

> Usually, when we comment on "book-banning" incidents, we take the side of the school board. . . . In the case of the Graves County school board's ban on the novel "As I Lay Dying," however, there's a sad difference. The board wasn't merely deciding not to include some writer's glitzy trash in its list of approved readings. It was denying its students the opportunity to read one of the milestone works of one of the finest writers America has produced. It has denied them, then, a part of their heritage.

The editorial concluded, "It's bewildering to see the book attacked by *a member of the school board* as pornographic. It suggests that the board not only doesn't know what literature is, but it doesn't know what pornography is."[52]

On the evening of September 11, 1986, the Graves County School Board met once more to determine the fate of *As I Lay Dying*. This time the meeting room was packed with spectators, including at least half a dozen Baptist ministers. When Chairman Jeff Howard called the meeting to order, he described the letters of support the board had received and read into the minutes the letter from the Graves County Baptist Association.

When the agenda reached the item titled "pending or proposed litigation," Chairman Jeff Howard announced that the meeting would now go into closed session. The room was quickly emptied of all but the five board members, Dan Sharp, and school administrators. Sharp immediately addressed the ACLU's letter and the threat of a lawsuit. He explained that by banning *As I Lay Dying* the school board had challenged the First Amendment. "You are clamping down on what people can read," he said. "You're interfering with the right to free expression." He read from Kentucky law books and demonstrated how other school boards had run afoul of the Constitution. "Unless you provide due process and right of appeal," he explained, "it's going to make trouble." One board member insisted that it was simply "our opinion against theirs." But Sharp replied, "I don't think the ACLU is kidding around. That book should go back on the shelves. All they need is one parent to come forward and agree to be the plaintiff."[53]

The board remained unconvinced. The closed session ended, and the crowd filed back into the meeting room. Superintendent Billy Wilkins then offered a compromise. He recommended that the teachers in the Language Arts Department review the books selected for use as assigned reading and that they consider replacing any book that would not serve the best interests of students. He also recommended that a seven-member review committee be established to consider any complaints about the books. Watkins said the committee, whose membership included two Parent-Teacher Organization (PTO) presidents, a counselor, a librarian, a minister, and two teachers, would first review the Faulkner book and report at the next regular board meeting. All five board members approved the recommendation.

The Graves High School English teachers met on Friday afternoon and decided to stand by their list of approved novels, including *As I Lay Dying*. "We felt we had spent many hours prior to the [board] meeting working on those novels and choosing what we thought were the best," said Alicia Brown, Language Arts Department chair. "We still feel the list intact is in the best interest of our students."[54] The next morning came the first sign that the board might be willing to compromise. Board member Andrew Goodman told a reporter that he expected the board would go along with whatever the review committee suggested. Even Board Chairman Jeff Howard said that the committee's recommendations would weigh heavily in the board's decision. Attorney Dan Sharp had recommended that the board establish the committee and return the book to the library. "It was not placed back," complained Sharp, who warned that the school board was "constitutionally vulnerable on the issue as it stands right now."[55]

Local preachers and church types were still anxious to get their moral position on the record. Baptist minister Terry Sims called the Faulkner book pornography. "As a parent, I wouldn't want my daughter reading this book," he said. "I feel like somewhere along the line people have to make a stand against this kind of thing." Minister Ronnie Stinson said, "It's something that if I caught my kid reading out of literature class, I would have to discipline him for it."[56]

Reporter Lonnie Harp described another Baptist preacher, "a moral-majority type," who claimed that he and some of the others saw the bookbanning as a way to step into the limelight and get in front on "the march for decency." Reverend Charles Simmons was particularly anxious to tell the press how distasteful he found *As I Lay Dying*. "If you hear that type of language, you would associate it with a rough, unruly group that is involved in a more worldly type of life than living a Christian life with the Lord. . . . Not only the Baptists but most all the religious groups would be against the blasphemy in the book where they take the name of the Lord in vain."[57]

But Bridges Holland, a junior high school teacher and minister, questioned whether removing books from the shelves wasn't an "infringement of a person's rights." He warned, "I think it is a very dangerous procedure, because who decides? Where do you draw the line? Are you going to pull out every Faulkner book? Is every book that has a cuss word in it going to be pulled off the shelf?"[58]

When the ACLU's Suzanne Post discovered that despite the board's conciliatory language *As I Lay Dying* remained banned from the school library shelves, she described the board's action as "illegitimate, mindless, anti-intellectual, authoritarian and extremely dangerous. . . . Rational people ought to be flying the flags at half mast for the Graves County board of education." Post said the board's action represented a "pre-fascist mindset—the kind of mind set that led to what the Nazis did in Germany."[59]

The *Lexington Herald-Leader* editorialized that the board's bookbanning was "an excuse in the kind of wanton logic that keeps so many Kentuckians from managing even the reading skills necessary for comic books."[60] Jim Paxton, editor of the *Paducah Sun,* wrote:

> [T]he action by the Graves board was ridiculous. It has already become state-wide news, and newspapers and editorial cartoonists are making a mockery of our region as a result of it. I predict that if the people of Graves County do not yank the board's chain soon, it's going to become national news and a national embarrassment for the state's educational system.[61]

A seventeen-year-old senior at the high school said that the school board wanted to prevent students from reading *As I Lay Dying,* but they would soon discover that the bookban produced the opposite effect. "It is idiotic. You can tell the guy [John Shelton] who proposed it isn't in school. If they tell us we can't read something, everybody is going to read it."[62] Indeed, almost overnight, area bookstores and libraries were deluged with requests. "It's unreal," said a clerk at a local bookstore. "We're getting probably about 20 [requests] a day. Everybody wants to read it and we are sold out."[63] The same heavy demand was seen in the local public libraries, where all copies of the book were on loan, with two or three requests each day.

Juanita Davis Elliott, a local resident, wrote to the Graves County Board of Education asking that the book be returned to the Graves County High School Library and curriculum. She warned that if the board did not lift its ban against *As I Lay Dying,* she would not rule out a suit against the board. "I want to handle it the right way," she explained. "But if they won't put it back, I'll take it from there." She called the bookbanning "an embarrassment," saying the board "reacted like a bunch of adolescent boys reading dirty words that had been printed on the outhouse wall."[64] Elliott added, "William Faulkner's book is not the main item here. The main item is that [the board members] are messing with our minds and our kids' minds. They are trying to control our minds. People got on boats and came over here a long time ago to get away from that."[65]

The school board decided to call a special meeting for the evening of September 18, 1986, at which time a "superintendents report" was to be presented. Once more, the meeting room was filled to overflowing. Chairman Jeff Howard opened by acknowledging Superintendent Billy Watkins, who began to read a prepared statement. After describing the school's book selection policy, Watkins recommended that the board's action to ban *As I Lay Dying* be rescinded. From the calm response of the board members it was clear that this recommendation had been discussed in advance of the meeting. Board member Andrew Goodman quickly moved that the recommendation be accepted. Robert Spaulding seconded the motion but explained that he had been advised to do so by Dan Sharp and Billy Watkins. He added that his second was not intended to endorse the use of books with foul language.

The board quickly voted 4 to 1 to rescind the banning of *As I Lay Dying*. Only Johnny Shelton voted to continue the ban, saying, "I still stand by what I said before. This hasn't changed my opinion."[66] After the vote, Chairman Jeff Howard read a prepared statement explaining the board's action and reassuring the audience and the media that he was still against indecent literature in schools. "We believed then as we believe now that books containing abusive language not be taught in our school system," stated Howard.

> However, since taking our actions we have been severely criticized by those who seem to feel that children may study any material available, so long as someone says it is valid or beneficial. The criticism does not bother us when we feel we are right. . . . Most significantly we have contacted constitutional lawyers throughout the state of Kentucky who tell us that our actions in excluding the book from our school were ill-advised. For this reason we have serious doubts as to successful litigation. . . . We therefore have made a motion rescinding our previous action taken on September 4 concerning the book "As I Lay Dying." We do feel, however, that our actions have brought attention to the books being taught in our schools. . . . We do believe that literature can be found which passes to our children all the ideas of Western Civilization that do not border on obscenity or in fact are obscene.[67]

The next day, *As I Lay Dying* was returned to the library shelves at Graves County High School, but LaDone Hill, the parent whose complaint initiated the ban, said the battle against the book would continue. "I'm not disappointed," she said, "but in my opinion the Graves County schools stand for better morals than this. I don't see it as being over; it's just starting. God has started moving and the book will come out."[68]

PANAMA CITY, FLORIDA: DARKNESS IN THE SUNSHINE STATE

One of the nation's more recent and disturbing bookbanning incidents occurred in Panama City, Florida, a beach town within what is called the "Redneck Riviera." Greater Panama City has a population of about 120,000, served by over 125 churches that advertise their healing powers in the Yellow Pages. This Bible Belt town has only grudgingly accepted the cosmopolitan influences of the local air force base, a navy research laboratory, several colleges, and a branch of the University of Florida. Panama City was to witness the familiar battle between religious fundamentalists, who wanted to teach children *what* to think, and teachers, who wanted to teach children *how* to think.

Gloria Pipkin was an eighth-grade English teacher in Panama City. When she first arrived at Mowat Junior High School, the English Department had the students spending most of their time identifying nouns and verbs in grammar workbooks, and the few textbooks that were used ignored all twentieth-century literature. Pipkin says the kids hated this arrangement, and so did the teachers. But then a new chairman of her English Department, Ed Deluzain, arrived from Florida State University (FSU), bringing with him new ideas for teaching English to kids, ideas that encouraged children to read and write, not just to learn grammar by rote. Gloria Pipkin and her friend ReLeah Hawks had heard of these teaching techniques, which utilized books that children actually enjoyed reading, including "young adult novels" written for and about adolescents. Soon all eleven teachers in the Mowat English Department were enthusiastically reading and discussing the novels.

In 1982, Gloria Pipkin became the chairman of the Mowat English Department, and under her leadership, the teachers introduced books by Mark Twain, George Orwell, Anne Frank, and Robert Cormier, while organizing paperback book swaps and book fairs at the school. The teachers created minilibraries within each classroom, purchased with their own money or income they earned from selling soft drinks at football games. Books from the classroom libraries were passed out to kids, allowing them to sample books at random and replace them as they wished. The students became excited over their reading, and they also began to write prolifically. The students in Pipkin's eighth-grade class even wrote and bound their own novels. In a countywide writing contest, Mowat students won all five first-place prizes, and eleven of fifteen prizes overall. Mowat ninth-graders soon achieved twelfth-grade reading comprehension, vocabulary, and grammar, well ahead of students at any other junior high school in the county. In 1985, the National Council of Teachers of English designated the Mowat English Department a "Center of Excellence," 1 of only 150 secondary schools in the United States and Canada to be so designated, and the only one in Florida.

Then the censors descended. In 1985, Marian Collins, grandmother of a Mowat Junior High School student, wrote to Bay County School Superintendent Leonard Hall, complaining that the novel *I Am the Cheese*, by Robert Cormier, contained vulgar language and advocated humanism and behaviorism. *I Am the Cheese* tells the story of a teenage boy whose family is put in a witness protection program after his father testifies against members of the Mafia. The book had been named as one of the best young adult books of 1977 by *Newsweek,* the *New York Times,* and *School Library Journal.* Hall immediately ordered Mowat principal Joel Creel to ban the book. Two months after Collins's original letter to Hall, she wrote again, complaining that *I Am the Cheese* was still being used at Mowat. She also wrote Principal Creel, asking why he had not complied with the superintendent's order to remove the book. Collins's daughter, Claudia Shumaker, then joined her mother's censorship campaign, and now mother, daughter, and granddaughter were in the fray. The Shumakers objected to the book's occasional profanity and the "subversive" suggestion that government agents could be involved in a murder plot.

Soon a few other parents began complaining about vulgarity in some of the books their children had acquired from the book fairs or borrowed from the classroom libraries. During the summer of 1985, the Mowat teachers did their best to accommodate them without altering the curriculum or their classroom libraries. They met regularly with concerned parents to explain their programs. They encouraged students whose parents objected to a book used in class to choose an alternative book. Also, written parental permission was required before any student could attend a book fair or read challenged books. But none of this could placate Claudia and Robert Shumaker, whose daughter was in ReLeah Hawks's English class. When they saw the classroom, with books lining the walls, they were dismayed. "It's like walking into a B Dalton with desks," complained Claudia Shumaker, who described some of the books as "immoral" and "blasphemous."[69] She said she didn't allow her children to see any movie they wished, so why should she have them exposed to books they shouldn't see?

The previous April, when ReLeah Hawks had assigned *I Am the Cheese* to her class, she sent a letter to parents, warning that the book was "difficult" and asking permission for their children to read it. If they disapproved of the book, an appropriate alternative would be assigned. When all parental responses were received, eighty-eight parents gave permission, and four, counting the Shumakers, rejected the book. Teacher Hawks saw the vote as an endorsement of Cormier's novel, and she anticipated no difficulty in assigning alternative reading for the other four students. Later she reflected, "How could I know that this was the first step in a long and terrible process that would lead to full-scale censorship and the virtual dismantling of our program?"[70]

The Shumakers were not willing to accept alternative books. They claimed that if their daughter read an alternative book, she would be ostracized. Therefore, on the advice of Superintendent Hall, Claudia Shumaker filed an official complaint against *I Am the Cheese* and another novel used at Mowat, Susan Pfeffer's *About David*. Creel immediately withdrew both books from use in all schools in the county, pending judgment by a review committee.

The teachers felt personally offended. "There was a lot of hurt and a lot of rage too," recalls teacher Sue Harrell.[71] ReLeah Hawks had to tell four classes that they couldn't read the book she had been touting all year. Gloria Pipkin warned, "If they take our books away and start giving us the books they want, then the kids won't read. We want to make them literate, life-long readers. We're co-learners. We're participating with the kids in the process of reading and writing."[72] But Pipkin was not discouraged. "I was really pleased," she says. "At last it was in the open, and there was a forum where it could be heard and we could respond."

In her formal challenge to *I Am the Cheese*, Claudia Shumaker stated that "the theme of the book is morbid and depressing. The language of the book is crude and vulgar. The sexual descriptions and suggestions are extremely inappropriate. Our children's minds are being warped and filled with unwholesome attitudes by reading worthless materials." She attached photocopies of offending passages containing words like *hell, shit, fart*, and *goddamn*. Her challenge to *About David*, a book about teenage suicide, said the subject should be handled through prayer at home, rather than in school. She added, "If the teaching of Christian morals and code of decency is illegal in the school system, then the teaching of the Humanist religion's code of immorality is also illegal."[73]

By the time the District Review Committee, composed of administrators, teachers, and parents, got around to judging *I Am the Cheese*, several Mowat English teachers had drafted a six-page rebuttal to Shumaker's challenge, signed by ten of the eleven members of the department. The rebuttal acknowledged that it was the right of parents to decide what their child may or may not read and that students were therefore free to choose an alternative to *I Am the Cheese*.

On May 20, 1986, the review committee issued its report, describing *I Am the Cheese* as a high-interest young adult novel that encourages reading, critical thinking, and class discussion. The committee recommended that the use of *I Am the Cheese* be continued with young adults. But the final judgment was left in the hands of Bay County School Superintendent Leonard Hall, who was in no hurry to make a difficult decision. He allowed the school year to pass without action on the challenge, thus effectively keeping *I Am the Cheese* out of the classrooms.

Even so, Charles Collins, Claudia Shumaker's father, was enraged over the recommendations of the review committee. Collins, a wealthy beach-front developer and former school board member, called the novels used in the Mowat schools "trashy" and "obscene," recommending instead the Nancy Drew mysteries and the Bobbsey Twins books. He regarded Mowat's book fairs and classroom libraries as part of the humanist conspiracy to take over American education. After the review committee recommended retention of *I Am the Cheese,* Collins stepped up his attacks on Mowat's schools, taking out a large ad in the local newspaper that began: "Your child's textbooks—Have you read them?" The ad printed a few excerpts from *I Am the Cheese* and another Cormier novel, *The Chocolate War,* and concluded by saying, "If you believe these books should be banned, mail in the attached coupon." School officials were quickly inundated with letters and phone calls.[74]

In a newspaper interview, Collins complained: "There's no respect in this county any more. You cannot go down the halls of the high schools and junior highs without hearing the dirtiest language you ever heard in your life. I believe these filthy little books are the cause."[75]

The Mowat teachers responded by calling a meeting on May 27, 1986, inviting all students, teachers, and parents. On the morning of the meeting, Superintendent Hall stormed into the Mowat English Department, accusing the teachers of inflaming the students. Hall told the teachers not to discuss the First Amendment with their students and not to answer any student questions on the book controversy. He then ordered the teachers to tell the students not to attend the meeting. "The issue is a parental issue," said Hall. "It is not a student issue. I think the parent should speak for his or her child. . . . We feel like they're at an impressionable age. They're not mature enough to recognize that the books are an invasion of their rights to have literature that is not full of obscenities in the classroom."[76] The meeting was attended by nearly 300 parents and an unexpected TV crew. There were some protesters present, but two thirds of the speakers expressed support for the school's English program. Many parents thanked the teachers for inspiring their children to read. One father told the crowd, "A strange thing has happened to my son since he's been going to Mowat. I've caught him reading. Sometimes on weekends. I also caught him writing a letter to his grandmother without my telling him to do it."[77] After the meeting, the teachers were optimistic, but they had no way of knowing what was in store for them.

On June 5, 1986, as summer vacation began, Hall announced that despite the review committee's recommendation to accept *I Am the Cheese* the book could not be used in Bay County schools, nor could any other material not specifically approved by the board be used in the future. Hall's announcement began with the statement that the school district would not use instructional materials that contain vulgar, obscene, or sexually explicit material. His proposal specifically required that all materials not formally adopted by the state be approved by the school superintendent and the principal before use in the schools. Even after approval, a challenged book would automatically be withdrawn from use until a series of review boards had decided its fate.

The edict not only banned the Cormier novel but eliminated virtually every book that had been used during the past year, as well as all classroom libraries. Even literary classics that had been taught for years were excluded under the new policy. All that remained for classroom use were a few old English textbooks. Many teachers were left with no books that could legally be used. ReLeah Hawks recalls: "Eleven dumbfounded, award-winning English teachers sat listening to our Superintendent tell us our program no longer existed. There was an overpowering feeling of helplessness as we realized that everything not on the state-adopted textbook list was being banned."[78]

In opposition to Hall's proposal, Gloria Pipkin organized a group of teachers, librarians, and book lovers calling themselves CHOICE (Citizens Having Options in Our Children's Education). To Pipkin, the forces recruited by Collins were fighting the concept of critical thinking. "They want kids to read well enough to follow directions and write well enough to take dictation," she said.[79] On the other side, Charles Collins began working full-time with church women circulating petitions against "obscene books."

On a hot August evening in 1986, the school board met to consider Hall's proposal and make the ultimate decision on the challenged books. Several hundred people packed the room, made all the hotter by the TV lights. After the board's attorney read the proposal, Hall himself presented the board with a stack of antiobscenity petitions that he claimed contained 9,000 signatures. Pipkin told the board of the successes of the English program. Another teacher pointed out that Bay County's program for children with learning disabilities used thousands of "unapproved" materials, each of which would now require a laborious review. The president of the teachers union noted that under the proposed guidelines, teachers would spend most of their time writing justifications for their books. An FSU professor read a long list of authors—from Shakespeare to Tennessee Williams—whose works would be banned under Hall's proposal. Several Mowat students spoke in defense of their teachers and the controversial books. But a woman opposing the challenged books rose to declare that she and her followers had prayed two hurricanes away during the previous year, and there would be grave consequences if the schools continued to profane the name of God.

After almost five hours of haggling, the board voted to approve Hall's policy, with a minor modification. Any books used during the previous year could be used in the coming year, after which they would all be subject to title-by-title official approval. Even that concession would not apply to two books—*I Am the Cheese* and *About David*. Those books remained banned.

Gloria Pipkin decided to submit a request to reinstate *I Am the Cheese* in ReLeah Hawks's class. She wrote a rationale and submitted it to Principal Creel. Creel rejected her request, saying the book was not appropriate for the age-group, that it contained vulgar or obscene language and might tend to encourage seventh- or eighth-graders to rebel against parental authority. Pipkin then wrote to Hall, asking him to override Creel, and when Hall refused, she wrote to the school board requesting a hearing.

But in the meantime, the bookbanning process proceeded apace. When the school year began in September 1986, Hall appeared in the library of the Lynn Haven Elementary School and browsed through the periodicals, looking for a magazine called *Young Miss*. Hall had heard that one issue of the magazine contained a story on abortion. After Hall left, the librarian received a phone call from the assistant principal, saying that Hall wanted the magazine removed from the shelf. The librarian picked three issues of *Young Miss* off of the shelves and threw them in the trash. Librarians at other elementary schools did the same. When the teachers' union protested the removal of library materials without following offical procedures, the local TV station, an NBC affiliate, assigned reporter Cindy Hill to cover the story. When her report was aired on TV, Hill received several irate phone calls, demanding that she drop the story. She was told to stop bothering Leonard Hall, a good, God-fearing man.

But Hill smelled a good story. She went to the school board to check on the 9,000 signatures Charles Collins had claimed during his petition drive. She reported that there were only 3,549 signatures, many of which were not registered Bay County voters. She also discovered that many people had signed the petition three or more times. In some cases, heads of family had signed the names of all family members, including children.

Immediately after Hill's report aired on the evening news, calls came in attacking her as a "Communist," "atheist," and the "daughter of Satan." One caller recited: "Roses are red, violets are black. You'd look good with a knife in your back."[80] The calls continued for several days, and on the morning of October 25, when Hill stepped out of her apartment, she came across a gasoline-soaked carpet with a burned match atop it. The following morning, at about 3:00 A.M., Hill was awakened by her smoke alarm to find her living room filled with smoke. She fled her apartment and called the police, who concluded that a flammable liquid had been poured under her door and then lighted.

A nervous Cindy Hill called Gloria Pipkin, who invited the young reporter to move in with her family for a few days. Soon thereafter, Pipkin's husband noticed the hood of Hill's car open in the driveway and discovered evidence of tampering. A few nights later, Hill's car suddenly stalled on a dark stretch of highway. When a policeman examined the engine, he noticed that three of the four sparkplug wires had been pulled loose.

After Hill received a phone call telling her, "Satan will get revenge," Pipkin staked out Hill's apartment to catch any intruders. She did surprise someone tampering with Hill's car, but the intruder fled to his car in the adjoining parking lot and disappeared. A note had been left on Hill's car warning, "Beware of the bomb." When the police arrived, they found a tape-covered device sitting on the engine, ticking. The police evacuated several apartments, sealed off the area, and summoned the bomb squad. The "bomb" turned out to be a fake, but that did not calm Pipkin's nerves. Charles Collins ridiculed the incident, first saying, "It may have been a practical joke."[81] He then announced: "I don't believe anything. The thing in her car was just a joke. The fire didn't burn anything. It just smoked. That's a good way to get your apartment painted by the landlord. I'm thoroughly disgusted with these trite little people in this county." Referring to the Mowat teachers, Collins said, "They ought to be fired, run out of the county and gotten rid of for insubordination."[82]

On a November afternoon, after a long day teaching and coaching the school's "Knowledge Bowl" team, Gloria Pipkin checked her school mailbox. There, amid the departmental notices and memos, Pipkin noticed an envelope addressed with letters crudely cut from magazines. She opened the envelope and unfolded a note, again written in letters cut from magazines. The note read:

> Woe to those who call evil good and good evil, who put darkness for light and light for darkness, who put bitter for sweet, for they have revoked the law of the Lord. For this you all shall DIE. One by one. Hill, Hawks, Farrell, Pipkin.[83]

Pipkin took the letter to the Panama City police. She later showed it to the other women threatened in the note. They were terrified. Hill talked of moving, and Farrell, a divorced mother of a teenage daughter, was worried that there was no one to protect them. Hawks, who was pregnant, wondered if she should send her five-year-old son to his grandparents. Pipkin said: "Three-quarters of me, the rational side, realizes that it's probably a trick to scare us, but part of me is afraid." She wondered if it was time for her to quit. After reflection, she concluded, "I'm in this to the bitter end."[84]

On November 12, 1986, when the school board met to consider her request to reinstate *I Am the Cheese,* Gloria Pipkin was not optimistic. Collins and the Shumakers were in the front row. There was some doubt about whether Pipkin would even be allowed to speak. The board chairman asked her if she was going to be speaking as a citizen or as a teacher, and Pipkin said it would be difficult for her to separate those roles. The chairman reminded her that as an employee of Mowat Junior High School she was obliged to follow the edicts of the principal and superintendent. Only after Pipkin said she had followed those edicts did the acting school board attorney state, "I think that since she's on the agenda, she has a right to speak." Pipkin then told the board, "Despite the fact that the board attorney . . . recently informed me that no right of formal appeal exists under the new policy, I am here today requesting that you restore this powerful tool to our curriculum. Make no mistake about it, *I Am the Cheese* has been banned in the Bay County School System because the ideas in it are offensive to a few." Charles Collins then attacked the book and suggested that Pipkin's actions might be cause for dismissal. "If teachers are unhappy then they should resign," said Collins. "We would ask this board to reprimand the teachers." Collins warned that if the teachers continued to oppose the bookban, "the board should dismiss the teachers and let them find another job."[85]

When all speakers had finished, the board chairman denied Gloria Pipkin's request to reconsider *I Am the Cheese.* In addition, the board approved a policy requiring all nontextbook materials to be formally approved by the principal, the superintendent, and the school board.

The next morning, Pipkin returned to her eighth-grade classroom. One of her students asked her if they could talk about censorship. Pipkin said they could if they wanted to. A number of students asked if Pipkin was going to be fired, and she assured them that a teacher couldn't be fired for simply talking to the school board. One student said, "I think they ought to keep you, not in spite of what you're doing but *because* you're doing it." Some students criticized Principal Creel, but Pipkin defended him, saying he was under enormous pressure.

"We lost *I Am the Cheese* and we're mad," said one girl.
"What would happen if we just started reading the book next Monday?" asked another student.

"I'd be fired," said Pipkin.
"I think you should take us to another state and teach us the book,"
suggested a girl.
"The sad thing about it," said Pipkin, "is that similar things are hap-
pening all over the country."
"About *I Am the Cheese?*"
"About a lot of different books," Pipkin said.[86]

Indeed, Superintendent Hall was not finished with his plan to
cleanse the Bay County schools of "bad language and ideas." Early in
1987, Hall cited a single vulgarity in Farley Mowat's *Never Cry Wolf* as
sufficient reason for banning it. "If you say a single vulgar word, you've
said it," proclaimed Hall. "If you steal a penny, you're still a thief, or is
it only when you steal $500,000?"[87]

In May 1987, Hall extended this purist notion of vulgarity by an-
nouncing a new three-tier book classification system by which all
schoolbooks would be judged. Hall's new system divided all the world's
literature into three categories: books with no vulgarity; books with a
"sprinkling" of vulgarity; and books with "oodles" of vulgarity. Hall
declined to define *sprinkling* or *oodles,* but he quickly issued a list of
sixty-one books in Category III, claiming they either contained vulgarity or the word *goddamn* and must henceforth not be taught or discussed in Bay County classrooms. Banned titles included classics by
Sophocles, William Shakespeare, Charles Dickens, Charlotte and Emily
Brontë, Ernest Hemingway, Geoffrey Chaucer, George Orwell, John
Steinbeck, Tennessee Williams, and a host of other prominent
writers.[88]

There was widespread concern that Hall's continuing crusade would
finally destroy Bay County's acclaimed English program. Some students
wore black arm bands to school as a protest, and the Panama City
Commission unanimously urged that the bookban be lifted. The Bay
County Public Library decided to assemble a "Banned Books" display,
prominently featuring the books that Hall had banned from classroom
use. The public librarian said Hall had moved his censorship to a new
level that required some response from the community. "[H]e's gone
beyond imaginative fiction for young people to the classics of our culture. The censorship craze has definitely moved from amusement to
concern, grave concern."[89]

On May 12, forty-four Bay County teachers, parents, and students
chose to file a class action suit in federal court against Superintendent
Hall, Principal Creel, and the school board, arguing that the bookban
was a violation of their First Amendment rights. A student, Jennifer
Farrell, was first among the plaintiffs, and the case went forward
as *Farrell v. Hall* (1988). The day after the suit was filed, the PAW,

which provided legal representation for the plaintiffs, met with the school board in an attempt to negotiate changes in the school's book review policy. A subsequent board meeting produced a revised policy, allowing teachers to assign any books that had been used in 1986–1987, as long as they were recommended by the principal.

Farrell v. Hall asked the court specifically to restore *I Am the Cheese* and the other books still excluded and to declare the ban on classroom libraries to be unconstitutional. The board claimed that their compromises on the book review policy now rendered *Farrell* moot, but the plaintiffs pointed out that *I Am the Cheese* and other books were still banned at Mowat because of Hall's earlier prohibitions. The plaintiffs noted that the new policy provided no time limits for board response to requests to use particular materials, thus allowing officials to effectively veto requests by delaying a decision. For example, while *Farrell* was in progress, Gloria Pipkin resubmitted a rationale for teaching *I Am the Cheese*. This time, Creel and the county curriculum officials approved the book, but Hall again rejected it, and the board upheld his action. The plaintiffs therefore asserted that it was disingenuous for Defendant Hall to claim the controversy over *I Am the Cheese* was moot or that the defendants' minds were open on these matters.

In particular, the plaintiffs argued that Hall had excluded books solely because they conflicted with his religious beliefs, and the new policy would not prevent such actions in the future. Hall's *motivation* in banning books thus became essential to the case, and the plaintiffs brought witnesses before the court to testify on Hall's religious agenda in the schools. Hall's public statements were cited to demonstrate his intention to bring Christian values to the schools of Bay County and remove library books and curricular materials that involve subjects such as feminism, consumerism, environmentalism, and racism. Hall had earlier stated that he had removed *I Am the Cheese* because it gave a negative picture of a department of the U.S. government, prompting a local journalist to ask, "What will they protect Bay County children against next? The depressing knowledge of the size of the federal debt?"[90] Even when Hall claimed to be banning books solely because of "vulgar" language, he failed to define what he meant by that characterization, allowing him to use language as a pretext to ban books on religious grounds. The plaintiffs concluded that the school board had acted improperly in allowing the superintendent to exercise such broad authority over the selection and rejection of books.

On July 18, 1988, Judge Roger Vinson of the U.S. District Court issued an order that supported some of the plaintiff's claims while rejecting others. Judge Vinson said Hall had admitted that his actions were motivated by his personal conservative beliefs, such as an obligation to restore Christian values to the county's schools. Vinson noted:

Hall thinks that one vulgarity in a work of literature is sufficient reason to keep the book from the Bay County school curriculum. Hall's opposition to *I Am the Cheese* arises solely from his personal opposition to the ideas expressed in the book. He believes it is improper to question the truthfulness of the government. Thus, students should not be presented with such ideas.[91]

Vinson refused to dismiss the case, ruling that the school board's use of the revised policy continued most of the activities to which the plaintiffs objected. On the other hand, Vinson continued the courts' long tradition of support for broad school board authority, finding that the removal of books on the basis of a single vulgarity was within the board's authority. Vinson said the review policy itself was acceptable to the court because school boards have the right to regulate the content of school libraries, including classroom libraries, in any way they wish. Their decisions can be challenged if they are made for illegal or arbitrary reasons, but the policy itself is legal. On the other hand, Vinson did *not* dismiss the complaint that *I Am the Cheese* and other books had been removed in an effort to suppress the ideas in them.

As both sides began preparing their arguments for trial, Leonard Hall announced that he would not run for reelection as superintendent, and on December 31, 1988, his term expired. Judge Vinson ruled that Hall's successor, Jack Simonson, automatically replaced Hall as a defendant, and a suspension was granted to attempt a resolution of the dispute out of court. By this time, the community was beginning to turn against Hall's draconian censorship. The Panama City mayor complained, "New business will not want to come to a place like this." The influential *St. Petersburg Times* warned:

Local control of schools is an important part of public education, but it has limits of reasonableness. Depriving students of knowledge by the widespread banning of books is not a reasonable element of local authority. Unless the book banners are stopped in Bay County, there's no telling how far they'll go.[92]

After three years of settlement negotiations between the school board and PAW, a further revision of the policy for approving instructional materials was approved by all. Time limits were set for each stage of the review process, and teachers were allowed to appeal denials of their requests for new materials. The new policy detailed a procedure for handling challenges to materials already in the classroom and ensured that parents would be notified of any complaints against materials in time for them to respond. The settlement negotiated under Vinson's order had the appearance of compromise, but the board's review policy was changed in a direction favorable to the *Farrell* plaintiffs *only* because the board agreed to it. In reality, Vinson's order had followed the decisions of other courts involved in textbook controversies, affirming the board's almost unlimited power over the curriculum.

Soon after Superintendent Hall left office, the terms of two of the five school board members expired, and their successors gave the board a potential 3–to–2 majority for a more liberal textbook policy. Fortunately, the reconstituted board countermanded Hall's exclusion of sixty-four literary classics in time to allow their use when classes began in September. But the educators who had endured this protracted censorship struggle were not around to savor the victory. Principal Creel had left Mowat Junior High School to head a brand-new junior high school in Bay County, and all eleven English teachers who had earned their department national awards had resigned. Today, the Mowat English Department is no longer listed as a "Center of Excellence" by the National Council of Teachers of English.

BLASPHEMY IN CHESHIRE, CONNECTICUT

On November 7, 1991, irate parents at a Cheshire, Connecticut, Board of Education meeting demanded that two award-winning books be removed from the Highland Middle School because of offensive language. The offending books were *The Alfred Summer,* by Jan Slepian, and *The Great Gilly Hopkins,* by Katherine Paterson. The most vocal parent, Sharon Kuehlewind, claimed that the books were filled with profanity, blasphemy, and obscenities. Kuehlewind also told the board that the authors had "dragged God and the church in the mud and slyly endorsed unwholesome values such as stealing, smoking, drinking and simply rebelling against authority." When Kuehlewind demanded an investigation into "who was pushing this filth on our kids," she received loud applause from supporters at the board meeting. Another parent said, "We don't need any more bureaucratic baloney. Pull it and pull it now. . . . I'd like to know who willfully introduced these books into our system."[93]

Board Vice-Chairman George Bowman was even more rash in his response, proclaiming that he would personally pull the books from the school library the next morning if something were not done. "I'll take them out myself, and you can arrest me," Bowman said. "Some of this language I hear on construction sites. I'm shocked these books are in our school. I want this trash removed from our school system, and find out who brought it in here and fire them. And I don't want to hear some warm fuzzy words about liberal ideas—it's trash."[94] Bowman concluded that the books had been written by perverted minds. Ironically, Paterson's book had received the 1980 American Book Award, the Newbery Medal, and the 1977 Christopher Award for novels representing the "highest human spiritual values." Slepian's book had been runner-up for the American Book Award.

Bowman waved copies of *Playboy* and the *National Enquirer,* asking if they, too, would be acceptable for fifth-graders. Though he had not read the books he was attacking, Bowman did say that he could safely recommend alternative books such as *Snow White and the Seven Dwarfs.* In response to the complaints, Board Chairman William P. Meyerjack announced that effective immediately a "moratorium" would be placed on the Paterson and Slepian books in all school libraries until the board could review the matter. The two books were therefore "temporarily" pulled from the language arts curriculum at Cheshire's four elementary schools.

Under cooler circumstances the following day, the complaining parents admitted that the books had positive themes but maintained that the language used made them unacceptable. Kuehlewind said she became aware of the problem books when her fifth-grader told her that he was reading a "bad book" in school. She later discovered that a neighbor's child was reading the other offending book. At that point, Kuehlewind and two other parents met with Highland Principal Diane Hartman, filled out the complaint forms, and listed the words that offended them. Hartman told them that she understood their point of view, but it was a district issue, not just a Highland one. Kuehlewind was not satisfied.

School Superintendent John Barnes said the offending words were "very much a part of reality for fifth-graders, and that using a book which contains them does not mean the school system is promoting obscene language."[95] He said the complaints were the first they had heard since the books were selected in 1987 by the school system's Language Arts Committee. He said no books had ever been pulled from the shelves in the Cheshire School District, but he gave assurances that the complaints would be reviewed. "I'll either come out and say they should be returned as literature in grade five, or the books are not appropriate for that grade," said Barnes.

> I read the books, and frankly it gave me some pause when it came to the language. But I also felt the books had strong messages about the lives the children lead and issues children need to come to grips with. I'm a realist. I know what language children this age use. The question is whether they should encounter this language with people their age in the classroom or in the back of the bus.[96]

Barnes emphasized the seriousness of the issue, warning that it would be regarded as censorship if the books were removed on the basis of personal biases or prejudices instead of good academic values.

Mrs. Kuehlewind insisted that parents had received forms at the beginning of the year, saying there would be no swearing allowed on the school bus or on the playground, yet profanity and blasphemy were being read in the classroom. She said, "No matter what 'phenomenal metaphors' or 'excellent themes' could be taught through these 'prizewinning' books, they are totally inappropriate and unacceptable for our public school system. They are filled with profanity, blasphemy and obscenities and utter gutter language."[97] She maintained that there were basic philosophical issues at stake in the book dispute. "We have the right to send our kids to public schools without having them bombarded with language and concepts counter to the moral standards upon which the country was founded," she said. "Who would have used books like these in the fifth grade, or any grade, 30 years ago?"[98]

Superintendent Barnes convened a special review board to assess the books' educational value before taking further action. "It could be," said Barnes, "that we don't want these books used because of these words, but I want to try to get a sense of perspective on this. The parents had a rather intense, emotional reaction to the books and I want to make sure they're not pulling the naughty words out of context."[99] Barnes invited board of education members, parents, PTA members, child psychologists, and others to attend the review board meeting, at which the Kuehlewinds submitted a complete list of the offending words, specifying book and page number.

*The Alfred Summer**	*The Great Gilly Hopkins***
1. Christ	2. Cripes
3. You Maniac	4. Jeez
6. Damn	8. God!
10. God	10. My God!
10. God	10. Stupid Kid
17. Hell	10. Good God—
19. Shit	12. Good God—
34. You little bums	12. Hell
39. Picks his nose with her finger	13. Jeez
41. Beer, Dirty jokes	19. Banged door and spit every obscenity
42. God	20. You dummy; What a dope
43. ½ man/ ½ woman; Tits; Wonder if it can do it to itself	21. Trotters huge breast; God!
44. Bridge; woman's skirt flying up; get good look; Saw hair	29. Dumb, stupid kids
45. God	30. One stupid minute

*The Alfred Summer**

46. Crap/Christ

49. Christ
54. You dope
61. Toilet seat up . . . fell in
76. Stealing . . . God
80. Kissing pig's ass better than praying
81. Damnedest
83. Drinking wine . . . like the idea
89. Damn money

*The Great Gilly Hopkins***

33. The Bible . . . afraid forced to read
37. Stupid
39. Stupid
40. What the heck
47. Put it down, stupid
50. Not as dumb as he looked

56. Dirty joke . . .
62. Blinking stupidly
69. Not as dumb as he looks; Acts stupid
70. Shut up; Shut up; Shut up
71. What the hell
72. God
74. Oh God; But Hell
78. Religious fanatic: read bible and prayed everyday; grace over food; church 9–12:30; peculiar Sundays—torture; Church didn't fit in modern world any more than people who went there
79. Saved—Who the hell; religious fanatics; religious fanatics
82. Good God
83. Shut up
84. Totally bustless; Hell
88. Oh God; Damn; Like Hell
89. Damn money
91. Stupid man
93. Don't give a spit
95. Damned cops
97. Smoothed pants over her rump
101. Get the hell out; best damn teacher
107. Dumbly Gilly stepped back
108. Damn
111. Dammit
113. Oh my God

115. Wet their stupid beds
117. This is so dumb
118. Hell
120. Oh Hell
120. Oh God
131. Oh Hell; How in the Hell; That damn letter
133. Shut up
147. God
148. Go to Hell

*New York: Macmillan, 1980.
**New York: Thomas Crowell, 1978.

Jan Slepian, who wrote *The Alfred Summer* in 1980 for an audience of nine- to twelve-year-olds, said she was saddened by the parents' reaction to her work. "These pitiful people who would point to a phrase and judge a whole book," Slepian said from her New Jersey home. "That's just what we don't want children to do." She said the main theme of the book—about the friendship of four boys, two of them handicapped—is acceptance and understanding. Slepian said the characters in her book are based on real children, including her retarded brother Alfred, and they talk the way real children do. "For them to say 'Gosh, darn,' it just wouldn't be true," she said.[100]

Katherine Paterson, author of *The Great Gilly Hopkins*, was similarly disappointed by the Cheshire controversy. "I'm sorry people are offended," she said, "but they're offended when they don't see what I'm trying to do." Paterson, the daughter of a missionary, said that her book about an eleven-year-old foster child was being misinterpreted by Cheshire parents who overlooked the book's positive themes. She said the book was "for those children who don't know if they have a place. . . . Gilly is a foster child who is very angry about being treated as a disposable commodity in the world. She lies, steals, bullies the handicapped and is racially prejudiced. Her mouth needs to reflect her state of anger and lostness."[101] Paterson said she wouldn't change a word in the book, her favorite of the eighteen she has written. As to the appropriateness of the language, she says fifth-graders should be the judge of that. She points out that virtually every time the main character, Gilly, curses, the other character, Trotter, corrects her.

Most of the Cheshire children reading the two books had no objection to them. Ten-year-old Elizabeth Abbate said of *The Great Gilly Hopkins*, "I really thought it was a good book. It was interesting, and it told kids how to behave. Most of those words you hear every day. They didn't really bother me."[102]

Highland School Principal Diane Hartman said both novels had been in the elementary schools' reading program since 1987 and were widely used in other schools and systems. Hartman said a curriculum committee had selected the books because they were outstanding examples of contemporary children's fiction and because they espoused strong values. She said the committee was aware of the language in the books, but the committee's goal was to get books for the children that have a strong message of acceptance of other people.

The *Meriden Record-Journal* editorialized:

> Clearly, the situation with these books is not black and white. The issue, really, is tolerance for rough if realistic language used at a given grade level. To one person, expressions seem blasphemous or obscene; to another, such usages shock no more than the casual use of "gosh." The attempt to remove such volumes from Cheshire's school libraries should be stoutly resisted. These books were not written to titillate or shock but to help kids work through problems and situations not unusual in real schools.

The editorial recommended that the children of the complaining parents be offered different reading assignments, but it concluded:

> In the long run, no significant book in the 4,000 years of Western civilization has failed to offend someone. The Bible contains some pretty racy scenes; Shakespeare has a number of gross physical jokes; racial language in Mark Twain can give offense; *The Wizard of Oz* has offended not only because it is fantasy but also because it deals with magic and witchcraft. If one were to start removing offending volumes from libraries upon the application of anyone who objected, it wouldn't be long before libraries no longer faced a space problem.[103]

Representatives of educational organizations around the state soon became involved in the Cheshire dispute. Mary Pellerin, president of the Connecticut Educational Media Association (CEMA), said that books, like people, should be given a fair trial and not censored without a thorough review. Harriet Selverstone, member of the CEMA and head of the group's Intellectual Freedom Committee, said she had notified other watchdog groups like the National Coalition against Censorship and the PAW. On November 21, Selverstone wrote to School Superintendent John Barnes to urge that the books not be pulled from the schools' libraries or curricula. Selverstone said that parents have a right to keep certain materials away from their children but not to prevent others from being exposed to the same material.

On December 4, Leanne Katz, head of the New York–based National Coalition against Censorship, sent a letter to Superintendent Barnes, expressing concern over the removal of the books before any inquiry had been made into the complaints. She stated that proper procedures were being ignored and that the professional opinions of educators were not being respected. Katz asked that her letter and an accompanying list of book selection procedures and principles be shared with the school board members and review committee. She urged the school board not to "cave in" to demands for bookbanning.

Connecticut state historian Christopher Collier wrote:

> Parents of Cheshire school children who see no beauty but only blasphemy and obscenity in a pair of books read by their fifth-graders should look again. And so should the hysterical Board of Education member who compared the books to a copy of *Playboy* which . . . he waved at citizens gathered at a Board meeting. Far from obscene or blasphemous, these books deal with family, love and mutual respect. They are exactly the books that parents concerned about old-fashioned family values should want their kids to read.

Collier, himself an author of historical novels for young adults, said that the words some have cited as objectionable in these books were being read out of context. To construct the dialogue in any other way, says Collier, would have left teenage readers "bored, uninvolved, and unmoved." He concluded, "Children lucky enough to have teachers perceptive enough and wise enough to choose such books as *The Alfred Summer* and *The Great Gilly Hopkins* should count their blessings."[104]

Most Connecticut schools have book selection policies and step-by-step procedures for handling complaints about books. If complaints cannot be resolved by the school principal or library media specialist, a review and decision by a Library Media Advisory Council would follow. If the complainant does not accept the council's decision, the school superintendent or, ultimately, the board of education would make a final review and decision. Materials are supposed to remain in use or on library shelves until a complaint is resolved. Such was not the case in the Cheshire incident, where the books were impounded, pending the recommendation of the supervisor's review panel.

The review panel was made up of about a dozen members, including school staffers, a board of education member, a parent, and a consultant on children's literature. The first two meetings of the panel were closed, and the third allowed public discussion of the issues. As the committee review of the Paterson and Slepian novels approached its conclusion, more books came under attack. Parents at a January 1992 school board meeting condemned the Newbery Medal–winning *Slave Dancer,* by Paula Fox, claiming it spoke disparagingly of blacks. Another novel, *My Brother Sam Is Dead,* by state historian Christopher Collier, was attacked for its "graphic violence" and "inaccurate depiction of the Revolutionary War." The board took no action on the request to remove these books from Cheshire schools. One parent, a former board member, said, "I understand the great fears parents have, but I submit that we have become a hysterical society when we review every single book and every single word."[105]

On February 6, 1992, the attempt to ban the Paterson and Slepian books came to an official end when the board of education, in response to the review panel's recommendation, voted unanimously to restore the two books to elementary school classrooms. In front of 300 residents packed into the council chambers at town hall, the board voted 6 to 0 to approve School Superintendent John Barnes's recommendation to retain the books. *The Great Gilly Hopkins* was retained as a fifth-grade reader, while *The Alfred Summer* was moved from the fifth- to the sixth-grade level.

The board's decision came after a final two-hour public debate on the books, during which about twenty people spoke. Those parents who spoke against the books at the final board meeting expressed disappointment at the outcome. "I am very concerned for the children of Cheshire," said Sharon Kuehlewind, "because what we teach at home will not be reinforced in the schools." She felt that the board's decision implied approval for the use of profanity in the classroom. But board member Robert Bown said the books were age appropriate, positive, and enriching. The audience responded with a standing ovation when he concluded, "Should a parent or well-organized group of parents dictate what should or should not be in the curriculum? I submit the answer is clearly no. Parents have no right to impose moral judgments and values on the children of others."[106]

NOTES

1. James Moffett, *Storm in the Mountains: A Case Study in Censorship, Conflict, and Consciousness* (Carbondale: Southern Illinois University Press, 1988), p. 15.

2. Ibid., p. 16.

3. Ibid., p. 19.

4. Thelma R. Conley, "Scream Silently: One View of the Kanawha County Textbook Controversy," *Journal of Research and Development in Education*, Spring 1976, p. 95.

5. Moffett, *Storm in the Mountains*, p. 24.

6. George Hillocks, Jr., "Books and Bombs: Ideological Conflict and the Schools," *School Review*, August 1978, pp. 632, 636.

7. Moffett, *Storm in the Mountains*, p. 26.

8. Robert Oscar Goff, *The Washington County Schoolbook Controversy: The Political Implications of a Social and Religious Conflict* (Ph.D. diss., Catholic University, Ann Arbor, University Microfilms, 1976), p. 47.

9. Ibid., p. 241.

10. Ibid., p. 300.

11. Ibid., p. 265.

12. Ibid., p. 82.

13. Frank R. Kemerer and Stephanie Abraham Hirsh, "School Library Censorship Comes Before the Supreme Court," *Phi Delta Kappan,* March 1982, p. 444.

14. Steven Pico, "An Introduction to Censorship," *School Library Media Quarterly,* Winter 1990, p. 84.

15. *Board of Education, Island Trees Union Free School District No. 26 v. Pico,* 102 S. Ct. 2799, 2803 (1982).

16. *Board of Education, Island Trees Union Free School District No. 26 v. Pico,* 474 F. Supp. 387, 390 (EDNY 1979).

17. Pico, "An Introduction to Censorship," p. 85.

18. Ibid., p. 87.

19. "Letters to the Editor: Sex Book Called Source of Immorality," *Prince Georges Journal,* March 17, 1978, p. A6.

20. Jacqueline Trescott, "An 'Our Bodies' for Our Times," *Washington Post,* October 3, 1992, p. D8.

21. Interoffice memorandum from Stephen C. Orenstein to Arthur A. Marshall, Jr., state's attorney for Prince Georges County, Maryland, September 15, 1977.

22. Memorandum from William R. Gordon to library board members, September 21, 1977.

23. Telephone interviews with William Gordon, spring 1992. Unless separately endnoted, all other Gordon quotes are from these interviews.

24. Letter from William Gordon, director, Prince Georges County Memorial Library System, to Winfield M. Kelly, Jr., county executive, Prince Georges County, December 14, 1977.

25. County Council of Prince Georges County, Maryland, Bill No. CB–42–1978, June 27, 1978, "An Act concerning Obscene Matter."

26. Peter D. Pichaske, "Libraries, Schools Attack Porno Ban," *Prince Georges Journal,* September 1, 1978, p. A5.

27. Ibid., p. A1.

28. "A Punch at Playboy May KO," *Prince Georges Sentinel,* August 17, 1978, p. A5.

29. "Libraries, Schools Attack Porno Ban," p. A5.

30. Quoted in Joan DelFattore, *What Johnny Shouldn't Read: Textbook Censorship in America* (New Haven: Yale University Press, 1992), p. 20.

31. "Intolerant Zealots Threaten Our Schools," *USA Today,* July 23, 1986, p. A8.

32. Beth McLeod, "Are These Textbooks Wrong?" *Johnson City Press Chronicle,* November 27, 1983, p. 41.

33. Quoted in David W. Dellinger, *"My Way or the Highway: The Hawkins County Textbook Controversy"* (Ph.D. diss., University of Tennessee, Knoxville, University Microfilms, May 1991), p. 86.

34. Ibid., p. 148.

35. David Brooks, "Hawkins School Board, Principals Focus on COBS," *Kingsport Times-News,* December 7, 1983, p. A6.

36. Quoted in Dellinger, "My Way or the Highway," p. 217.

37. Quoted in ibid., p. 224.

38. *Mozert v. Hawkins County Board of Education,* 827 F.2d 1058, 1069 (1987).

39. DelFatorre, *What Johnny Shouldn't Read,* p. 75.

40. "County Board Bans Faulkner Book," *Mayfield Messenger,* September 5, 1986, p. 1. This censorship incident has been dramatized in detail in William Noble's *Bookbanning in America: Who Bans Books and Why,* Middlebury, Paul S. Erickson, 1990.

41. Noble, *Bookbanning in America* pp. 10–11.

42. Ibid., pp. 8–9.

43. "County Board Bans Faulkner Book," p. 1.

44. "Book's Loss Doesn't Kill Controversy in Graves," *Louisville Courier-Journal,* September 11, 1986, p. B3.

45. "Graves Board Bans Faulkner Book from School Library," *Paducah Sun,* September 5, 1986, p. A1.

46. "ACLU Letter Addressed to Book-Banning Topic," *Mayfield Messenger,* September 10, 1986, p. 1.

47. "Graves Board Bans Faulkner Book from School Library," *Paducah Sun,* September 5, 1986, p. A1.

48. "Book's Loss Doesn't Kill Controversy in Graves," p. B3.

49. "Graves School Board to Take 'Further Action' in Bookbanning Case," *Paducah Sun,* September 11, 1986, p. A12.

50. Ibid.

51. "Graves Sticks to Ban," *Paducah Sun,* September 12, 1986, p. A18.

52. "Faulkner Wasn't a Pornographer," *Paducah Sun,* September 11, 1986, p. A4.

53. Quoted in Noble, *Bookbanning in America,* p. 29.

54. "Ban-Fighter Says She's Getting Lots of Support," *Paducah Sun,* September 14, 1986, p. A16.

55. "Graves Sticks to Ban," p. A1.

56. Ibid., p. A18.

57. Quoted in Noble, *Bookbanning in America,* pp. 32–33.

58. "Graves Sticks to Ban," p. A18.

59. Ibid., p. A1.

60. "Ban-Fighter Says She's Getting Lots of Support," p. A16.

61. Jim Paxton, "Graves' Theatre of the Absurd," *Paducah Sun,* September 14, 1986, p. C2.

62. "Ban-Fighter Says She's Getting Lots of Support," p. A16.

63. "Graves Ban Makes 'As I Lay Dying' a Hot Item," *Paducah Sun,* September 14, 1986, p. A1.

64. "Ban-Fighter Says She's Getting Lots of Support," p. A1.

65. "Book-Banners Having 2nd Thoughts: Lawyer," *Paducah Sun,* September 17, 1986, p. A1.

66. "Publicity, Legal Questions Reverse Book Ban Decision," *Paducah Sun,* September 19, 1986, p. A18.

67. "Text of Statement by Jeff Howard, Board Chairman," *Paducah Sun,* September 19, 1986, p. A1.

68. "Graves Teachers Praise End of Ban on Faulkner Book," *Louisville Courier-Journal,* September 20, 1986, p. B5.

69. Peter Carlson, "A Chilling Case of Censorship," *Washington Post Magazine,* January 4, 1987, p. 13.

70. ReLeah Hawks, "The Year They Came to Arrest the Books," *Florida English Journal,* Fall 1986, p. 14.

71. Peter Carlson, "A Chilling Case of Censorship," p. 14.

72. "Book Ban Issue: Parents Rights vs. Censorship," *Panama City News-Herald,* June 1, 1986, p. A2.

73. Ibid.

74. "Everyone Seeks the Last Word in Book Battle," *Miami Herald,* May 26, 1987, p. A6.

75. Ibid.

76. "Book Ban Issue: Parents' Rights vs. Censorship," p. A2.

77. Ibid.

78. Hawks, "The Year They Came to Arrest the Books," p. 14.

79. Peter Carlson, "A Chilling Case of Censorship," p. 16.

80. Ibid., p. 17.

81. "A Tumultuous Chapter in Fla.," *Atlanta Journal and Constitution,* June 7, 1987, p. A21.

82. Peter Carlson, "A Chilling Case of Censorship," p. 40.

83. Ibid., p. 10.

84. Ibid.

85. "Teacher Vows Fight," *Panama City News-Herald,* November 13, 1986, p. B2.

86. Peter Carlson, "A Chilling Case of Censorship," p. 41.

87. Ken Kister, "Censorship in the Sunshine State," *Wilson Library Bulletin,* November 1989, p. 29.

88. "Everyone Seeks the Last Word in Book Battle," p. A6.

89. "Library Takes Stand on Censorship," *Panama City News-Herald,* May 13, 1987, p. A2.

90. DelFattore, *What Johnny Shouldn't Read,* p. 109.

91. *Farrell v. Hall,* Order, July 18, 1988, U.S. District Court for the Northern District of Florida.

92. Kister, "Censorship in the Sunshine State," pp. 29, 32.

93. Patrick Dilger, "Author Laments 'Pitiful People' in Book-Ban Flap," *New Haven Register,* November 9, 1991, p. A10.

94. Marianne Cipriano, "Cheshire Parents Want 'Filthy' Books Yanked from Schools," *Meriden Record-Journal,* November 8, 1991, p. A4.

95. "Editorials: Cheshire Books," *Meriden Record-Journal,* November 13, 1991, p. A16.

96. Jacqueline Weaver, "A Mother Calls Two Books Inappropriate for Fifth Grade," *New York Times (Connecticut Weekly),* January 12, 1992, Section 12, p. CN9.

97. "Parents Ask for Ban on 2 'Obscene' Kids' Books," *New Haven Register,* November 8, 1991, p. A19.

98. Marianne Cipriano, "Couple Battles Books for Being 'Abusive' of Kids," *Meriden Record-Journal,* November 18, 1991, p. A13.

99. "Disputed Books Out of Classes," *Meriden Record-Journal,* November 9, 1991, p. A9.

100. Dilger, "Author Laments 'Pitiful People' in Book-Ban Flap," pp. A1, A10.

101. Marianne Cipriano, "Author Defends Her Book," *Meriden Record-Journal,* November 13, 1991, p. A1.

102. "Efforts Grow to Censor Books," *New Haven Register,* December 1, 1991, p. A17.

103. "Editorials: Cheshire Books," p. A16.

104. Christopher Collier, "Two Objectionable Books Are Not Obscene," *New Haven Register,* December 15, 1991, p. B3.

105. "Board Withholds Comments as More Books Come Under Fire," *New Haven Register,* January 20, 1992, p. A16.

106. Patrick Dilger, "Board Refuses to Ban Two Books from Schools," *New Haven Register,* February 7, 1992, pp. A1, A10.

| 2 |

The Law on Bookbanning

BACKGROUND

As we saw in the previous chapter, some of the censorship conflicts in schools and public libraries have precipitated violent and extended social convulsion, leaving the competing sides exhausted and embittered and their conflict unresolved. Some disputes have been resolved through negotiation and compromise. But the final option available to the contending parties is litigation, an appeal to the courts to sort out the competing rights and interests of readers, teachers, parents, and administrative officials.

An examination of the litigation involving bookbanning in schools and libraries reveals two interesting surprises. First, the major legal precedent relates *exclusively* to public school censorship, rather than public library censorship. Second, most of the early case law on such bookbanning does not deal directly with books at all, concentrating more generally on the authority of school officials to control the curriculum and the libraries as part of the process of inculcating and socializing students. As we saw in Chapter 1, school boards are as often the victim as the villain in bookbanning incidents. Sometimes school officials exercise administrative authority to repudiate censorship attempts by religious or political pressure groups. Other times, they invoke seemingly arbitrary authority to impose their own taste or ideology on the local curriculum or school library. We will see that the latter has become more likely since the 1988 *Hazelwood School District v. Kuhlmeier* decision, which gave almost unlimited authority to school officials to control curricular expression.

The virtual absence of major litigation concerning censorship in public libraries is probably attributable to their more diverse clientele and the relative ease with which disputes can be resolved in this less sensitive environment. Deanna Duby, an attorney for the PAW, says that some degree of public school censorship for "educational purposes" is tacitly accepted by the law and the community. This is in part due to mandatory school attendance, the homogeneous curriculum, and the absence of parental oversight within the classroom. On the other hand, it is assumed that parents monitor their children's use of the public library. For all of these reasons, there is much more law regulating public schools than public libraries; and where there is law, there is litigation. For example, the Education Code in California covers school library books and curriculum materials in great detail. The very existence of such law means that disputes tend to be resolved by the courts, not by local officials or citizens. The statutory detail on the process of acquiring or removing materials in public libraries is minute in comparison. In fact, in California a recent attempt was made to reduce the legal restraints on school libraries to the same level as those on public libraries. That attempt failed.

School censorship cases go to court because the conflicts are sensitive, legalistic, and intractable. The decisions rendered on these "hard" cases, as the First Amendment attorneys call them, trickle down to public libraries and even to university libraries. But how are teachers and librarians to sort out the legal precedent that protects them from book-banning? Today, *Hazelwood School District v. Kuhlmeier* (1988) is regarded as the benchmark of legal doctrine toward school and library censorship. It appears to have established a greater authority for school officials to control the content of the curriculum, including school libraries, than had been previously accepted. However, from *Meyer v. Nebraska* (1923) to *Hazelwood* (1988) and beyond, the body of legal precedent concerning bookbanning in schools and libraries is often contradictory and inconclusive, and the current status of First Amendment protection therein may seem unclear. What was the doctrinal path by which the courts reached *Hazelwood,* and where will that path lead in the 1990s? This chapter analyzes the major legal precedent concerning bookbanning in schools and libraries to reveal its evolution and current status.

APPROPRIATE MEANS AND LEGITIMATE PURPOSES

The earliest cases from which current constitutional guidelines on bookbanning in schools and libraries are derived are *Meyer v. Nebraska* (1923) and *Bartels v. State of Iowa* (1923).[1] In these two "companion cases," the Supreme Court struck down state laws against teaching subjects in any language other than English prior to the eighth grade. The decision demonstrated that the Supreme Court, when treating an appropriate case, will interfere with a curricular decision made by state or local authorities.

Justice James Clark McReynolds's opinion in *Meyer* suggests a "means test" for judging the constitutionality of state control over schools: "Perhaps it would be highly advantageous if all had ready understanding of our ordinary speech, but this cannot be coerced by methods which conflict with the Constitution—a desirable end cannot be promoted by prohibited means."[2]

Two years later, in *Pierce v. Society of Sisters* (1925), an Oregon military academy challenged a state law requiring all children between the ages of eight and sixteen to attend public school in the district where they reside. The lower court ruled that the conduct of schools was a property right and that parents, as a part of their liberty, may direct the education of their children by selecting reputable schools and teachers outside the public schools. Enforcement of the Oregon statute, therefore, not only would deprive parents of their liberty but would destroy the business and property of private school owners. The Supreme Court subsequently affirmed that decision.

In striking down mandatory public school attendance, the Court in *Pierce* stated:

> The fundamental theory of liberty upon which all governments in this Union repose excludes any general power of the state to standardize its children by forcing them to accept instruction from public teachers only. The child is not the mere creature of the state; those who nurture him and direct his destiny have the right, coupled with the high duty, to recognize and prepare him for additional obligations.

This statement has been interpreted as condemning the state's *purpose* in attempting to standardize its children. More particularly, in writing for the Court in *Pierce*, Justice McReynolds declared:

> Under the doctrine of *Meyer v. Nebraska*, 262 U.S. 390, we think it entirely plain that the Act of 1922 unreasonably interferes with the liberty of parents and guardians to direct the upbringing and education of children under their control. As often heretofore pointed out, rights guaranteed by the Constitution may not be abridged by legislation that has no reasonable relation to some purpose within the competency of the State.[3]

This suggests that legislation abridging these guaranteed rights may be found unconstitutional if its *purpose* goes beyond the limited competency of the state, or if the state's *means* to accomplish a legitimate purpose is not reasonably related to that purpose. Both *Meyer* and

Pierce have been interpreted as applying a First Amendment test based on the purpose or motivation behind the disputed actions of school authorities. Justice Oliver Wendell Holmes, dissenting in *Meyer,* clearly favored a means test rather than a motivation test. Indeed, though he was writing in dissent in *Meyer,* Holmes's opinion is still cited by modern writers as support for a constitutional means test. For example, years later in *Board of Education, Island Trees Union Free School District No. 26 v. Pico,* Justice Harry Blackmun invoked *Meyer* in rejecting the view that a state might so conduct its schools as to foster a homogeneous people.

Pierce established the states' authority over the public school curriculum but maintained that such authority is limited by the constitutional protections for individual rights. Unfortunately, neither *Meyer* nor *Pierce* provided grounds for deciding the limits on state power. Not until 1940, in the flag salute case *Minersville School District v. Gobitis* did the Court go beyond *Meyer* and *Pierce* in clarifying these limits. Here, the children of a Jehovah's Witnesses family had refused to join the flag salute ceremonies at their school, claiming that they were following the biblical prohibition against bowing down to graven images. After the Gobitis children were expelled from school, their parents brought the suit decided by the Supreme Court in 1940. The Court ruled that the school authorities *did* have the right to require participation in the flag salute and that the religious beliefs of the Jehovah's Witnesses did *not* represent a First Amendment exemption.

In proclaiming that our flag summarized all the values of our free society, Justice Felix Frankfurter wrote for the Court: "A society which is dedicated to the preservation of these ultimate values of civilization may in self-protection utilize the educational process for inculcating those almost unconscious feelings which bind men together in a comprehending loyalty." Once more addressing the *means* by which the state may control educational expression, Frankfurter claimed that the issue before the Court was "whether the legislatures of the various states and the authorities in a thousand counties and school districts of this country are barred from determining the appropriateness of various means to evoke that unifying sentiment without which there can ultimately be no liberties, civil or religious." Frankfurter concluded that

the courtroom is not the arena for debating issues of educational policy. It is not our province to choose among competing considerations in the subtle process of securing effective loyalty to the traditional ideals of democracy, while respecting at the same time individual idiosyncracies among a people so diversified in racial origins and religious allegiances. So to hold would in effect make us the school board for the country.[4]

Justice Harlan Stone, dissenting in *Gobitis*, declared:

> The state concededly has the power to require and control the education of its citizens, . . . [but] there are other ways to teach loyalty and patriotism . . . than by compelling the pupil to affirm what he does not believe. . . . Without recourse to such compulsion, the state is free to compel attendance at school and require teaching by instruction and study of all in our history, . . . including the guarantees of civil liberties which tend to inspire patriotism and love of country.[5]

Justice Stone's dissenting opinion in *Gobitis* laid the foundation for the majority in *West Virginia State Board of Education v. Barnette* (1943), just three years later, in which *Gobitis* was overruled. The challenge in *Barnette* was again brought by Jehovah's Witnesses, but Justice Robert H. Jackson's statement went beyond any religious claims: "If there is any fixed star in our constitutional constellation, it is that no official, high or petty, can prescribe what shall be orthodox in politics, nationalism, religion, or other matters of opinion or force citizens to confess by word or act their faith therein." Jackson sharply distinguished the bureaucratic authority of school boards from that of, say, a public utility, which has the power to impose legislatively adopted restrictions. He concluded that "freedoms of speech and of press, of assembly, and of worship may not be infringed on such slender grounds."

In overruling *Gobitis, Barnette* established a legal restraint on the power of school officials to impose their "socialization" process on students. Justice Jackson's repudiation of Justice Felix Frankfurter's *Gobitis* opinion reinforced the notion of a "means test" for judging the limits of the state's authority: "National unity as an end which officials may foster by persuasion and example is not in question. The problem is whether under our Constitution compulsion as here employed is a permissible means for its achievement." Jackson suggested clear limits on the authority of school officials to impose their ideas on students. "That they are educating the young for citizenship is reason for scrupulous protection of constitutional freedoms of the individual, if we are not to strangle the free mind at its source and teach youth to discount important principles of our government as mere platitudes."[6]

This doctrinal debate over means and ends continued in subsequent cases like *Keyishian v. Board of Regents, Epperson v. Arkansas,* and *Tinker v. Des Moines Independent Community School District* (1969). In *Keyishian* (1967), the Supreme Court professed broad First Amendment protection for academic freedom, striking down sections of a New York law that disqualified members of "subversive" organizations from teaching. Writing for the majority, Justice William Brennan declared that the

First Amendment "does not tolerate laws that cast a pall of orthodoxy over the classroom." Brennan explained:

> The vigilant protection of constitutional freedoms is nowhere more vital than in the community of American schools. The classroom is peculiarly the "marketplace of ideas." The Nation's future depends upon leaders trained through wide exposure to that robust exchange of ideas which discovers truth "out of a multitude of tongues," [rather] than through any kind of authoritative selection.

Brennan concluded: "Our Nation is deeply committed to safeguarding academic freedom, which is of transcendent value to all of us and not merely to the teachers concerned. That freedom is therefore a special concern of the First Amendment."[7] However, because the circumstances in *Keyishian* concerned college faculty, the extension of academic freedom to elementary and secondary education was left to two cases addressed by the Court during the following year.

Epperson v. Arkansas (1968) and *Tinker v. Des Moines Independent School District* (1969) were argued within four weeks of each other, and none of the justices siding with Frankfurter in *Gobitis* remained on the Court. Though *Epperson* and *Tinker* did not focus on the socializing function of schools that had been emphasized in *Meyer* and *Barnette,* the cases did involve disputes over the appropriate extent of legislative and administrative discretion in controlling school operations, including libraries. *Epperson* threw out an Arkansas law against teaching evolution and indicated that the principles of academic freedom established in *Keyishian* should also apply to precollegiate levels of education. Writing for the Court in *Epperson,* Justice Abe Fortas quoted *Keyishian*'s rejection of "laws that cast a pall of orthodoxy over the classroom." In dissent, Justice Hugo Black accused Fortas of applying a "motivation test" in *Epperson,* claiming, "[T]his court has consistently held that it is not for us to invalidate a statute because of our views that the 'motives' behind its passage were improper." Black concluded:

> I am not ready to hold that a person hired to teach school children takes with him into the classroom a constitutional right to teach . . . subjects that the school's managers do not want discussed. . . . I question whether it is absolutely certain, as the Court's opinion indicates, that "academic freedom" permits a teacher to breach his contracted agreement to teach only the subjects designated by the school authorities who hired him.[8]

But Justice Potter Stewart, in his concurring opinion, stated:

> It is one thing for a state to determine that the subject of higher mathematics, or astronomy, or biology shall or shall not be included in its public

school curriculum. It is quite another thing for a state to make it a criminal offense for a public school teacher so much as to mention the very existence of an entire system of respected human thought.[9]

The decision in *Epperson* was based on the First Amendment prohibition against religious establishment and was not, strictly speaking, a precedent for free speech rights of elementary and secondary school students. But *Keyishian* and *Epperson* prepared the way for the momentous First Amendment decision in *Tinker v. Des Moines Independent Community School District* (1969). Like *Epperson, Tinker* involved disputes over the limits of legislative and administrative discretion in controlling school operations. Indeed, *Epperson* and *Tinker* were considered almost contemporaneously by the Court. Four weeks after the Court heard arguments in *Epperson,* the decision in that case was announced on the same day that *Tinker* was argued.

Tinker arose when a number of students in Des Moines chose to demonstrate their objection to the Vietnam War by wearing black arm bands to school. The principals of the Des Moines schools announced that any student wearing such an arm band would be asked to remove it, and if the student refused, he or she would be suspended from school. One group of students, including John and Mary Beth Tinker, wore the arm bands to school, where they were told to remove them in accordance with the principals' edict. They refused and were ordered to leave school. The students subsequently returned to school without their arm bands, but only after filing suit in federal court.

The Tinkers lost their case at both the district court level and in the U.S. Court of Appeals, but the U.S. Supreme Court reversed these decisions. In the Supreme Court's first affirmation of First Amendment rights for schoolchildren, the majority opinion held that school officials may not place arbitrary restraints on student speech in public schools. In *Tinker,* Justice Fortas wrote: "First Amendment rights, applied in light of the special characteristics of the school environment, are available to teachers and students. It can hardly be argued that either students or teachers shed their constitutional rights to freedom of speech or expression at the schoolhouse gate." Quoting heavily from Brennan's opinion for the Court in *Keyishian,* Fortas emphasized the classroom as the "marketplace of ideas" and declared "In our system, students may not be regarded as closed-circuit recipients of only that which the State chooses to communicate."[10]

Though the courts after *Tinker* continued to examine the state's means and motives for suppressing educational expression, they were soon to test the notion of a student's explicit right to receive ideas.

THE RIGHT TO RECEIVE IDEAS

The courts have long acknowledged a citizen's right to receive information. In *Martin v. City of Struthers* (1943)[11] the Supreme Court gave the first explicit recognition of the right to *receive* information. Justice Hugo Black wrote: This freedom [of speech and press] embraces the right to distribute literature, and necessarily protects the right to receive it." In Black's view, the right to receive information was "vital to the preservation of a free society." In *Lamont v. U.S. Postmaster General* (1965),[12] the Court gave implicit support for the right to receive information, stating: "The dissemination of ideas can accomplish nothing if otherwise willing addressees are not free to receive and consider them." Justice Brennan noted that it would be a barren marketplace indeed that allowed only sellers and not buyers. The Court's opinion in *Virginia State Board of Pharmacy v. Virginia Citizens Consumer Council* (1976)[13] has become a cornerstone in the protection of the right to receive information. Here the Court extended First Amendment protection to commercial speech, declaring: "Freedom of speech presupposes a willing speaker. But where a speaker exists as in the case here, the protection afforded is to the communication, to its source and to its recipients both."[14] This statement was the Court's first explicit recognition of First Amendment protection for *both* the dissemination and reception of information.

Despite the clarity of these pronouncements, the courts have never unequivocally affirmed such rights within the classroom or school library. In *Wisconsin v. Yoder* (1972) and *San Antonio Independent School District v. Rodriquez* (1973), it was argued that in order for Americans to exercise their right to participate in a democracy, they must have the right to universal education. The Court majority in both cases dismissed this argument, so it cannot be regarded as precedent for a student's First Amendment right to receive information.

In *Yoder,* Chief Justice Warren Burger wrote for an almost unanimous Court in affirming the right of Amish parents to have their children exempted from compulsory schooling beyond the age of fourteen. Burger claimed that Amish children must acquire "Amish attitudes" and the specific skills to be an Amish farmer or housewife. In clarifying the purposes and powers of public education, Burger concluded: "Indeed it seems clear that if the State is empowered as *parens patriae,* to 'save' a child from himself or his Amish parents by requiring an additional two years of compulsory formal high school education, the State will in large measure influence, if not determine, the religious future of the child." In rejecting Wisconsin's claim that mandatory public education beyond the eighth grade was necessary to protect Amish children from ignorance, Burger rejected the notion that students had a constitutional "right to know."[15]

In dissenting in *Yoder*, Justice William O. Douglas warned: "It is the student's judgement, not his parents, that is essential if we are to give full meaning to what we have said about the Bill of Rights and of the right of students to be masters of their own destiny." Douglas expressed concern that the child's choices and judgments be respected before allowing the imposition of Amish attitudes:

> Where a child is mature enough to express potentially conflicting desires, it would be an invasion of the child's rights to permit such an imposition without canvassing his view. . . . And, if an Amish child desires to attend high school, and is mature enough to have that desire respected, the State may well be able to override the parents' religiously motivated objections.[16]

In *Rodriguez* (1973), the Court rejected a claim that the Texas school finance system violated the equal protection clause because of severe inequalities in educational spending. Emphasizing the importance of education to the realization of the right to free speech, the plaintiffs argued that a "strict scrutiny" standard was required to justify state-sponsored inequalities. Writing for the majority, Justice Lewis Powell argued that *if* children have a fundamental right to education, it would not be violated simply by relative differences in spending levels.

Justice Thurgood Marshall's dissenting opinion in *Rodriguez* invoked *Yoder* in arguing, "Education directly affects the ability of a child to exercise his First Amendment rights, both as a source and as a receiver of ideas, whatever interests he may pursue in life." But Marshall's claim that a student's right to education is derived from a First Amendment right to *receive* ideas was again rejected by the majority in *Rodriguez*, for whom Justice Powell wrote:

> The Court has long afforded zealous protection against unjustifiable government interference with an individual's rights to speak and vote. Yet we have never presumed to possess either the ability or the authority to guarantee to the citizenry the most *effective* speech or the most *informed* electoral choice.[17]

When addressing bookbanning in schools, the courts have usually held that a student's right to receive information is subject to a school board's authority to determine the curriculum, including the library's collections. Sometimes this authority may be exercised to deny students' access to information, but it also has been used to deny demands to censor library and curricular materials. Among the earliest major opinions that directly addressed the right of a school board to remove books from a school library was the 1972 decision in *Presidents Council District 25 v. Community School Board No. 25* (1972). After receiving several complaints about offensive language in a junior high school library book,

Down These Mean Streets, by Piri Thomas, a school board acted to prevent access to the book. The board took this action over the objections of parents, teachers, librarians, students, the local PTA, and a junior high school principal. Nonetheless, the U.S. Court of Appeals for the Second Circuit deferred to the school board's judgment, upholding its action in denying access to the Thomas novel.

The court in *Presidents Council* declined to review either the wisdom or the efficacy of the determination of the board, saying that *Epperson* precluded the court's intervention "in the resolution of conflicts which arise in the daily operation of school systems and which do not directly and sharply implicate basic constitutional values." Judge William H. Mulligan, writing for the court, stated:

> Since we are dealing not with the collection of a public book store but with the library of a public junior high school, evidently some authorized person or body has to make determination as to what the library collection will be. . . . The ensuing shouts of book burning, witch hunting and violation of academic freedom hardly elevate this intramural strife to first amendment constitutional proportions.[18]

The court thus ruled that since school boards are statutorily empowered to operate the schools and prescribe the curriculum, they are the appropriate body to assume responsibility for book selection. Indeed, the court reduced the issue to the level of shelving books:

> The administration of any library, whether it be a university or particularly a public junior high school, involves a constant process of selection and winnowing based not only on educational needs but financial and architectural realities. To suggest that the shelving or unshelving of books presents a constitutional issue, particularly when there is no showing of a curtailment of freedom of speech or thought, is a proposition we cannot accept.[19]

The court in *Presidents Council* did not regard the removal of the book from the library as an effort by the state to aid or oppose religion, as was at issue in *Epperson,* nor did it consider the removal to be a restraint on nondisruptive silent expression, which was prohibited in *Tinker.*[20] But *Presidents Council* did provide some guidelines by which the legitimacy of bookbanning in schools may be judged. For one, school authorities are expected to follow established procedures when removing books. Indeed, the court noted that such procedures did exist and that the school board had followed them properly. School authorities are also required to demonstrate proper motivation in removing books, showing economically justified or politically neutral reasons for such action.

In 1975, the lengthy Kanawha County (West Virginia) textbook dispute, described in Chapter 1, found legal resolution in *Williams v. Board of Education of County of Kanawha* (1975). The plaintiffs alleged that the board of education had adopted textbooks containing "both religious and anti-religious materials offensive to Christian morals, matter which defames the Nation and which attacks civic virtue, and matter which suggests and encourages the use of bad English." Plaintiffs sought injunctive relief restraining the board from using the textbooks, which they alleged violated the state's neutrality in religious matters and inhibited the free exercise of their religion as guaranteed by the First Amendment. In rejecting these complaints, the court, quoting heavily from *Epperson,* declared:

> A complete loosening of imagination is necessary to find that placing the books and materials in the schools constitutes an establishment of religion contrary to the rights contained in the Constitution. Further, the Court finds nothing in defendant's conduct or acts which constitutes an inhibition on or prohibition of the free exercise of religion. These rights are guaranteed by the First Amendment, but the amendment does not guarantee that nothing about religion will be taught in the schools nor that nothing offensive to any religion will be taught in the schools. . . . In the absence of bases for relief in the courts, where no violation of constitutional rights is found, plaintiffs . . . may find administrative remedies through board of education proceedings or ultimately at the polls on election day.[21]

The following year in *Minarcini v. Strongsville (Ohio) City School District* the court seemed to reverse the *Presidents Council* opinion by denying a school board's authority to remove books from the curriculum and library. When high school teachers recommended the use of Joseph Heller's *Catch-22* and Kurt Vonnegut's *God Bless You, Mr. Rosewater* in the school curriculum, the Strongsville City Board of Education not only rejected their recommendation but also ordered that those books plus Vonnegut's *Cat's Cradle* be removed from the library. No official reason was given for the removal, but the minutes of a board meeting described the books as "completely sick" and "garbage." Five high school students, through their parents, brought class action against the city school district, members of the board of education, and the school superintendent, claiming violation of their First and Fourteenth Amendment rights. On appeal, the Sixth Circuit ruled against the school board, upholding the First Amendment right of teachers and librarians to disseminate information and the students' right to receive it.

In an affirmation of the students' right to know, the appeals court stated:

A public school library is also a valuable adjunct to classroom discussions. If one of the English teachers considered Joseph Heller's *Catch-22* to be one of the more important modern American novels (as, indeed, at least one did), we assume that no one would dispute that the First Amendment's protection of academic freedom would protect both his right to say so in class and his students' right to hear him and to find and read the book. Obviously, the students' success in this last endeavor would be greatly hindered by the fact that the book sought had been removed from a school library.

The court made reference to Justice Harry Blackmun's earlier opinion that "where a speaker exists . . . the protection afforded is to the communication, to its source and to its recipients both."[22]

The court in *Minarcini* said that the school board had removed the books "because it found them objectionable in content and because it felt it had the power, unfettered by the First Amendment, to censor the school library for subject matter which the Board members found distasteful." In rejecting the absolute right of a school board to remove books from the library, even when those materials are available outside the school, the court held that the removal of books from a school library was a much more serious burden on the freedom of classroom discussion than the action found unconstitutional in *Tinker*. The court concluded:

> A library is a storehouse of knowledge. When created for a public school, it is an important privilege created by the state for the benefit of students in the schools. That privilege is not subject to being withdrawn by succeeding school boards whose members might desire to "winnow" the library for books the contents of which occasioned their displeasure or disapproval.[23]

The opinion in *Minarcini* was soon applied to resolve a Chelsea, Massachusetts, bookbanning. In 1976, the Chelsea School Committee banned the use of poetry anthology *Male and Female under 18*, describing it as "objectionable," "obnoxious," "filthy," and "vile and offensive garbage." The committee's actions were challenged in federal court by the Chelsea school librarian, Sonja Coleman, and a support group, the Right to Read Defense Committee of Chelsea. The complainants contended that the use of *Male and Female under 18* was fully protected under the First Amendment, that students possess a right to have access to such materials, and that the school committee's objections to the book did not constitutionally justify its suppression.

In *Right to Read Defense Committee v. School Committee of the City of Chelsea* (1978), the school committee argued that under Massachusetts law it had clear authority to approve or disapprove materials used in the schools, but the U.S. District Court relied on *Minarcini* in requiring the school committee to return the anthology to the high school library. The *Chelsea* court found that the book was "tough but not obscene," and "no substantial government interest was served by cutting off student access to 'Male and Female' in the library." School officials were enjoined from removing *Male and Female under 18*, which was to be made available to students "in accordance with standard library procedures." Judge Joseph L. Tauro ruled:

> The library is "a mighty resource in the marketplace of ideas." There a student can literally explore the unknown, and discover areas of interest and thought not covered by the prescribed curriculum. The student who discovers the magic of the library is on the way to a life-long experience of self-education and enrichment. That student learns that a library is a place to test or expand upon ideas presented to him, in or out of the classroom. The most effective antidote to the poison of mindless orthodoxy is ready access to a broad sweep of ideas and philosophies. There is no danger from such exposure. The danger is mind control. The committee's ban of the anthology *Male and Female* is enjoined.[24]

Again, as in *Minarcini,* the court distinguished between the authority of school boards to control curriculum content as opposed to library collections and also between the board's authority to *select* library books as opposed to *removing* them.

The following year, in *Cary v. Board of Education Arapahoe School District* (1979), the court seemed to recognize both a teacher's right to independently select curricular materials and a school board's authority to remove them, though they were stipulated to be "non-obscene." A Colorado school board banned ten books from use in high school English courses, giving no written reasons for banning the books. The board also declared that no books could be purchased or used for class assignment without board approval, and no student could be given credit for reading such books. The ten banned books were to be given to the department chairman, who was to hold them pending further directions. Teachers were subject to dismissal if they violated any of these stipulations. Five teachers brought action against the board, claiming rights under the First and Fourteenth amendments. The trial court found that the teachers had a First Amendment right to choose the contested books for their high school English courses but said their rights were waived under a collective-bargaining agreement previously reached with the school district.

The teachers appealed, and the U.S. Court of Appeals declared: "Thus we are presented with a conflict between the school board's powers over curriculum and the teachers' rights to classroom expression in a context somewhat different and more sharply drawn than any case which has arisen heretofore." The court claimed that "the board was acting within its rights in omitting the books, even though the decision was a political one influenced by the personal views of the members." Because the board gave no reasons for banning the books, the appeals court considered remanding the case for trial to determine if the board's purpose was constitutionally permissible. But the court chose not to remand for trial after concluding that the board's seemingly indiscriminate censorship showed no systematic effort to exclude any particular kind of thought. In a ruling that seemed to tolerate the banning of individual titles, as long as comparable alternatives were available, the court concluded: "No objection is made by the teachers that the exclusions prevent them from studying an entire representative group of writers. Rather the teachers want to be freed from the 'personal predilections' of the board. We do not see a basis in the Constitution to grant their wish."[25]

In *Salvail v. Nashua Board of Education* (1979), the Federal District Court for New Hampshire followed the *Chelsea* analysis, requiring the Nashua Board of Education to return to the high school library copies of *Ms.* magazine, which had been removed because of alleged advertisements for "vibrators, contraceptives, materials dealing with lesbianism and witchcraft and gay material" as well as procommunist advertising. Here the court found that the board had failed "to demonstrate a substantial and legitimate government interest sufficient to warrant the removal of *Ms.* from the Nashua High School Library."[26]

Another 1979 case, *Ambach v. Norwick*,[27] affirmed the role of public schools as socializing agencies and the state's authority in performing that role. Here, two teachers challenged the constitutionality of a New York statute that denied teaching certification to aliens not in the process of acquiring citizenship. The teachers cited *Meyer, Pierce, Barnette, Keyishian, Epperson,* and *Tinker,* among other cases, to support their argument that the New York statute should be subject to strict scrutiny on First Amendment grounds because it directly affects academic freedom. The district court agreed in an opinion emphasizing the First Amendment values involved, yet when the Supreme Court considered the case, it found no First Amendment violation. *Ambach* upheld discrimination in occupations, such as public school teaching, that "go to the heart of representative government," as long as the state could show that it was "reasonably related" to the legitimate public purpose for which it was employed. Although *Ambach,* like *Rodriguez,* was decided on equal protection grounds, it later became a pivotal case for First Amendment doctrine in the schools, cited in cases such as *Board of Education, Island Trees Union Free School District No. 26 v. Pico* (1982), *Bethel v. Fraser* (1986), and *Hazelwood School District v. Kuhlmeier* (1988).

In *Zykan v. Warsaw (Indiana) Community School Corporation and Warsaw School Board of Trustees* (1980), the court addressed the school board's removal of several books from a high school library, including *Growing Up Female in America, Go Ask Alice, The Bell Jar,* and *The Stepford Wives.* A student brought suit to reverse the school officials' decision to "limit or prohibit the use of certain textbooks, to remove a certain book from the school library, and to delete certain courses from the curriculum." The suit, which charged that school officials had violated constitutional guarantees of academic freedom and the "right to know," was dismissed by the district court. On appeal, the Court of Appeals for the Seventh Circuit upheld the school board's right to establish a curriculum on the basis of its own discretion, as long as it did not impose a "pall of orthodoxy" on the classroom.

In *Zykan,* the court once more refused to acknowledge a student's right to *receive* information, and the shocking court record in *Zykan* revealed that the school board turned the offending books over to complaining citizens who had them publicly burned. The court condemned this ceremony as "contemptible" but nonetheless held that

> two factors tend to limit the relevance of "academic freedom" at the secondary school level. First, the student's right to and need for such freedom is bounded by the level of his or her intellectual development. . . . Second, the importance of secondary schools in the development of intellectual faculties is only one part of a broad formative role encompassing the encouragement and nurturing of those fundamental social, political, and moral values that will permit a student to take his place in the community.

Following this argument, the court concluded that "complaints filed by secondary school students to contest the educational decisions of local authorities are sometimes cognizable but generally must cross a relatively high threshold before entering upon the field of a constitutional claim suitable for federal court litigation."[28]

At the same time that *Zykan* was being decided, the Second Circuit was reconsidering its 1972 *Presidents Council* opinion through two cases: *Board of Education, Island Trees Union Free School District No. 26 v. Pico* and *Bicknell v. Vergennes Union High School Board of Directors.* The two cases, both of which involved the removal of books from a school library, were decided on the same day and by the same panel, and the opinions invoked both the court's earlier concern with motivation as well as its more recent debate over a "right to know." The dismissal of the complaint in *Bicknell* was affirmed, while the dismissal of the complaint in *Pico* was reversed, both by 2-to-1 majorities. The deciding vote in each case focused on the school board's *motive* in removing books from the library. In *Bicknell,* the deciding judge approved the board's action, saying it had been motivated by the desire to remove vulgar and indecent language from the library, but in *Pico,* the deciding judge said the board had removed the books in order to suppress "ideas," not language. The latter was held to be an unconstitutional attempt to purge the library of ideas, whereas the former was considered an appropriate part of the school's process of value inculcation.

In *Bicknell,* U.S. District Judge Albert W. Coffin dismissed a complaint filed by librarian Elizabeth Phillips and several students to protest the school board's removal of *The Wanderers* and *Dog Day Afternoon* from the library and a freeze on library acquisitions. The district court declared:

> Although the Court does not entirely agree with the policies and actions of the defendants we do not find that those policies and actions directly or sharply infringe upon the basic constitutional rights of the students of Vergennes Union High School. . . . [N]either the board's failure to purchase a work nor its decision to remove or restrict access to a work in the school library violate the First Amendment rights of the student plaintiffs before this Court. . . . Nor do we believe that school librarians have an independent First Amendment right to control the collection of the school library under the rubric of academic freedom.[29]

Bicknell relied heavily on the *Presidents Council* decision in rejecting the notion of academic freedom for librarians, suggesting that any claims of academic freedom made in library censorship cases must be linked in some way to the classroom and curriculum. The court ruled that the rights of neither the students nor the teachers had been violated, since the board removed the books because it viewed them as vulgar and in bad taste.

In *Pico* (see Chapter 1 for further discussion of this case), the court addressed the action of a school board in Long Island, New York, which removed nine books from the school library shelves after three members of the school board saw the titles on a list of "objectionable books" distributed at a meeting of a conservative educational organization. The board claimed the books were "anti-American, anti-Christian, anti-Semitic, and just plain filthy" and cited its "duty, or moral obligation, to protect the children in our schools from this moral danger as surely as from physical and medical dangers." Five of the books were removed despite a report by the board's own Book Review Committee, which noted the books' educational suitability, good taste, relevance, and appropriateness for age and grade. Five students from the local junior high school and high school brought suit to challenge the school board's action, but the district court initially followed the *Bicknell* approach, granting summary judgment in favor of the board of education. The district court concluded:

> [T]he issue is whether the First Amendment requires a federal court to forbid a school board from removing library books which its members find to be inconsistent with the basic values of the community that elected them. . . . In the absence of a sharp, focused issue of academic freedom, the court concludes that respect for the traditional values of the community and deference to the school board's substantial control over educational content preclude any finding of a First Amendment violation arising out of removal of any of the books from use in the curriculum.[30]

The plaintiffs in *Pico* appealed, and in October 1980, the U.S. Court of Appeals for the Second Circuit reversed the judgment of the district court and remanded the action for trial on the plaintiffs' allegations. The three-judge panel was badly split, but Judge Charles B. Sifton, who wrote the opinion, maintained that while the school board may have broad authority to remove books from the library, their removal cannot be for the purpose of suppressing ideas contained in them. Noting the board's procedural irregularities and absence of specific criteria for removing the books, Judge Sifton concluded that

> the school officials' concern is less to cleanse the libraries of all books containing material insulting to members of one or another religious group or which evidences an inaccurate view of the nation's history, than it is to express an official policy with regard to God and country of uncertain and indefinite content which is to be ignored by pupils, librarians, and teachers at their peril.[31]

Judge Walter R. Mansfield dissented, arguing that the majority was, in effect, overruling the *Presidents Council* decision. Judge Mansfield wrote: "Absent some evidence that speech or ideas by anyone are likely to be suppressed, I believe this court should keep its hands off. The effect of the majority's decision is improperly to substitute a court's view of what student curriculum is appropriate for that of the Board."[32] Mansfield noted that the teachers remained free to discuss the ideas in the books in class and on school grounds. Judge John O. Newman, however, pointed out that removing a book from the library because of its ideas would inevitably have a chilling effect on students' and teachers' rights of expression. He added, "I wonder how willing members of the school community are to discuss the virtues of Malcolm X after the School Board has condemned a book . . . because it equated Malcolm X with the founding fathers of our country."[33]

The school board responded in 1981 by requesting that the Supreme

Court review the *Pico* case, and certiorari was granted. By a vote of 5 to 4 the Supreme Court affirmed the Second Circuit's ruling that the board's removal of books from the libraries denied the students their First Amendment rights. Justice William Brennan wrote the plurality opinion, with Thurgood Marshall and John Paul Stevens joining, Byron White concurring, and Harry Blackmun concurring in part. Chief Justice Warren Burger and Justices Lewis Powell, William Rehnquist, and Sandra Day O'Connor dissented in four separate opinions. The argument centered on the motivation behind the board's actions. If the board *intended* to deny the students access to ideas with which the board disagreed, then the board had violated the Constitution. The plurality said the case should be tried in district court to determine whether the school board had acted to suppress ideas with which it disagreed, or whether it had removed the books simply because they were vulgar. In his concurring opinion, Justice Blackmun, while not sharing the plurality's opinion, agreed that the case should be tried to determine the school board's reason for removing the books. "In my view," wrote Blackmun, "we strike a proper balance here by holding that school officials may not remove books for the *purpose* of restricting access to the political ideas or social perspectives discussed in them, when that action is motivated simply by the officials' disapproval of the ideas involved."[34]

In writing for the plurality in *Pico,* Brennan said that the current action did not require the Court to reenter the difficult terrain that *Myer* and *Epperson* had traversed. Brennan explained:

> For as this case is presented to us, it does not involve textbooks, or indeed any books that Island Trees students would be required to read. [The students] do not seek in this Court to impose limitations upon their school Board's discretion to prescribe the curricula of the Island Trees schools. On the contrary, the only books at issue in this case are *library* books, books that by their nature are optional rather than required reading. Our adjudication of the present case thus does not intrude into the classroom, or into the compulsory courses taught there. Furthermore, even as to library books, the action before us does not involve the *acquisition* of books. Respondents have not sought to compel their school Board to add to the school library shelves any books that students desire to read. Rather, the only action challenged in this case is the *removal* from school libraries of books originally placed there by the school authorities, or without objection from them.[35]

Thus, Brennan established a hierarchy of censorship that distinguished between curricular controls, library acquisitions, and the removal of library materials.

Brennan acknowledged that all First Amendment rights accorded to students must be construed in light of the "special characteristics of the school environment," but he said school boards had no authority "to extend their claim of absolute discretion beyond the compulsory environment of the classroom, into the school library and the regime of voluntary inquiry that there holds sway."[36]

The *Pico* plurality attempted to establish that the Constitution protects the right to receive information and ideas, but there were opinions within both the majority and dissenting justices that specifically denied a "right to access." The plurality nonetheless proclaimed that "a right to receive ideas follows ineluctably from the *sender's* First Amendment right to send them" and "the right to receive ideas is a necessary predicate to the *recipient's* meaningful exercise of his own rights of speech, press, and political freedom." They concluded:

> In sum, just as access to ideas makes it possible for citizens generally to exercise their rights of free speech and press in a meaningful manner, such access prepares students for active and effective participation in the pluralistic, often contentious society in which they will soon be adult members. . . . The special characteristics of the school *library* make that environment especially appropriate for the recognition of the First Amendment rights of students.[37]

In his *Pico* dissent, Justice Rehnquist was joined by Burger in rejecting such rights within the special circumstances of the school:

> When it acts as an educator, at least at the elementary and secondary school level, the government is engaged in inculcating social values and knowledge in relatively impressionable young people. . . . In short, actions by the government as educator do not raise the same First Amendment concerns as actions by the government as sovereign.[38]

Rehnquist distinguished between the First Amendment rights of high school students as opposed to college students, drawing on the conclusion in *Zykan* that high school students lack the intellectual skills necessary to take full advantage of the marketplace of ideas. Their need for academic freedom is therefore bounded by their level of intellectual development. Burger, Rehnquist, and Powell rejected any constitutional right to receive information as having no application to the public school, which they regarded as a place for the selective conveyance of ideas.

Rather than go to trial, as the *Pico* plurality ordered, the school board voted to return *all* of the banned books to the library shelves, effectively ending the dispute. But the fractured and relatively feeble judgments in *Pico* showed the depth of the Court's philosophical change since 1943, when it held in *Barnette:*

Probably no deeper division of our people could proceed from any prov-
ocation than from finding it necessary to choose what doctrine and whose
program public educational officials may compel youth to unite in em-
bracing. . . . The First Amendment to our Constitution was designed to
avoid these ends by avoiding these beginnings.[39]

Because the decision in *Pico* was fractured, with seven of the nine
justices writing separate decisions, the application of the First Amendment to the schoolbook issue remained ill-defined. However, *Pico* was
significant not so much for the precedent established as for the clarity
with which it revealed the doctrinal dichotomy within the Burger Court
and its predecessors. The opinions in *Pico* documented a fundamental
philosophical dispute between two entrenched factions within the
Court. The faction led by Justice Brennan regarded education as having an analytic objective that should not be subordinated to indoctrination. Such education would require that teachers and students together
examine information and values in a joint search for truth. On the
other hand, the faction led by Chief Justice Burger regarded elementary and secondary education to be indoctrinative or prescriptive in
purpose. The function of the teacher and the curriculum is thus to
convey prescribed truths.

William D. North, former general counsel for the Freedom to Read
Foundation, reminds us:

The concept that secondary schools can, consistent with the First Amendment, be reduced to a purely indoctrinative function serving the will of
any transient political majority which might gain control of the system
appears as a repudiation of the very purpose for which this amendment
was adopted. That purpose was not to protect the rights of the majority,
but rather to protect the rights of the minority *from* the majority.[40]

North notes that the narrow view of the school as an inculcating mech-
anism will guarantee that secondary schools become political and ideological battlegrounds, allowing the "winner" of this battle to control the
curriculum and purge the library of competing ideas. "This," says
North, "is an opportunity no demagogue or ideologue can or will resist,
and the Kanawha County chaos will be the norm, not the exception."[41]

Still, the *Pico* plurality saw nothing incompatible between the students' "right to know" and the inculcative function of secondary
schools, as long as that function was performed by persuasion and example rather than intellectual force-feeding, by selection rather than
suppression. But Chief Justice Burger's characterization of schools as
vehicles for inculcating the fundamental values of our political system
caused Brennan to fear that students would become nothing more than

"closed circuit recipients of only that which the State chooses to communicate." Burger's primary concern was with the "social interest in order and morality," and he was inclined to grant school authorities broad discretion to fulfil their inculcative function, including the right to make "content based decisions about the appropriateness of retaining school materials in the school library and curriculum." Burger did not share Brennan's fear of a pall of orthodoxy in the classroom, except for the possibility that the orthodoxy imposed might not be representative of community values. As for those in the community who might not be represented in the curricular orthodoxy imposed by school officials, Burger simply advised: "They have alternative sources to the same end. Books may be acquired from book stores, public libraries, or other alternative sources unconnected with the unique environment of the local public schools."[42]

Burger placed his faith in local political control of school boards, whereby "parents influence, if not control, the direction of their children's education." He concluded that "a school board reflects its constituency in a very real sense and thus could not long exercise unchecked discretion in its choice to acquire or remove books." Burger therefore advised, "[I]f parents disagree with the decisions of the school board, they can take steps to remove the board members from office."[43]

This glib assurance has been questioned by attorneys like William D. North, who points out that less than 20 percent of voters are parents of elementary and secondary school children. In addition, the usual six-year term of school board members makes changes in the board's composition and orientation a long and problematic struggle with a bureaucracy whose budget and manpower exceeds that of any other government activity. It should also be noted that bookbanning is often initiated without the participation of parents or, indeed, against their wishes. In *Zykan*, the bookbanning was demanded by an organization of senior citizens, who proceeded to burn the books. In *Chelsea*, a book was removed on the demand of one parent over the objections of many parents. In *Pico*, the books were removed from the library, not at the request of local parents but on the basis of an "objectionable book list" prepared in another state and promoted by a national conservative organization.

Following the *Pico* decision, the court once more considered the notion of a student's right to receive information in *Sheck v. Baileyville School Committee* (1982). *Sheck* addressed the banning of the book *365 Days*, by Ronald Glasser, which had been acquired by the Woodland High School library in 1971 and used frequently for a decade before being banned by the Baileyville School Committee in 1981. The action arose from a complaint by parents whose daughter borrowed the book from the library, after which the school committee voted 5 to 0 to re-move *365 Days* from the library. Michael Sheck, a Woodland High School senior, brought a copy of the book to school, where he was informed by the principal that mere possession of the book on school property would result in its confiscation. The plaintiffs asked redress of the First Amendment "rights of freedom of speech [and] freedom of access," and the court declared that "[t]he burden of persuasion that there has been no *unnecessary* abridgement of first amendment rights rests with the defendants."

The court advised:

> The first amendment right of secondary students to be free from govern-mental restrictions upon nondisruptive, nonintrusive, silent expression in public schools was sustained by the Court in *Tinker* notwithstanding full awareness of the "comprehensive authority" traditionally afforded local officials in the governance of public schools. . . . Book bans do not di-rectly restrict the readers' right to initiate expression but rather their right to receive information and ideas, *the indispensable reciprocal of any meaningful right of expression*. . . . The information and ideas in books placed in a school library by proper authority are protected speech and the first amendment right of students to receive that information and those ideas is entitled to constitutional protection.[44]

The court concluded that the bookban was overly broad, applying to adults as well as students and to mature as well as immature students, and the plaintiffs were provided injunctive relief.

The following year, in *Johnson v. Stuart* (1983),[45] public school teach-ers, students, and parents brought suit against the Oregon State Board of Education, challenging the constitutionality of Oregon's textbook se-lection statute, which prohibited the use of any textbook that speaks slightingly of America's Founders or of those who preserved the Union or that belittles or undervalues their work. The case was appealed to the U.S. Court of Appeals, Ninth Circuit, which concluded that the teachers did not have standing to challenge the constitutionality of the statute, since they failed to show that they had suffered some actual or threatened injury. On the other hand, the court accepted the students' claim that the schoolbook screening system restricted their First Amendment right of free access to information. The appeals court af-firmed the standing of the students and the ripeness of their claims, applying that conclusion as well to the parents, who may assert claims of constitutional violation affecting their children's education.

SECULARISM AND SEX: THE TWIN THREATS TO AMERICA

In 1985, *Grove v. Mead School District No. 354* rejected a parent's claim that a book should be removed from the curriculum because it fostered a belief system called "secular humanism." After Mrs. Grove complained to her daughter's eighth-grade teacher about the use of *The Learning Tree,* by Gordon Parks, the daughter was assigned another book and given permission to leave class during discussions of the book. Still, the mother filed a formal complaint with the school district, claiming that the book embodied the philosophy of secular humanism and thereby violated her religious beliefs. A school textbook evaluation committee subsequently concluded that *The Learning Tree* was an appropriate element of the sophomore English curriculum, and after a hearing, the board of education denied the request to remove the book. Plaintiffs then brought a civil rights suit against the school district, seeking damages and injunctive relief. They contended that use of *The Learning Tree* violated the religion clauses of the First Amendment. After a hearing, the judge granted summary judgment for the defendants.

With respect to the establishment clause, the court in *Grove* stated:

> It is true that *The Learning Tree* poses questions and ponders doubts with which plaintiffs may be uncomfortable. Yet to pose questions is not to impose answers. Since the first amendment is designed as much to protect the former as prevent the latter, I cannot conclude, on the record presented, that the use of *The Learning Tree* inhibits religion.

The court also ruled that the burden on the free exercise of religion was "minimal," since the child was assigned an alternate book. In this regard, the court concluded: "The state interest in providing well-rounded public education would be critically impeded by accommodation of Grove's wishes. . . . In light of the absence of coercion and the critical threat to public education, we conclude that the school board has not violated the free exercise clause."[46]

Two years later, in a similar judgment, *Mozert v. Hawkins County Board of Education* (1987) concluded a lengthy controversy (see Chapter 1) by rejecting parents' demands to remove a textbook series from the curriculum. Tennessee parents were plaintiffs in a civil rights action in U.S. District Court seeking damages and injunctive relief, based on their objections to the requirement that all Hawkins County public school children through the eighth grade must read from the Holt *Basic Readings* textbooks. The plaintiffs alleged that the textbooks taught nine different objectionable things, including witchcraft, magic and the occult, relative values, disrespect and disobedience to parents, idolatry, generalized faith in the supernatural, humanism, and Darwinism. The plaintiffs claimed, in essence, that the First Amendment freedom to believe as they choose was meaningless if the state could force their children to read books that contain ideas and values to which they did not subscribe. The court decided that only one of the nine complaints (that the texts accept any type of faith as an acceptable method of salvation) might represent a constitutional violation but said that the plaintiffs had not specified which parts of which books substantiated their complaint. The court concluded that no basic constitutional values were implicated in the allegations against the Holt *Basic Readings,* saying: "The First Amendment does not protect the plaintiffs from exposure to morally offensive value systems or from exposure to antithetical religious ideas."[47] The court thereby decided against the plaintiff's request for an injunction to prohibit compulsory use of the Holt *Basic Readings.*

That same year, another challenge to secular education was rebuffed in *Smith v. Board of School Commissioners of Mobile (Ala.) County* (1987). Here 624 Christian Evangelicals in Mobile, Alabama, brought suit against a school board, charging that the school system was teaching an antireligious religion called "secular humanism." The complainants asked that forty-four different textbooks, from elementary through high school, be removed from the curriculum. They claimed that the texts contained passages about one-parent families and divorce, offending their belief in the sanctity of traditional families. The case grew out of Alabama's earlier adoption of silent prayer in schools, upheld in court by Federal District Judge W. Brevard Hand. When silent prayer was overturned by a higher court, and declared unconstitutional by the Supreme Court, Judge Hand responded by approving the ban of the forty-four textbooks. In ruling in favor of the fundamentalist plaintiffs, Judge Hand declared: "If this Court is compelled to purge 'God is great, God is good, We thank him for our daily food' from the classroom, then this Court must also purge from the classroom those things that serve to teach that salvation is through one's self rather than through a deity."[48]

The U.S. Court of Appeals for the Eleventh Circuit reversed Judge Hand, ruling that as long as the school was motivated by a secular purpose, its curriculum and textbooks could present ideas held by one or more religious groups. The appeals court ruled that the textbooks neither endorsed theistic religion as a system of belief, nor discredited it, but rather promoted important secular values, such as tolerance, self-respect, and logical decision making. The answer to the fundamentalists' complaint, said the court, was not less speech but more.

Cases like *Kanawha, Grove, Mozert,* and *Smith* reveal the courts' reluctance to endorse fundamentalist attempts to censor school materials, suggesting that vulgarity or indecency remains the most acceptable legal basis on which to ban books in schools. Interestingly, vulgarity and indecency are not constitutionally justifiable reasons for banning books in *public libraries,* where a higher standard, obscenity, must be met. But virtually every act of school censorship upheld by the courts has turned on the sexual content of the material, and the special characteristics of the school environment have allowed the age of the school audience to be a deciding factor. This has been seen in cases like *Presidents Council, Zykan, Bicknell,* and *Seyfried v. Walton.*[49] Even Justice Brennan in *Pico* noted: "[R]espondents implicitly concede that an unconstitutional motivation would *not* be demonstrated if it were shown that petitioners had decided to remove the books at issue because those books were pervasively vulgar." Justice Blackmun's concurring opinion in *Pico* stated that "First Amendment principles would allow a school board to refuse to make a book available to students because it contains offensive language."[50]

In *Bethel School District No. 403 v. Fraser* (1986), a high school student was suspended for making sexually suggestive remarks at a student-government assembly. Here the Court rejected the student's claim that his First Amendment rights were violated when he was disciplined for an alleged sexual innuendo in his speech nominating another student for school office. *Fraser,* like *Pico,* was decided as a First Amendment case, with Chief Justice Burger invoking *Ambach* for a doctrinal definition of public education as the inculcation of "fundamental values necessary to the maintenance of a democratic political system." In supporting the school board, Burger advised:

> The undoubted freedom to advocate unpopular and controversial views in schools and classrooms must be balanced against the society's countervailing interest in teaching students the boundaries of socially appropriate behavior. . . . It does not follow . . . that simply because the use of an offensive form of expression may not be prohibited to adults making what the speaker considers a political point, that the same latitude must be permitted to children in a public school.

Writing for the majority, Burger concluded:

> Surely it is a highly appropriate function of public school education to prohibit the use of vulgar and offensive terms in public discourse. . . . Nothing in the Constitution prohibits the states from insisting that certain modes of expression are inappropriate and subject to sanctions. . . . The determination of what manner of speech in the classroom or in school assembly is inappropriate properly rests with the school board.[51]

From cases like *Fraser,* Robert S. Peck, legislative counsel of the ACLU, concludes that if there is a legal and societal consensus on any free speech issues, it is that children should not be exposed to sexual content. This would mean that children's rights to free expression in this area are clearly less than for adults, an approach seemingly endorsed by the benchmark *Hazelwood* decision.[52]

HAZELWOOD: A CHILL WIND FOR THE 1990S

In the 1988 *Hazelwood School District v. Kuhlmeier* decision, the Court affirmed the principle of judicial restraint in educational affairs by stating that "the education of the Nation's youth is primarily the responsibility of parents, teachers, and state and local school officials, and not of federal judges." Here the Court saw no constitutional restraint on a Missouri school principal who removed portions of a student newspaper produced as part of a high school journalism class. When the principal removed pages containing articles on pregnancy and divorce from the high school newspaper, the student staff filed suit, claiming violation of their First Amendment rights. The school principal claimed he was properly protecting the privacy of pregnant students described, but not named, in the articles and also protecting younger students from inappropriate references to sexual activity and birth control. The principal also claimed that since a school-sponsored newspaper could be perceived as an expression of official school opinion, censorship was justified to protect the school from possible libel action. The Supreme Court held that the principal acted reasonably and did not violate the students' First Amendment rights. The Court declared that a school need not tolerate student speech "that is inconsistent with its 'basic educational mission,' even though the government could not censor similar speech outside the school."[53]

Because the newspaper was part of the journalism curriculum, it was held to be subject to control by a faculty member. The newspaper was thus regarded not as a forum for the free expression of ideas but "as supervised learning experience for journalism students." The Court ruled that "educators do not offend the First Amendment by exercising editorial control over the style and content of student speech in school-sponsored expressive activities so long as their actions are reasonably related to legitimate pedagogical concerns." The Court did caution, however, that this authority does not justify school action

> to silence a student's personal expression that happens to occur on the school premises. . . . It is only when the decision to censor a school-sponsored publication, theatrical production, or other vehicle of student expression has no valid educational purpose that the First Amendment is so "directly and sharply implicate[d]" as to require judicial intervention to protect students' constitutional rights.

Hazelwood therefore established that teachers, principals, and school boards may take action within the school's educational mission that might otherwise be unconstitutional.[54]

Hazelwood, like virtually all the relevant cases that preceded it, attempted to define the mission of the public education system and the authority vested in its officials. In many ways it contradicted the Court's declaration in *Tinker* that students do not shed their constitutional rights at the schoolhouse gate. But there is a strong suggestion in *Hazelwood* that postsecondary educational institutions or libraries outside the school system (e.g., public libraries) would receive greater First Amendment protection than do the elementary and secondary school curriculum and libraries. In fact, the courts following *Hazelwood* appear to have established different levels of constitutional protection for books and other publications, depending on whether they are removed from a classroom, a school library, or a public library.

Within a year of *Hazelwood*, the fears that it would lead the courts to place school censorship outside of First Amendment protections seemed realized. In *Virgil v. School Board of Columbia County* (1989), the Eleventh Circuit applied the Supreme Court's approach in *Hazelwood*, upholding a school board's removal of a previously approved textbook because of alleged vulgarity and sexual explicitness. For a decade, the Columbia County High School had been offering an elective course using the state-approved text *The Humanities: Cultural Roots and Continuities*. In addition to the optional status of the course itself, parents were allowed to request alternative readings if they found any of the assignments objectionable. During the 1985–1986 school year, the daughter of a fundamentalist minister took the course and objected to two selections in the text: "The Miller's Tale," by Chaucer, and *Lysistrata*, by Aristophanes. Neither selection was assigned reading, though portions of *Lysistrata* were read aloud in class. In *Lysistrata*, a fifth-century Greek drama, an Athenian woman persuades other women to stop sleeping with their husbands until the men promise to stop fighting wars.

The complaint form filled out by the minister cited vulgar language and "promotion of women's lib," and the complaint was pursued even after his daughter had completed the humanities course. An advisory committee made up of Columbia County teachers read the two challenged selections in *The Humanities* and recommended retaining the text but not assigning either of the challenged works. The superintendent of schools rejected the recommendation, saying that "any literature in which God's name is used in vain is not appropriate for use in the classroom."[55] The school board then felt obliged to vote unanimously to ban the book from the curriculum.

The parents of some Columbia High School students objected to the fact that the views of a small number of people, led by the minister, had determined what could be read by all of the students in the school. Under threat of a lawsuit, the school board voted 4 to 1 to put one copy of *The Humanities* in the school library, although the book remained banned from the curriculum. Nonetheless, on November 24,

1986, the ACLU brought suit against the board on behalf of a parent named Moyna Virgil. The case, *Virgil v. School Board of Columbia County*, argued that the removal of the textbook suppressed free speech and free thought while advancing religion through the public schools. The defense claimed that despite the superintendent's comments, the board had rejected the book solely because it contained sexually explicit scenes and inappropriate language. The defense relied on *Hazelwood*, while the ACLU relied on *Pico*, arguing that if the Supreme Court had intended to supersede *Pico* with *Hazelwood*, it would have said so.

U.S. District Judge Susan Black concluded that *Hazelwood* was the relevant Supreme Court precedent, saying:

> In light of the recent decision of the United States Supreme Court in *Hazelwood* . . . , this Court need not decide whether the plurality decision in *Pico* may logically be extended to optional curriculum materials. *Kuhlmeier* resolves any doubts as to the appropriate standards to be applied whenever a curriculum decision is subject to first amendment review. . . . Although it did not specifically refer to textbooks, the Court [in *Hazelwood*] evidently sought to address a wide realm of "curriculum decisions," including those affecting textbooks.

Judge Black admitted, "The Court finds it difficult to apprehend the harm which could conceivably be caused to a group of eleventh- and twelfth-grade students by exposure to Aristophanes and Chaucer,"[56] yet she concluded that the *Hazelwood* interpretation of the limited scope of students' First Amendment rights compelled her to decide in favor of the school board.

The ACLU appealed, arguing that *Hazelwood* applied to student writing, not literary classics, and that the board's action was "rooted, indeed steeped, in philosophic valuing rather than pedagogical concern." The ACLU brief argued, "There must be some First Amendment recourse against the tyranny of bad taste. Literary classics generally considered part and parcel of a liberal arts education cannot be constitutionally bannable because a board doesn't 'like' them."[57] The Florida Department of Education, along with many national educational organizations, filed amici curiae briefs supporting the ACLU position, but the U.S. Court of Appeals for the Eleventh Circuit upheld Black's decision, stating:

> Of course, we do not endorse the Board's decision. Like the district court, we seriously question how young persons just below the age of majority can be harmed by these masterpieces of Western literature. However, having concluded that there is no constitutional violation, our role is not to second guess the wisdom of the Board's action.[58]

The decision in *Virgil*, as in *Hazelwood*, had repercussions in lower court decisions around the country. We saw in Chapter 1 that a Florida bookbanning incident produced litigation (*Farrell v. Hall*, Order, July 18, 1988, U.S. District Court for the Northern District of Florida)[59] and subsequent compromise contemporaneously with the deliberations in *Virgil*. During the course of negotiations overseen by the court in *Farrell*, the announcement that *Virgil* was lost despite what appeared to be a strong First Amendment case had a sobering effect on the *Farrell* plaintiffs. The secondary school teacher who was prominent among the plaintiffs admitted that their willingness to settle out of court was heavily influenced by the outcome of *Virgil*.

Although the trend since *Hazelwood* has been for lower state and federal courts to reject claims of First Amendment protection against official censorship of the curriculum, this view has been contested in cases like *McCarthy v. Fletcher* (1989). There, a teacher, a student, a parent, and a taxpayer brought suit against the administrators and trustees of the Wasco Union High School District after school officials banned the use of two novels, *Grendel*, by John Gardner, and *One Hundred Years of Solitude*, by Gabriel García Márquez, from use in a twelfth-grade English class. In response to an initial complaint about the books, the school superintendent and the principal had restricted their use to only those students whose parents gave written permission. But when *all* students produced signed permission slips, the school board decided to ban the books formally.

The school officials filed suit for summary judgment, claiming that their action was "cloaked with a legislative immunity preventing judicial inquiry into the board members' motives or intent in excluding the books."[60] The trial court granted summary judgment in favor of the school officials, ruling that the plaintiffs had not shown sufficient cause to even hold a trial. The court ruled that even if all the allegations of bookbanning by school officials were proved, those officials were still permitted to take such actions without violating the First Amendment. The teacher appealed to the California Court of Appeals, which reversed the lower court's judgment, interpreting *Hazelwood* in a way that recognized the possible violation of First Amendment rights for teachers and students, depending on the outcome of a trial clarifying the board's motivation in banning the books.

In *McCarthy* the court found that the school officials' evaluations of the banned books included statements suggesting that the books were removed for religious reasons. For example, the superintendent's evaluation of *Grendel* said it "was designed to break down a student's belief in God," and the vice-principal's evaluation charged that *Grendel* "contains many anti-government, anti-God, and anti-religion statements." Similar comments were made by the superintendent at a public school board meeting. Based on such information, the court concluded that religious motives were behind the deletion of the two books. The court therefore remanded the case for a trial to determine whether "the administrators were acting to protect and advance the Christian ideology on behalf of the Wasco religious community—a patently illegitimate educational purpose."

In remanding the case for trial, the court said that even under the broad *Hazelwood* standard, school officials may not be motivated by an intent to "prescribe what shall be orthodox in politics, nationalism, religion, or other matters of opinion." The court in *McCarthy* revealed its skepticism about the school board's real reason for banning the books when it stated that "the educational unsuitability of the books . . . must be the true reason for the books' exclusion and not just a pretextual expression for exclusion because the board disagrees with the religious or philosophical ideas expressed in the books." *McCarthy* thus made clear that *Hazelwood* did not authorize school officials to ban books on the mere *claim* of a valid educational purpose. Allowing such an interpretation, said the court, would enable school officials to "camouflage religious 'viewpoint discrimination' . . . which we do not believe *Hazelwood* intended."[61]

The decision in *McCarthy* suggests that even *Hazelwood* can be read as providing First Amendment limitations on official power to interfere with intellectual freedom in the public schools. The ruling depended on the judge's argument that the legal doctrines in *Hazelwood* still allow the courts a substantial role in reviewing the constitutionality of actions by local school officials, beyond the limited role recognized in *Virgil*.

The prospects for defeating religiously motivated challenges to school and library materials thus remain good, even under the *Hazelwood* standard. A very recent California case concerning the most frequently banned (and litigated) book of the 1990s, the *Impressions* textbook set from Holt, Rinehart and Winston, may suggest the future for that series and other modern textbooks. During the 1989–1990 school year, several parents of schoolchildren in the Woodland Joint Unified School District filed a formal written request to "reconsider," that is, remove, the *Impressions* series from the curriculum. They initially contended that the text contained too many references to Canadian culture, that it intruded on the privacy of children and their families, that it contained excessive violence and morbidity, and that it emphasized the occult. The school district had earlier conducted a lengthy piloting and review process, including field testing and public comment, from which *Impressions* emerged as the overwhelming favorite of teachers and students. At the conclusion of the process, nine of the twelve elementary schools in the district had selected *Impressions* as part of their language arts curriculum.

Nonetheless, in response to the parents' complaints, Woodland School Superintendent Robert Watt appointed a review committee consisting of a school administrator, two teachers, the librarian of the Woodland Public Library, a parent, and a local fundamentalist minister. After a comprehensive review, the committee concluded that the parents' complaints were unwarranted and recommended retention of *Impressions* in its entirety.

On January 8, 1991, the complaining parents initiated legal action in the U.S. District Court. In *Brown v. Woodland Unified Joint School District,* plaintiffs requested injunctive and declaratory relief, now alleging that the school district's acquisition and use of portions of the *Impressions* series endorsed and sponsored the religions of "Witchcraft" and "Neo-Paganism," in violation of federal and state constitutional requirements of separation of church and state. The school district contended that the case was controlled by *Grove v. Mead School District No. 354,* which upheld a school board's refusal to remove a book from the curriculum on the basis of plaintiffs' religious objections to the book. U.S. District Judge William B. Schubb wrote:

> Factually, this case bears a strong similarity to *Grove.* Here, plaintiffs, Evangelical Christians, bring a religiously based challenge to a public school's use of a reading series. Here, as in *Grove,* plaintiffs argue that the religion at issue denigrates or inhibits their own religion and establishes a somewhat novel religion. As in *Grove,* the challenged material serves secular goals. Similar to *Grove,* plaintiffs object to isolated and small portions of all the activities in the *Impressions* series. . . . The *Impressions* series, like *The Learning Tree,* is only one part of the two part language arts curriculum utilized in the School District.[62]

The plaintiffs claimed that *Grove* only addressed the relatively passive act of reading a book, whereas *Brown v. Woodland* also involved exercises that convert neutral reading into sponsorship of witchcraft and neopaganism. Judge Schubb rejected this claim, stating:

> A school district may incorporate folk traditions into learning exercises. The convergence of a School District and religious organization on the same exercise or practice does not necessarily suggest that the former is conveying a message of government endorsement of the religious aspects of the practice. The School District's purchase and use of certain prescribed exercises within the *Impressions* series does not suggest a religious preference for Witchcraft or Neo-Paganism. . . . As the court has previously indicated, the exercises, like the excerpts in *Grove,* played only a minute role in the entire *Impressions* series, and *Impressions,* in turn, is only one part of defendant's language arts curriculum.[63]

In ruling that the school district was entitled to summary judgment, Judge Schubb stated: "While the court is not unsympathetic to plaintiffs' concerns, there is no constitutional basis [for] the court to order that the activities in question be excluded from the classroom simply because isolated instances of those activities may happen to coincide or harmonize with the tenets of two relatively obscure religions." Schubb concluded:

> Finally, there is no evidence that *Impressions* was initially selected or retained by the School District out of hostility toward Christianity or fealty to any Wiccan or Neo-Paganist credo. . . . [F]ar from preferring one religion over another, *Impressions* materials were chosen in part to reflect the cultural diversity of North American society.[64]

Later in 1992, an Illinois case treated a similar complaint and relied heavily on the decision in *Woodland*. In *Fleischfresser v. Directors of School District No. 200* (1992), Judge James B. Moran wrote:

> The *Impressions* series has, apparently, generated a certain amount of controversy around the country, with parents having views similar to the plaintiffs complaining to other school boards about the contents. . . . It is not the province of this court, however, to sit as some sort of reviewer of the decisions of local school boards. Plaintiffs must be able to establish that the series fosters a particular religious belief, and a review of the series establishes that it cannot be reasonably concluded that it does so.

Judge Moran noted that Judge Schubb in *Woodland* had analyzed both the series and the applicable law in granting summary judgment to the defendants, and Moran said it was not necessary to revisit that analysis. He concluded, "Whether or not it [*Impressions*] is the best available educational medium is up to defendant to decide. It certainly passes constitutional muster."[65]

Although the courts have not usually been sympathetic to the censorship demands of religious fundamentalists, local school boards have been intimidated into changing their policies. For example, in Hawkins County, Tennessee, the *Diary of Anne Frank* was among the books accused of being "anti-Christian." The fundamentalists claimed that a passage in *Anne Frank* suggested the equivalence of all religions, contradicting the notion of one true religion. Though the fundamentalists were eventually unsuccessful in their lawsuit, *Mozert v. Hawkins County* (1987), the school chose to cancel the performance of *Anne Frank* as a play, rather than face further complaints and litigation.

Charles Halpern, director of the Institute for Public Representation, feels that the courts may no longer be the most appropriate battleground for combating school censorship, and he recommends caution in initiating litigation toward that end. "We are talking about extremely difficult cases," he warns.

> School libraries strike me as an incredibly difficult problem. It is very much harder, for example, than taking books off the shelves in a general library. Before we go all out and say we should get these issues before the courts, let's ask whether we really want to focus on the *school* library, as we're asking the courts to do. . . . [P]eople should be discouraged from taking on very hard cases, particularly since there can be a real down side to this litigation. You can make bad law, you can win cases on grounds which can lead to results and consequences that you don't like.[66]

Halpern also questions whether litigation is the most effective support for the people on the First Amendment battle lines.

> How do you provide for support and encouragement for the librarians, the school teachers, and others who are out there waging the day-to-day, low visibility struggle against censorship efforts? Litigation backup might not be available to each of them in each of their travails. That is holding out a false promise and it is, to my way of thinking, also a strategy which in the long-term is counterproductive. The dilemma of supporting and encouraging these people is one in which nonlegal strategy should be emphasized.[67]

Whether or not one regards *Hazelwood* as a green light for official suppression of expression in schools and libraries, there is an increasing view that the courts can never be the ultimate protector of our First Amendment rights. James Anthony Whitson, a legal and educational scholar, warns:

> [A]s scholars, researchers, and educators, we have responsibilities of our own for protecting intellectual freedom, independently of whatever protection is afforded by the courts. For another thing, we now see that the judicial interpretations of Constitutional rights are not arrived at simply through a top-down process of rule-governed deduction from the written document itself. Instead, they reflect at least tacit interpretations of the realities of language, learning and freedom of thought, things that come within the realm of special expertise of educators and educational researchers and scholars, as distinct from that of judges and lawyers. To interpret First Amendment rights, therefore, the legal process needs input from the education community, input that is not unduly prejudiced by the parameters of the judicial discourse.[68]

NOTES

1. *Bartels v. State of Iowa*, 43 S. Ct. 628 (1923).
2. *Meyer v. Nebraska*, 262 U.S. 390, 401 (1923).

3. *Pierce v. Society of Sisters,* 286 U.S. 510, 535 (1925).

4. *Minersville School District v. Gobitis,* 310 U.S. 586, 598 (1940).

5. *Minersville School District v. Gobitis,* 310 U.S. 586, 604 (1940).

6. *West Virginia State Board of Education v. Barnette,* 319 U.S. 624, 637, 640 (1943).

7. *Keyishian v. Board of Regents,* 385 U.S. 589, 603 (1967).

8. *Epperson v. Arkansas,* 393 U.S. 97, 105, 113, 114 (1968).

9. *Epperson v. Arkansas,* 393 U.S. 97, 115–116 (1968).

10. *Tinker v. Des Moines Independent Community School District,* 395 U.S. 503, 506, 511 (1969).

11. *Martin v. City of Struthers,* 319 U.S. 141 (1943).

12. *Lamont v. U.S. Postmaster General,* 381 U.S. 301 (1965).

13. *Virginia State Board of Pharmacy v. Virginia Citizens Consumer Council,* 425 U.S. 748 (1976).

14. Mary Elizabeth Bezanson, "The Right to Receive through the School Library," *Communication Education,* October 1987, pp. 340–41.

15. *Wisconsin v. Yoder,* 406 U.S. 205, 234, 240 (1972).

16. *Wisconsin v. Yoder,* 406 U.S. 205, 242, 245 (1972).

17. *San Antonio Independent School District v. Rodriguez,* 411 U.S. 1, 36 (1973).

18. *Presidents Council District 25 v. Community School Board No. 25,* 457 F.2d 289, 291–92 (1972).

19. *Presidents Council District 25 v. Community School Board No. 25,* 457 F.2d 289, 293 (1972).

20. *Presidents Council District 25 v. Community School Board No. 25,* 457 F.2d 289, 291 (1972).

21. *Williams v. Board of Education of County of Kanawha,* 388 F. Supp. 93, 96 (1975).

22. *Minarcini v. Strongsville (Ohio) City School District,* 541 F.2d 577, 582, 583 (6th Cir. 1976).

23. *Minarcini v. Strongsville (Ohio) City School District,* 541 F.2d 577, 581 (6th Cir. 1976).

24. *Right to Read Defense Committee v. School Committee of the City of Chelsea,* 454 F. Supp. 703, 707, 713 (1978).

25. *Cary v. Board of Education Arapahoe School District,* 598 F.2d 535, 542, 544 (1979).

26. *Salvail v. Nashua Board of Education,* 469 F. Supp. 1269, 1272, 1275 (1979).

27. *Ambach v. Norwick,* 441 U.S. 68 (1979).

28. *Zykan v. Warsaw Community School Corporation and Warsaw School Board of Trustees,* 631 F.2d 1300, 1304, 1306 (1980).

29. *Bicknell v. Vergennes Union High School Board of Directors,* 475 F. Supp. 615 (1979).

30. *Board of Education, Island Trees Union Free School District No. 26 v. Pico,* 474 F. Supp. 387, 396–97 (1982).

31. *Board of Education, Island Trees Union Free School District No. 26 v. Pico,* 638 F.2d 404, 416 (1982).

32. *Board of Education, Island Trees Union Free School District No. 26 v. Pico,* 638 F.2d 404, 419 (1982).

33. *Board of Education, Island Trees Union Free School District No. 26 v. Pico,* 638 F.2d 404, 437 (1982).

34. *Board of Education, Island Trees Union Free School District No. 26 v. Pico,* 457 U.S. 853, 879–80 (1982).

35. *Board of Education, Island Trees Union Free School District No. 26 v. Pico,* 102 S. Ct. 2799, 2805–6 (1982).

36. *Board of Education, Island Trees Union Free School District No. 26 v. Pico,* 102 S. Ct. 2799, 2809 (1982).

37. *Board of Education, Island Trees Union Free School District No. 26 v. Pico,* 457 U.S. 853, 867–8 (1982).

38. *Board of Education, Island Trees Union Free School District No. 26 v. Pico,* 102 S. Ct. 2799, 2829–30 (1982).

39. *West Virginia State Board of Education v. Barnette,* 319 U.S. 624, 641 (1943).

40. American Library Association, Office for Intellectual Freedom, *Intellectual Freedom Manual,* 4th ed. (Chicago: ALA, 1992), pp. 182–83.

41. Ibid., p. 183.

42. *Board of Education, Island Trees Union Free School District No. 26 v. Pico,* 102 S. Ct. 2799, 2808, 2821 (1982).

43. *Board of Education, Island Trees School District No. 26 v. Pico,* 102 S. Ct. 2799, 2821 (1982).

44. *Sheck v. Baileyville School Committee,* 530 F. Supp. 679, 684–85, 689 (1982).

45. *Johnson v. Stuart,* 702 F.2d 193 (1983).

46. *Grove v. Mead School District No. 354,* 753 F.2d 1528, 1534, 1541 (1985).

47. *Mozert v. Hawkins County Board of Education,* 579 F. Supp. 1051, 1053 (1987).

48. *Smith v. Board of School Commissioners of Mobile (Ala.) County,* 827 F.2d 684, 688 (1987).

49. *Seyfried v. Walton,* 572 F. Supp. 235 (D. Del. 1981).

50. *Board of Education, Island Trees Union Free School District No. 26 v. Pico,* 457 U.S. 853, 870, 871, 880 (1982).

51. *Bethel School District No. 403 v. Fraser,* 478 U.S. 675, 681, 682 (1986).

52. American Library Association, Office for Intellectual Freedom, *Intellectual Freedom Manual,* 4th ed., Chicago, ALA, 1992, p. 188.

53. *Hazelwood School District v. Kuhlmeier,* 108 S. Ct. 562, 571 (1988).

54. *Hazelwood School District v. Kuhlmeier,* 108 S. Ct. 562, 571 (1988).

55. *Virgil v. School Board of Columbia County,* 862 F.2d 1517, 1522 (11th Cir. 1989).

56. *Virgil v. School Board of Columbia County,* 677 F. Supp. 1547, 1551–52 (M.D. Fla. 1988).

57. *Virgil v. School Board of Columbia County,* Appellants' Initial Brief, submitted by the American Civil Liberties Union on April 29, 1988, pp. 13, 25.

58. *Virgil v. School Board of Columbia County,* 862 F.2d 1517, 1525 (11th Cir. 1989).

59. *Farrell v. Hall,* Order, July 18, 1988, U.S. District Court for the Northern District of Florida.

60. *McCarthy v. Fletcher,* 254 Cal. Rptr. 714, 718 (1989).

61. *McCarthy v. Fletcher,* 254 Cal. Rptr. 714, 720, 724 (1989).

62. *Brown v. Woodland Joint Unified School District,* E.D. Cal. Case No. Civ. 5–91–0032 (April 2, 1992).

63. *Brown v. Woodland Joint Unified School District,* E.D. Cal. Case No. Civ. 5–91–0032 (April 2, 1992).

64. *Brown v. Woodland Joint Unified School District,* E.D. Cal. Case No. Civ. 5–91–0032 (April 2, 1992).

65. *Fleischfresser v. Directors of School District No. 200,* 805 F. Supp. 584 (1992).

66. American Library Association, Office for Intellectual Freedom, *Censorship Litigation and the Schools,* proceedings of a colloquium held January 1981 (Chicago: ALA, 1983), p. 117.

67. Ibid., p. 118.

68. James Anthony Whitson, *Constitution and Curriculum* (New York: Falmer Press, 1991), p. 254.

| 3 |

Voices of Banned Authors

Judy Blume

Several years ago, the head librarian of the New York Public Library's Children's Room said she had never seen a children's author as popular as Judy Blume. Indeed, Blume's novels became so popular with adolescents that one critic observed that "there is, indeed, scarcely a literate girl of novel-reading age who has not read one or more of Blume's books."[1]

Judy Blume has written more than twenty books, including *Are You There God? It's Me, Margaret; Deenie; Blubber;* and her most recent, *Here's to You, Rachel Robinson.* Among her books for younger readers is the popular "Fudge" series: *Tales of a Fourth Grade Nothing; Otherwise Known as Sheila the Great; Superfudge;* and *Fudge-a-mania.* She has also written books for young adults (e.g. *Forever* and *Tiger Eyes*) and for adults (e.g. *Wifey* and *Smart Women*). With this broad readership it is not surprising that over 50 million copies of her books are in print, and her work has been translated into fourteen languages.

Blume has received numerous awards for her books, including Children's Choice Awards in thirty states, Australia, England, and Germany. She is a board member of the Society of Children's Book Writers and a member of PEN American Center, and she serves on the Council of the Authors Guild, Planned Parenthood Advocates, and the Council of Advisors of the National Coalition Against Censorship. She has been the recipient of the Carl Sandburg Freedom to Read Award, the Civil Liberties Award, and the John Rock Award, and has been chosen as a

"Hero of Young America" for eight of the past nine years in the annual World Almanac poll award. Nonetheless, her candid treatment of mature issues, including adolescent sexuality, and her frank use of language has caused some schools and libraries to ban her books.

Blume thinks she writes about sexuality today because it was uppermost in her mind when she was a child. There was the need to know but no easy way to find out. Like most kids, she *never* asked her parents. Blume told the *New York Times* magazine: "I don't believe that sex is why kids like my books. The impression I get from letter after letter, is that a great many kids don't communicate with their parents. They feel alone in the world. Sometimes, reading books that deal with other kids who feel the same things they do . . . makes them feel less alone." [2]

When I asked if her parents had attempted to control or censor her reading habits, Blume quickly answered, "No, they didn't. I was very lucky. My father had a fairly extensive library, and no one ever told me what I could read or what I could not read. Not that my mother discussed the subjects in those books, but I never felt that I couldn't read them. My mother was very shy, but she was a reader, and reading was always considered a good thing in my house." [3]

When Judy Blume began writing, she had traditional models among the children's and young adult authors: Elaine Konigsburg, Beverly Cleary, Louise Fitzhugh. Indeed, Blume's first two books bore little resemblance to the controversial works that followed. When she wrote *The One in the Middle is the Green Kangaroo* and *Iggie's House*, she was learning her trade, but after they were done, she said to herself, "Now that I've figured out how to write books, I'm going to write what I know to be true." At that point, she began *Are You There God? It's Me, Margaret*. During this period, she was taking a writing course with Lee Wyndham, a children's writer during the late 1940s and 1950s, who gave Blume her first professional encouragement. Wyndham had absolute rules and regulations for writing children's books, and Blume says many students in the class may have felt that they couldn't get anything published if they didn't follow the rules. Blume recalls saying to herself, "Never mind these rules. This isn't what it's really like." [4] She says she was not breaking rules in a hostile or rebellious way. She was simply determined to write about what she remembered. When Wyndham saw the manuscript to *Margaret*, she wrote Blume a long letter about it, questioning some of the sensitive or intimate subjects. But Wyndham was also the first to write to congratulate her when the *New York Times* gave *Margaret* a good review.

While Blume was writing *Iggie's House*, she came across an announcement in a magazine that a new publishing company was interested in realistic books about childhood and adolescence. Through this ad, she contacted Bradbury Press and met Dick Jackson and Bob Verrone. They took a big chance on her when they agreed to publish *Iggie's House* and, after that, *Margaret*. Blume says she always had the happiest publishing experiences with Bradbury Press, where Dick Jackson taught her how to revise and rewrite her books on her own.

Did it take courage for Blume to write candidly about topics like menstruation, not previously covered in young adult books? She says, "It was not courage. It was naivete. I had absolutely no idea I was writing a controversial book. There was nothing in it that wasn't a part of my sixth grade experience."[5] She recalls that she and her friends talked endlessly about menstruation and breast development, just as Margaret and her friends do in the book.

Blume was shocked when I told her that public libraries were increasingly banning her books. She had assumed bookbanning was primarily confined to school libraries. She added, "It's difficult keeping track of these events, because the authors don't find out unless someone else notifies them. More recently, thanks to the National Coalition against Censorship, we are hearing more promptly about when and where our books are being banned. I don't think any school board or school library or teacher has ever tried to contact me directly. In the past, that information has usually been communicated to me through the newspapers, but today it is more effectively documented in publications by the American Library Association, People for the American Way, and the organization I'm most involved with, the National Coalition against Censorship. As soon as they hear of any book that's been challenged, they will contact the author and try to work with everyone involved. They're a small but wonderfully effective organization, located in New York. Their executive director, Leanne Katz, is up to date on everything. ALA is terrific on censorship issues, and People for the American Way is, too, but they are involved in many other activities. The National Coalition deals only with censorship."

When Blume talked to the National Council of Teachers at their 1991 annual meeting in Seattle, she discovered that the classroom teachers and school librarians knew surprisingly little about how to respond to censorship, how to prepare for it, and the need to have policies in place. She says, "When I gave them the names and phone numbers of the organizations available to help them, most of them didn't seem to know how to proceed, how to get help. I told them that the National Coalition against Censorship was just a phone call or fax away, and the sooner they were informed of a challenged book, the better they would be able to help. I'm not aware of what may be going on in public libraries, but the school librarians, teachers, and principals who are under fire should know that they are not alone, that there is a support group. That is very important. A lot of the censors out there claim that a challenged book can be harmlessly removed from a classroom or school library, because a reader can always go to a public library to find it. That's one way the censor is able to get a book out of a school."

The first act of censorship that Judy Blume recalls against one of her books was initiated by her children's elementary school principal. Blume had given the school some copies of *Margaret* when it first came out, but the principal refused to allow the books in the school's library. Blume thought the principal was "a nut," and it never occurred to her that this sort of thing would happen again. In the beginning, her publishers tried to protect her from controversy, and as a result, she never saw the letters or heard about the phone calls. Today she realizes that was wrong.

When I asked Blume if she was offended or angered when one of her books was banned, she responded: "Years ago a woman called me on the phone and asked me if I had written *Are You There God? It's Me, Margaret.* When I said yes, she called me a communist and hung up. But this was a long time ago, perhaps twenty years ago. I was bewildered and perplexed in the beginning, and I was personally hurt. Now I understand that this is something much bigger than any kind of personal attack on any one of us. It's like a grieving process. One goes through different stages. Of course, all of those angry feelings cross your mind. What is wrong with these people? How can they possibly think this is something to be afraid of? But I don't feel that way anymore, because I'm too familiar with it. I'm glad I'm beyond that.

"This kind of bookbanning has been going on for a long time, but in 1980, after the election of Ronald Reagan, it really took off. I was very lucky because I wrote all of these books that are now under fire before any of the broader controversy arose. Aside from the phone call I mentioned, I really had no early contact with any of the bookbanners. They weren't yet organized the way they are now. The major censorship groups that now exist didn't exist then. There were the occasional frightened parents who came into the library, waving a book that they didn't want their children to read, but today it is organized in a way that is much more dangerous. I feel badly for the children because it sends a message to them that there is something wrong with reading, that we don't want them to read this book because there's something in it that we don't want them to know."

Like most writers for young people, Judy Blume receives a good deal of mail from her readers. She says: "About 99.9 percent of the letters I receive from children are positive. The negative ones will list the curse words and the pages where they appeared. Such letters are curiously similar, though they come from different parts of the country. I have no doubt that they are written by children, but one can't be sure whether an adult requests that they be written. You never know how some of these censorship groups operate. I had my secretary subscribe to the newsletter of one of these organizations, and they were advertising a pamphlet titled *How to Rid Your Library of Books by Judy Blume*."

The most painful letter she ever received from a child was addressed to "Jewdy Blume." It was from a nine-year-old child who referred to her as "Jewdy" throughout the letter, underlining the letters *JEW* in crayon. The letter attacked the book *Starring Sally J. Freedman as Herself*, complaining of its reference to Jewish angels. Blume says that although she is used to objections about sex and language in her books, that kind of hate from a young child was particularly disturbing.

Judy Blume believes that because many adults are uncomfortable with their own sexuality, they can't begin to deal with their children's. They are embarrassed and uneasy when their children ask them questions about sex, and they are often unable to answer those questions. She says the letters she receives indicate that most parents grew up without ever talking about sex. The message they got from their parents was that sex was neither good nor enjoyable, and that pattern may continue generation after generation. Blume notes that adults are suspicious of any books that kids like, and even some children's librarians tend to tell kids which books they *should* read, rather than encouraging them to read what they enjoy.

Blume says parents find it much harder to listen to their children than to impose rules. She believes censorship grows out of fear, and there is a tremendous amount of fear on the part of parents who wish to control their young children and shield them from the world. She points out that children are inexperienced, but not innocent, and their pain and unhappiness do not come from books. They come from *life*.

Blume says parents should ask themselves what harm is likely to occur if their child browses through the books at the library and happens to pick up a book for older children or even adults. The child may ask the parents a question, and if the child does, the parents should answer it. Blume says children have problems not just with sex but with death, with money, with feelings and emotions—everything that is most important in life. Like all age-groups, children simply want people to be honest with them. Blume says children learn from adults, yet many adults do not know how to talk to kids about anything personal. She grew up hating secrets, and she still hates secrets.

I asked Blume what it was that the censors found so objectionable in her books. She said, "I think in the old days the complaints concerned language and sexuality, but perhaps the censors have become more sophisticated. With respect to *Blubber*, which I think may be my best book for younger kids, the complaints focused on something called 'lack of moral tone,' which I now understand to mean that the bad guys go unpunished or, as the bookbanners put it, evil goes unpunished. In other words, I don't beat the kids over the head with the 'message.' When I lecture and refer to 'lack of moral tone,' I always add, 'whatever that means,' and the audience always laughs. But I have read enough of the forms filled out challenging school library books to know that 'lack of moral tone' is used as a justification for banning books. There is also the claim that my books do not show sufficient respect for authority. But the letters of complaint that I have received are much more specific about offensive language, often specifying a particular curse word."

A school librarian once told Blume that the male principal of her school would not allow Blume's book *Deenie* to be put in the library because Deenie masturbated. He said it would be different if the character were a boy. Interestingly, the only time Blume's editors tried to soften her work, the sensitive passages involved masturbation. "I have a story that I tell on my favorite editor," she said. "It pains me to tell it, and it pains him to hear it. But it happened. When *Tiger Eyes* was published about eleven or twelve years ago, it was shortly after the 1980 elections. The censors were all over the place, and my editor said to me, 'We want this book to be read by as many young people as possible, don't we?' And I said yes. He said, 'Well, then, we don't want to make this a target for the censors, do we? Is it really necessary to include this one passage?' He agreed that the passage was psychologically appropriate to the character but asked whether it was necessary.

"I took it out, and I have regretted it ever since. Was the passage essential to the book? Well, every appropriate passage helps you to know the character. This character was a girl who turned herself off, didn't allow herself to feel emotion after her father was killed. She was beginning to get her feelings back as she explored her body. She masturbated. That's the passage that I was asked to take out, because masturbation is far more threatening than intercourse in a book about young people. I'm sorry that I took it out, and I have done nothing of the sort since then. The last time that I was asked to delete material from one of my books, the publisher's concern was with specific language rather than sexuality. There were just three words involved, but the publisher felt that their inclusion would reduce the paperback book club sales. I thought about it long and hard, but I concluded that the characters would not be real with sanitized speech. The book was eventually published without change."

Blume, like some of the other authors interviewed for this book, is uncomfortable with the attempts to narrowly define her audience: "I hate to categorize books. . . . I wish that older readers would read my books about young people, and I hope that younger readers will grow up to read what I have to say about adult life.[6] She is concerned that, increasingly, children's books that deal realistically with life are being published as adult books or young adult books. She is still angry with Bradbury Press for advertising *Forever* as her first book for adults. She says *Forever* was not intended for adults, but the publishers hoped to protect themselves and her from controversy by suggesting that younger people were not the primary audience.

Blume says some teachers have told their students that if they use her books for a book report, they will automatically have points taken off their grade. She says, "When I began writing, I never thought of my books as classroom materials. I've always hoped that my books would be read the way I read books, which is to become involved in a story that I can't put down, to be swept away by a character, to be entertained and shown how other people live and solve their problems. All the reasons that I read fiction are the very reasons that I write fiction and hope what I write will be read. None of that involves the classroom. Over time, I've become used to the fact that teachers read my books aloud. But in the beginning, it bothered me because I thought of reading as a personal experience between the reader and the book, the kind of thing that you go away in the corner to do. You don't have to talk about it, you don't have to do a book report on it, you're never going to be graded on it, and you don't have to share it if you don't want to. On the other hand, if handled sensitively, my books can be useful classroom tools. I know of one teacher who begins his course each year by reading *Blubber* aloud. He then proceeds to a careful, often intense, discussion of the book and the issues it addresses. Of course, my 'Fudge' books are probably the most commonly used in class because they are fun."

The controversy surrounding her books has also discouraged their inclusion in textbooks and anthologies. She notes, "I've turned down a lot of book club editions, and the like, because they asked me to remove this, this, and this. Some of my material for younger kids has been excerpted, for example, *Tales of a Fourth Grade Nothing*, but not much of my work has been included in anthologies. Frankly, I would prefer that a child read an entire book rather than excerpts. Most schools today are moving away from traditional anthologies and texts, toward the creation of genuine classroom libraries. That's very positive." When asked to analyze the First Amendment implications of school and library censorship, Blume commented: "Obviously, school officials, teachers, and librarians engage in a selection process. But do they select under fear and intimidation or under professional guidelines? Do they select books that the students really want to read and need to read? There is a good deal of censorship by selection, by 'avoidance/selection,' one might say. But once the book has been selected for sound reasons, once it's there, then there are First Amendment rights to protect its availability. Children have rights, too, and in some places, children are beginning to understand that they have a right to choose what they want to read. I think it's very positive that they become involved in these struggles within their community. I encourage young people to become involved."

Judy Blume says her books have been defended by teachers, librarians, concerned citizens, and the kids themselves, the people she believes must be encouraged to take a stand to protect the books that they want to read. She told me: "I frankly feel that my job is to write the books, not to defend them. It is always the reader's job to defend the books, to ensure that they are available. What I try to do now is offer all the support I can to those who are under fire by the bookbanners, whether it is the teachers, librarians, or parents, or students. I feel that I should help by making available any information I can, so I send them letters from readers, letters from teachers, letters from parents. In the case of *Forever,* I send my personal letter describing how I came to write the book and why it is dedicated to my daughter. But I don't travel to the scene of the conflict in an attempt to defend my books."

Like Robert Cormier, Judy Blume feels that the more time she spends defending her books, the less time she has to write. "Cormier and I are of an age where suddenly we realize there isn't all that much time remaining. I don't really see the point of entering the fray, interceding in conflicts over my books. I think that should be done without the author present. I don't believe the issue should be personalized. It's not about the author—it's about the book. I cannot defend my books. I wouldn't even know how to do it. How do you explain why you wrote what you wrote when you wrote it? I just don't think that's part of the job. I love to read letters from kids, because it always seems to me that they make the point so much better than I could. I remember when *Deenie* was under fire, and a seventh-grade girl went before the school board and read a letter she had prepared, explaining why the book was important to her and how it had helped her and her friends to talk about scoliosis [curvature of the spine]. She said that if there was something bad in this book, she didn't know what it was— and maybe they could explain it to her. Such comments are far more persuasive and more important than anything Judy Blume or Robert Cormier could say before a school board.

"I'm not saying that no writer should go before a school board and put himself or herself on the line. I just don't feel it's right for me. I once put myself in the position of having to debate the Moral Majority on television, and I came away saying I'm never going to do that again. It's not what I want to do. On the other hand, I can think of many wonderful experiences, like the group of people in Gwinnett County, Georgia, who came together when a group of my books was banned.

They came together without me, because they cared about reading and about choosing. Even people who had no children in the school became involved because they were readers. They became strong, and even though they lost their case and *Deenie* was banned, it will never happen there again. Not to those people. I came to talk to them after the event, and, even now it makes me cry because it was so moving an experience to meet them and talk with them.

"The point I would like to make is that it is the kids who are the losers in all these battles. We're really talking about what they have a right to know, what they have a right to read. The adults' fears prevent them from talking to their children about subjects that all kids have a right to discuss and learn about. You know, puberty is not a dirty subject, but the censors seem to feel that it is, and that message is sent to the kids. When books are taken away from them because the natural events of puberty are discussed, the message is that these biological processes must not be anticipated or discussed, even though they are going to occur. This is bowing to fear. This is giving the censors power. That bothers me more than anything."

Daniel Cohen

Fundamentalist Pat Robertson, former presidential candidate and recent fund-raiser for George Bush, issued a 1992 fund-raising letter attacking, among other things, radical feminism. "The feminist agenda," wrote Robertson, "is not about equal rights for women. It is about a socialist, anti-family political movement that encourages women to leave their husbands, kill their children, practice witchcraft and become lesbians."[7] Does anyone take this sort of thing seriously? Many librarians do, because there is no hotter topic among today's bookbanners than the devil and witchcraft. The American Library Association's 1992 conference featured an Intellectual Freedom program entitled "Witches, Devils and Demons: Legitimate Resources or a Satanic Force?" The moderator began by telling the assembled librarians that materials about witchcraft and the occult account for the largest number of challenges to resources in libraries today. She then introduced the two authors who would speak on the topic, Robert Hicks, a law enforcement specialist for the Virginia Department of Criminal Justice Services, and Joanna Michelson, author of two books on satanism and the occult, which together have sold over 500,000 copies.

Hicks told how his concern with popular terms like *satanic crime* or *occult crime* led him to track down the source and reliability of such characterizations. He discovered that within the law enforcement community, professional development seminars were being conducted under the guidance of clergy, social workers, and concerned citizens, to convince police officers that not only was satanism pervasive in our society, but it was actually the source of an epidemic of crime. The overt manifestations of these satanic influences, the officers were told, could be seen in everything from Ouija boards to fantasy role-playing games like Dungeons and Dragons, from graffiti on school walls to the lyrics of heavy metal rock groups. In addition, the law enforcement seminars told of "covert entrenched" satanists who secretly operate from positions of power and trust throughout our country, while engaging in kidnappings, child abuse, sexual assault, and sacrificial murder.

Hicks saw an immense danger in the willingness of some law enforcement officers, under the guise of maintaining public order, to confiscate library materials, books, magazines, and music whenever they consider them to be "cult related." He described one example in Louisiana where the sheriff's office tried to acquire a list of library patrons who had checked out books on the occult, and another where police attempted to influence school and library officials to remove such materials. When an Illinois school board recently met to decide on the purchase of textbooks, the local police chief wrote to warn the board of the danger of witchcraft and demons in the books. Hicks says such actions on the part of police are the result of the growing number of law enforcement seminars designed for police officers by people who have no knowledge of law enforcement.

The model of criminality proposed in these seminars was the subject of Hicks's book *In Pursuit of Satan: The Police and the Occult,* in which he debunked their bizarre claims. In summarizing his findings for the assembled librarians, he declared that there was no basis in fact for this model of criminality. "We have no evidence that there is any kind of continuum of behavior from those kids who listen to heavy metal rock music or play Dungeons and Dragons to [those who] end up being covert Satanists," he said. "I am not arguing that a Satan exists or does not exist. I'm simply saying that we cannot lasso him in as a law enforcement problem."[8]

Joanna Michelson followed Hicks to the speaker's podium and provided the assembled librarians with an emotional, almost apocalyptic picture of the cancerous spread of satanism in our public schools and libraries. She began by proclaiming that we must purge from our public schools the religions of witchcraft, spiritism, shamanism, Hinduism, and humanism. Michelson told the librarians of the dangers posed by satanism, wicca (the name preferred by witches for the religion of witchcraft), neopaganism, astrology, divination, magic, and even scientology, all of which were being foisted on unsuspecting children through transpersonal education, yoga, relaxation techniques, self-esteem programs, meditation, and guided imagery. "These people are using techniques," said Michelson, "that I used to become a medium. I worked with one of the few psychic surgeons in the world. . . . This woman could literally split people open with a rusty hunting knife and a pair of scissors. . . . Can I prove it to you in a court of law that she did these things? No. . . . But I will give you my personal testimony . . . that these things happened, there is power to be had there."[9]

Michelson said that many "Gifted and Talented" programs in the public schools teach Dungeons and Dragons, a popular fantasy game that she believes satanists use to recruit members. She said real witches had told her that they wouldn't let their children play Dungeons and Dragons because there are "real spells in there and they might end up with lower elementals on their doorstep." Michelson explained that *lower elementals* was a Christian euphemism for demons. She held up a book on witchcraft that she had found in a local school district, exclaiming, "You had kids who were coming to me and saying, 'Look, we've got friends who are literally skinning little rabbits alive and hanging their blood to drip down in the center of the school courtyard, because [these books] . . . are in their school libraries.' Allowing free access to books on witchcraft teaches them how to deny their Christian faith, deny the creator in heaven, . . . swear allegiance to the Devil and promise to offer child sacrifice. I don't care whether there's an international conspiracy or not, the fact is, that while not necessarily every kid who reads *The Headless Cupid* is gonna wind up sacrificing chickens on mama's dining room table, the fact is you are . . . desensitizing him to the occult thing."[10]

Michelson demonstrated the legitimacy of her contentions by reading from the Scriptures, Deut. 18:9–11, where God says that divination, astrology, and the like, are "abominations." She warned that authors or teachers who indulged in such activities were abominable to the Lord. "Do you wonder why, when parents come across these books, . . . books that have been banned, books that have been challenged, maybe you've got an idea why?"[11]

This message may have been strong stuff for the assembled librarians, but there are many people who are inclined to see the devil throughout our curricula and in our libraries. They are disturbed by any stories about witches, goblins, demons, and the like, and authors like Daniel Cohen, who specializes in such stories, finds his books frequently banned. Cohen writes nonfiction for young adults, drawing heavily on folktales about superstition and fantasy. Like Robert Cormier, he began his career as an editor and journalist, serving as managing editor of *Science Digest* from 1960 to 1969. He is an amazingly prolific writer, having published about 150 books covering everything from computers to biorhythms to *The Monsters of Star Trek*. No sex, no profanity here. The trouble is, many of Cohen's books have titles like

Masters of the Occult, Superstition, In Search of Ghosts, Magicians, Wizards and Sorcerers, and *Curses, Hexes, and Spells.* He lends no credence to occult beliefs, writing only to inform and entertain. In fact, a common theme in his books is that superstition is nonsense. Still, his books are frequently banned because they address such topics at all.

I asked Daniel Cohen if he knew that one of his books had appeared on PAW's ten most frequently banned books. He answered: "Yes, I indeed am aware of it. Apparently it was on the AP wire, because I received a call from my local newspaper asking me if I was aware of this. I was surprised to hear it. The same book was also on a *New York Times* list a year or two ago, a list of the most frequently stolen books. The book ranked just beneath *The Joy of Sex.*" When I pointed out that another Cohen book, *The Restless Dead: Ghostly Tales,* was on the American Library Association's most banned list, he responded with surprise. "Really? I didn't know about that at all. I had not heard about that, but I guess it shouldn't surprise me anymore."[12]

Did Cohen feel that this kind of censorship entered First Amendment territory? "My gut reaction is that they are certainly getting into First Amendment territory, but not being a lawyer, I simply do not know. What disturbs me about this far more than the occasional school board that wants to pull a book off of the shelves is the chilling effect that this has on authors. The effect is particularly insidious on children's books which appear primarily in libraries. Once a book or an author or a subject acquires the reputation of being controversial, you don't have to worry about pulling it off the shelves, because it's not going to appear on the shelves in the first place. The library is not going to buy it, and that effect moves up the chain. The publishers are less likely to accept manuscripts by that author or about that subject. I can give you an example from my own experience. For years I have been writing a series of books on folklore and ghost tales that has been very, very well received. *The Restless Dead* was one of them. Right now I'm doing a book for Putnam, and it's going to be called *The Demon Lover.* There is a whole series of folktales warning that if you grieve too much, you will call down the evil spirit in the form of the deceased, and the spirit will take you away. There is a cycle of legends and tales on that theme, particularly in Central Europe. The "Demon Lover" is a well-known phrase. I was going to include such tales in my book and call it *The Demon Lover.* It sounded like a great idea, but when the book salesmen heard about it, they all said, 'Oh, my God, you can't call this book *The Demon Lover.* That will not only get you thrown out of the Bible Belt, but it'll get you thrown out of Oregon as well.' So we changed the title of the book. The upshot is, the book is now called *Ghostly Tales of Love and Revenge.* Same book.

"I'll give you another example, from something I'm working on now for a new publisher that handles a lot of schoolbooks and is publishing a series for school libraries. They handle reasonably controversial topics, and given their audience, that takes a certain amount of guts. The editor there is one of the best in the business, a woman I've known for many, many years. I said, 'Look, how about a book on the alleged influence of satanism? That's something that kids talk about all the time, and it has aroused fears in the media.' She thought that was a terrific idea. But when she brought it up before her editorial board, they practically fell over dead. They said, 'My God, you can't do that! It'll get you thrown out of all the libraries in the country.' So, in the end we actually changed the entire concept of the book. It will focus on cults. It will cover the subject, but it will be a different book and not as strong a book. It represents a compromise, and that's what I mean by the chilling effect."

Cohen explained that although he has done a good deal of writing on the supernatural and the occult, he is not an occultist. "I think it's a bunch of crap, and I say so in my books. In the book that got in all the trouble, I say this kind of superstition is nonsense. But the people who challenge my books—*they actually believe it!* They believe in it, and they think that if you say anything about it, other than their particular line, you are somehow opening the door to hell, and all these spirits are going to rush out and suck the brains out of the kids. You know this is a great fund-raiser for the fundamentalist religious groups. I gather that books on satanism and the occult are the best-sellers in Christian bookstores. I've heard the subject labeled 'Christian pornography.' I think there is a certain manipulation that's going on here, and it does present real problems for a writer."

I described my conversation with the director of the Prince Georges County Public Library, who said the hot topic this year in bookbanning is the devil. Cohen recalled that one of his books had been challenged there. "You know, they get tired of one hot topic and they go on to another. What bothers me is that I often don't know when a book is being challenged. I'm never told. I pick it up in the newspapers, or someone sends me a clipping, or a newspaper reporter will call me up, or I'll hear about it years later when someone publishes a list. But when my books are challenged, no one from any school or library board has ever contacted me and asked for a reaction. Never."

I asked if that meant he was usually outside the fray. Cohen said: "I'm not usually outside the fray—I'm *always* outside the fray. I just don't know anything about it. For example, the People for the American Way list came out in September and was played up in our local newspaper, because I've been here for a long time. I'm very well known. People came up to me on the street and said, 'Oh, God, isn't this nonsense? We don't take this sort of thing seriously.' But usually around Halloween I get a dozen or more calls from schools, asking me to tell ghost stories to the kids. I keep the kids amused for an hour and, as a favor to the community, I don't charge anything. This year, perhaps because of the bookbanning publicity, I did not receive a single call. Do you think that's coincidence? The people here know better, but they're frightened."

I asked whether Cohen regarded all of this fuss about witches and goblins as more of a farce than a conspiracy. He answered: "It's certainly not a sinister conspiracy, but it has not been a laughable farce either. When people truly believe in this sort of thing, for or against, it can be dangerous. In a society where people deeply believe in magic, magic will work. Not because there is any power emanating from a spell but because a person who believes that he can be killed by magic will sicken and die. It's not something that you can take lightly. But in modern America, to think that some kid is going to sprinkle salt around a candle and reverse the course of nature is absolute nonsense. My books explain this kind of thinking and reveal it as primitive. Yet they are banned from schools, while children can go to the drugstore and pick up books that pander to these beliefs. The kids are given no choice. They either get books that pander to occultism or they get nothing. Any attempt to present these matters responsibly for kids is shut out of the schools. The fundamentalists are against it, and the school boards and librarians are simply afraid to confront this. They have enough problems with the budget and community support, and they figure, 'We don't need this. Just take it off the shelf.' Look, *Curses, Hexes, and Spells* is not one of the world's great contributions to literature. It was a relatively lighthearted, simple, easy-to-read book which created no problems at all when it first came out. Over the years, as this fear of satanism has grown among certain groups, this book has loomed larger. Why this book, and not any one of a hundred other books? I really do not know why this rather nondescript book has gained this kind of notoriety."

Has Cohen ever had the opportunity to intercede on behalf of his challenged books? "Never. Not once. Not ever. No one who has ever challenged the books, no school board that ever faced such a challenge, has ever had the decency to call me up and ask what I think. We had an incident in this area a few years back when one of my books was challenged. These people knew who I was. They knew my phone number, yet they never called me. It wasn't until I called them and really yelled at them that I received any response from them at all. If you call yelling at the school principal interacting, then I suppose I did interact. I'm not the kind of person who takes these things quietly. The response of the principal was, 'I guess I ought to look at the book. Besides, I'm only here temporarily.' So I sent him a copy of the book, and in the end, I think the problem just sort of faded away. After the controversy erupted, the teenager who had complained about the book didn't bother to fill out the form necessary to initiate a formal challenge, so the controversy just sort of petered out. But I would not be willing to bet that if you went to that school you would still find that book on the shelf."

When asked if he felt common cause with the other banned authors interviewed for this book, Cohen said: "I wish I felt common cause with their sales. I'm by far the most obscure member of that group, let me tell you. But I do invoke this commonality. I'm just sorry that authors do not always express themselves aggressively on the issue of censorship. Judy Blume does, but the publishers don't. They are too frightened. It's a bottom-line situation for them. They don't want trouble. You can have two or three people in a school, a small handful of people in an area, and their effect goes right to the editorial offices in New York where books get killed before they're born. That's where the real chilling effect is felt, not in libraries."

Robert Cormier

Robert Cormier began his career as a radio writer, newspaper reporter, wire editor, and associate editor, before becoming a successful author. While still a journalist, he earned prizes for the best human interest stories of the year (Associated Press) and best newspaper column. But his literary career began with a bang in 1974 when *The Chocolate War* won the *New York Times* Outstanding Book of the Year award. Cormier won the same award in 1977 for *I Am the Cheese* and in 1979 for *After the First Death*. He has also won a host of other awards, including several of ALA's Best Book for Young Adults citations. His most recent book, *We All Fall Down*, has been lauded by reviewers.

Although Cormier claims he writes *about* adolescents, not for them, his books have come to be characterized as young adult literature, a category within which *Newsweek* calls him a "best-selling heavyweight writer, an equivalent to Saul Bellow or William Styron." Because any written material aimed at America's youth arouses fear and anxiety in our *adult* population, Cormier's work has been criticized, and sometimes banned, because of its uncompromisingly realistic portrayal of life. Yet Cormier says his young readers are themselves not troubled by the messages in his novels. "They're not upset about the world I portray because they're in that world every day and they know it's war, psychological war." Cormier insists, "I'm not worrying about corrupting youth. I'm worrying about writing realistically and truthfully to affect the reader."[13]

Cormier was about a third into his first important book, *The Chocolate War,* when his agent called and asked what he was working on. When Cormier said he was writing a book about kids selling chocolates in a high school, the agent said it sounded like a young adult book, a term Cormier had not heard before. Four major publishers refused the book, one complaining that it was neither a children's book nor an adult book. The other three publishers wanted Cormier to change the ending, and he was tempted to oblige them. He was offered a $5,000 advance and major promotion of the book if he would give it a more upbeat ending, but he couldn't bring himself to make the change. His agent sent the book to Fabio Coen at Pantheon, who agreed to publish it without change.

Cormier's books appear to have aroused controversy, not just on matters of sexuality or vulgarity but on his depiction of human nature. His novels underscore the fact that good guys do not always win, and as a result, his work has sometimes been criticized for an absence of hope. He has also been accused of being critical of authority and presenting subject matter that could upset children. In short, he tends to write realistically. Perhaps this stems from the fact that Cormier spent much of his life as a journalist. He told me: "I was a reporter, editor, columnist. I started from a police beat and went right up to associate editor over a period of about thirty years. I left in 1978 when things reached the point that I could support my family and send my kids to college on my writing." [14]

Cormier was initially quite surprised to discover that much of his audience was made up of young adults. "I was flabbergasted. When I wrote *The Chocolate War,* about a high school chocolate sale, I regarded the high school as a metaphor for the world. It could just as easily have been set in, say, the business world. When it came out and the *New York Times* had it as the lead review in the children's book review section, I was immediately hailed as a brilliant 'young adult' author writing a landmark book. And I wasn't. I had just written this book and wondered who would ever read it. Ostensibly it was about high school kids, but I thought it had a deeper meaning. It was immediately controversial. I don't write for the kids, but I know they're my audience, although in recent years I've had an increasingly adult audience. Today, when I go out to speak, there are sometimes more adults than children in the audience. It's great. I can write to the full extent of my ability. I believe that I'm accepted by young people because they are a very tough audience. They know when you're pandering or writing down to them or patronizing them. And I don't do that. My books are complex and hard-hitting, and they're fully characterized. The kids know that I'm not just patting them on the back. They are tough books, and I think the kids respect me for that."

Cormier chooses to characterize his novels not as young adult fiction but as books with young adults in them. His early novels were about adults, but since the 1970s he has written mostly about adolescents. A few years ago he decided to write a novel in which the main character was a middle-aged man, but he says he soon became bored with the character, with his personality, and with his reactions to things. He put the book aside and went back to writing about adolescents.

When *The Chocolate War* came out, the critics seemed to think that Cormier had set out to write an unhappy ending in order to break some taboo. He says he was just writing a novel about the adolescent experience. *Booklist* presented a prepublication review of *The Chocolate War*, criticizing the book for being cynical and undermining moral values. Soon after the book came out in paperback, there were censorship attempts, such as the request in Groton, Massachusetts, that the book be removed from a school reading list. A compromise was reached, placing warning labels on the book. Cormier concludes, "That's why I say that in censorship cases, even when you win you lose." [15]

When nervous school officials across the country made early attempts to ban *The Chocolate War*, Cormier was not reassured that the book survived. "The book always triumphed, but even when you won, you lost," he told *Publishers Weekly*. "They'd say, 'Well, okay, but we'll put a mark on it indicating there's special permission needed to read it, or we'll put it in a special section.' And the narrowness of the victories always bothers me—a three-to-two committee vote isn't any resounding triumph. And I'm just a minor part of it all, when you consider the great books that are being attacked." [16]

Cormier says he spends a good deal of his time answering the hundreds of letters he receives from young readers. "They are supportive, because they say I tell it like it is. This is the way life is, and they are tired of books where everyone walks off into the sunset together. My books don't always have happy endings. There is a lot of psychological violence, more psychological violence than physical violence." Cormier is not sure where this preoccupation with happy endings comes from. Perhaps from fairytales, though he points out that many tales and nursery rhymes have disastrous endings. He believes that happy endings should not be one of the requirements of children's books. He says, "*The Chocolate War* was a big battle over selling chocolates in school. I have received letters from students saying, 'Hey, chocolates are mild. You ought to see what's going on in my school.' So you're not shocking the students, because the kids live with this. You're shocking the parents."

Until 1986, *The Chocolate War* was the only one of Cormier's books that attracted the censors, but then *I Am the Cheese* came under attack. It had gone unchallenged for almost ten years, but suddenly it was criticized for being too complex and too critical of government. In 1986 there were at least three attempts to censor it—two in Massachusetts and one in Florida—and all three of these attempts succeeded.

Cormier is amazed that people believe they can obliterate certain words from their children's lives by banning books. He says such people would be in for a shock if they rode a school bus or walked down a corridor in any junior high school. It is in these locations, not in books, that children learn the words that offend their parents. He warns that when writing dialogue, an author's personal taste can easily conflict with the speech patterns of real children. In such an event, the author should not impose his personal standards onto his characters.

I asked Cormier what it was that the self-appointed censors found so objectionable in his books. Was it vulgarity? "That's the least of it," he said. "What they don't like about my books is the absence of role models, the fact that the bad guy often wins in the end, that the heroine may be killed. But this is the way life is. Sometimes it's almost absurd. You'd laugh if it weren't so serious. One fundamentalist objected to *I Am the Cheese* because the parents in the book would not tell their child that they were in the federal government's witness protection program. That was the last thing I would have thought would upset anyone. The man complained that the book was virtually an essay on lying to one's children. He could never allow his son to read the book because he might conclude that parents lie to their children. The parent wasn't concerned about the language, or that the book was antigovernment or antiauthority. It was a bad book to read because his son would get the message that parents lie to their kids. Well, it happens that parents do lie to their kids. Lying is part of our daily life. If we all told the truth, people would stop talking to each other. We lie to them to protect them."

Cormier says some critics charge that his books are antigovernment and antibusiness. "*I Am the Cheese* is looked upon as critical of the United States government. *The Chocolate War* is considered critical of authority. The strange thing is, teachers aren't painted in a very positive light in this book, yet the books are requested by teachers around the country because there are teachable values in it. The book is selling more today than it ever has, and it came out in 1974. That's astonishing to me. Recently, a teacher in Connecticut wrote a defense of *The Chocolate War* for use as a teaching tool. He submitted this document to the school board and convinced them that the book had value for the curriculum."

When asked if there were any benefits from being a banned author, Cormier answered: "Just one, and that's that you find yourself in pretty good company."[17] He recalled reading a list of books that had recently been banned, with *The Chocolate War* in the middle of many classics.

Robert Cormier and Katherine Paterson, another frequently banned author, are old friends who have appeared on many anticensorship programs together. When I told Cormier that Paterson had been unable to recall a single example of a school administrator contacting her directly after one of her books had been banned, Cormier said that, on the contrary, it happens to him frequently.

"In fact, that's how I usually learn about one of my books being banned. For instance, just outside of Hartford, Connecticut, recently, the head of the Curriculum Department at the high school called to notify me of a school board hearing the following week. He wanted to know if I had any 'supportive materials.' So I sent some materials immediately, by overnight mail, and the school board voted 8 to 1 to keep *The Chocolate War* in the classroom. We don't always win. Sometimes I'm contacted by a journalist who gets wind of it while doing a story, and he wants my side of it. You see, when bookbanning occurs in a small town, it's not just a one-shot thing. It goes on and on and on. There are hearings and new hearings; there are decisions and appeals."

Cormier has mixed feelings about his personal involvement in anticensorship work. He feels it is important to resist censorship pressures, and he has spoken out on numerous occasions, lending his support to the people who are defending his books. But, in a way, he resents having to do it, saying that anything that diverts an author from writing is a victory for the censors. Cormier says his biggest frustration in fighting censorship is that the cards are stacked in favor of the censors. He describes a man in Florida who took out a newspaper ad in which he reprinted lines from *The Chocolate War* and *I Am the Cheese* with the so-called dirty words left blank. Cormier says he felt like taking out an ad urging people to read the whole book, but he knew it wouldn't work.

When his books are under fire, Cormier tends not to focus on the broader First Amendment implications. He told me: "I concern myself with the individual case that we're battling at the time. I seldom worry about the broader legality or ethics of it. I can't afford to do that much worrying, you know? Here's what I *can* do. I flew down to Panama City a few months after the violence surrounding the bookbanning had receded somewhat. [See Chapter 1.] They sequestered me in a hotel way out in nowhere. But we had a good talk with all of the concerned parties down there. So I do this sort of thing, but then I think, this is exactly what the would-be censors want me to do. That is, stay away from the typewriter. I mean, the last place they want me to be is at the typewriter. So if I spend a lot of time and energy away from writing, that plays right into their hands."

When I observed that he appeared, nonetheless, to be active in the fray, Cormier responded, "Frankly, that's why I'm a little weary, because just a few months ago there was another battle, also in Connecticut. I've gone to the fray so many times, and I've been interviewed so many times that . . . , you know. First of all, I'm irritated and upset when the censorship problem does come up, so I'm not in the best of moods when I'm called and asked to defend my books. I always feel that the books speak for themselves. I wrote them. Why should I have to defend them? Of course, the proper thing to do is to try to defend the book, to help these poor teachers who sometimes put their jobs on the line. How can I be indifferent? But I do resent it. I could tell you some horror tales that are documented down in Florida. I don't know if you are familiar with the debacle down there, right outside of Panama City. There were death threats and firebombings. It was so inflammatory that Gloria Pipkin, the teacher who led the battle, was honored in Washington, D.C. last year by the Courage Foundation. The *Washington Post* did a major cover story in their feature magazine, and *60 Minutes* even went down to investigate it. The battle was over *I Am the Cheese,* but it concerned a lot of other books as well. There were numerous death threats to the teachers. One teacher, Gloria Pipkin, went to her locker one afternoon and found one of those ransom-type notes, with words cut out of newspapers to avoid detection. In addition, a young female reporter who had gone on TV to challenge the book-banning petition had her car firebombed. You know, this is America. I received a recent letter from Gloria Pipkin in which she said that all of the challenged books have been restored to the school except *I Am the Cheese.* But they're teaching another one of my books that the censors haven't caught up with yet." [18]

Why was *I Am the Cheese* the only one of the challenged books that was not returned to the school? Cormier told me: "I suppose the original objection is still maintained. Mr. Collins, who led the opposition to the book, ran a large ad in the newspaper, listing selections from the book, with the objectionable words excised, of course. For example, in one selection a girl complains that her breasts are too large. The word *breast* is blacked out. In reality, that selection was not written in a titilating way. The girl was simply complaining that she had to lug her large breasts all over town. *I Am the Cheese* has very little in it that anyone could object to. Perhaps it remains out of the school because the curriculum was built around it, and it was the first book that was challenged."

Cormier described the typical pattern of censorship that he has experienced. "Here's the way it usually happens. One of my books is assigned to a student. The student brings the book home. The parent picks it up, doesn't read it, but looks through it and finds bad words or a sexual scene. Though it's quite mild compared to what's really out there, the parent complains to the school. Most times, when the school deals alone with a parent, they come to some accord. Frequently, if the child doesn't want to read the book, another book may be assigned to that child. Or once the book and its purpose in the curriculum is explained and discussed, the parent will sometimes agree that there are teachable aspects to, say, *The Chocolate War*." I asked Cormier if he considered the assignment of a different book to the children of complaining parents to be "caving in." He responded: "It's not caving in, because there are so many, many books out there that may be as good as *The Chocolate War*. The main thing is to get the child reading. If a different book from mine is chosen for a particular child, fine. The teachers are just trying to get the kids interested in reading. Censorship just gets in the way of teaching, and that's the tragedy of it all."

Cormier says he often has trouble with fundamentalist groups. "When a fundamentalist organization enters the picture, that's where the issue becomes intractable and reasonable negotiation becomes impossible. For me and a lot of other authors, the fundamentalists have become the major problem. Yet I really sympathize with these people because of their complete sense of righteousness." The fundamentalists remind Cormier of the young terrorist he wrote about in *After the First Death*. Like that character, they are so convinced of the righteousness of their cause that they don't consider what they are doing to other people when they ban a book. Cormier says, "They really believe that they're protecting their children from the world, though that's an impossible thing. That's why they're so hard to fight, because they are so sincere and well-meaning."

Has Cormier ever convinced fundamentalist critics that they were wrong about a challenged book? He says, "No, the most I can do is what I did when I went to Panama City to speak to these people. Charles Collins, the man who led the forces against me, a born-again Christian and wealthy businessman, was in the audience. I spoke for about forty-five minutes and received a standing ovation, even from the fundamentalists. My only reason for going down there was to show them that I wasn't a monster from New England trying to corrupt their children. And that what I was writing, whether they objected to it or not, was sincere and to the best of my ability. I was not trying to corrupt their children but to open their eyes to certain things. I'm a human being, I'm a father, I'm a husband. Right now I'm a grandfather, too. After my talk, Charles Collins came up to me and shook my hand. He said, 'I can't agree with what you write, but I can see where you're coming from. I can admire what you're doing by your own standards.' That's the closest I ever came to a meeting of the minds with such people, but then, I haven't met many of them. I only know them through their petitions and the material I receive in the mail."

Cormier sympathizes with a parent's impulse to shelter children. He admits that as a father he has tried to keep his children from being hurt or from being exposed to disturbing sights. But, he says, this impulse often leads parents to attempt to control the entirety of their children's lives, which is an impossible task. He says children begin thinking on their own while they are still in the sandbox, and if we try to control their fantasies, thoughts, and emotions, we will only drive them away from us. He argues that children have already heard of corruption, terrorism, and sexuality, and he sees no reason to expunge those subjects from children's books. Yet he points out that he does not consciously consider these issues when he writes a book, concentrating instead on realistically developing his characters and their situations. Cormier says he doesn't write his books worrying about what a four-teen- or fifteen-year-old can absorb. As he sees it, he owes his readers an honest story that is neither exploitative nor sensational, and if some kid finds that upsetting, he says that's just too bad.

Cormier told me of an incident in the Cape Cod schools, where a child brought home *The Chocolate War* and her parents objected to it. "It became a big brouhaha out there. As you may know, when a book is challenged and a hearing scheduled, the book is sometimes kept in the curriculum until the hearing. In other cases, the book is removed until the hearing. In this particular case, the book was maintained in the classroom, so the complaining parents insisted that when the book was being discussed, their daughter must go to the library to avoid being affected. Well, I received a letter from the daughter's classmate who said that by being removed from the classroom in this way, the girl was being ostracized and poked fun at. Now, as an adolescent, at a time of life when you want to belong, this isolation from her classmates was more harmful to her than reading the book. In a postscript to her letter, the classmate confided that her ostracized friend had read *The Chocolate War* the previous year, anyway. She had already read the book. So you see, there are kids being hurt by a kind of ricochet effect of censorship. The parents who thought they were protecting their child were separating her from her peers, perhaps exposing her to ridicule."

Textbook publishers, always a hypersensitive lot, have borrowed sparingly from Cormier's work. "A lot of my short stories have been in textbooks," he says, "but my short stories are very innocent. Nothing inflammatory. The only excerpt from my novels that I can recall was part of a Russian exchange project, where they excerpted a chapter from *The Chocolate War*."

Aside from some mutually agreed editing on *The Chocolate War,* Cormier says he has felt no pressure from his publisher to avoid controversy. I wondered whether his publisher had ever asked him to tone things down just a bit? "Never," he said. "Never with me. They wouldn't dare. My last book begins with a terrible act of violence, and I wrote it in language designed to shock the reader. I didn't use polite words, because I wanted the reader to feel it. You can see that I'm not bending over backwards to soften my work." Indeed, that book, *We All Fall Down,* received a starred review from *School Library Journal* and a glowing review from *Hornbook,* a major children's review journal. It received similar commendation from *Kirkus,* and *Publisher's Weekly,* which said it was one of the seven best young adult books of the year.

In March 1992, Robert Cormier sent me a small package of materials containing a letter from an angry parent, some letters of support from teachers, some newspaper clippings on censorship, and a sheet of paper signed by Cormier and titled "Some Thoughts on Censorship." Among those thoughts were expressions of sympathy for parents who sought control over what their children should do, see, and read, and objections to such control over other people's children. Cormier noted: "The irony of book-banning attempts is that the publicity often causes people to read the books for the wrong reasons. If a book is controversial, perhaps the best place for it is the classroom where, under the guidance of a teacher, the book can be discussed and evaluated, where each student will be free to proclaim how he or she feels about the book and, in fact, can even refuse to read the book. The point is that free choice must be involved."

Cormier concluded: "I try to write realistic stories about believable people, reflecting the world as it is, not as we wish it to be. I think there is room in the great halls of reading for this kind of book. The hundreds of letters I receive each year from both teachers and young people are what sustain me at moments when censorship threatens my work. I owe a great debt to the many teachers, librarians and parents who support my work. The blessing is that in doing so they also strike blows for freedom." [19]

Katherine Paterson

Katherine Paterson is the daughter of a clergyman and wife of a clergyman, a woman who has spent much of her life serving as a missionary. In 1966, the United States Presbyterian Board of Education asked her to write a church schoolbook from a child's point of view. The text she produced, *Who Am I?,* was widely used by the church, and its success encouraged Paterson to try her hand at professional writing. She enrolled in a course geared specifically to writing for children, and by the end of the course, she had written her first novel, *The Sign of the Chrysanthemum,* the first of her three children's historical novels set in Japan. Next came *Bridge to Terabithia,* her first book set in contemporary America, and then *The Great Gilly Hopkins.* Both books have been major targets of censorship.

Among the many honors that have been accorded to Katherine Paterson's books are ALA's Notable Children's Book Award, the National Book Award for Children's Literature, and the John Newbery Medal. Paterson has received the Irvin Kerlan Award "in recognition of singular attainments in the creation of children's literature" and the Catholic Library Association's Regina Medal Award for demonstrating "the timeless standards and ideals for the writing of good literature for children."

Who would have thought that this award-winning author and Christian educator could possibly write books that spark controversy around the country? Yet her books are sometimes banned in schools and libraries on the grounds that her stories contain "unhappy" endings and realistic language that might be damaging to children. She responds, "The books ended the way I thought the books had to end. That's not satisfying to everybody, but it seems to me that if you're really 'in' a story then the story seems to have a life of its own. The story seems to have necessities and its own ending. . . . If you try to change what is the inevitable ending of that story, you violate the story and the reader will recognize that."[20]

I asked Katherine Paterson about the recent attempt to ban *The Great Gilly Hopkins* in Cheshire, Connecticut (see Chapter 1). She said, "I just received a letter indicating that they voted in Cheshire to keep the book in the curriculum. Have you seen the letters that the children wrote in support of the book? The *Hartford Courant* Sunday Magazine recently published the children's letters describing their own experience with the book. They are the most eloquent defense of literature that you would ever hope to see, on First Amendment grounds, on the need to read a book before judging it, and much more."[21]

Given the extreme sensitivity of publishers to these censorship controversies, has Paterson been pressured to alter her writing? "Certainly not by my editor. Never. I have received no pressure at all from my publishers or editors. I'm totally free to write exactly the way I want to write. I put the book out, and when the challenge to it arises, it's the teachers and librarians who have to put their jobs and reputations on the line to defend what I've done. I had a teacher who, after seeing an early draft of one of my books, suggested that I reconsider using the word *Jesus* in the mouth of a black child. I reconsidered it and decided that it was so inconsequential that it was not worth causing a problem over. So I dropped it. But I would not consider changing the words in the mouth of Jesse Aarons or Gilly Hopkins [in *The Great Gilly Hopkins*]. That would be quite a different proposition."

When I suggested that it was part of the professional obligation of librarians and teachers to defend against bookbanning, Paterson said, "Sure, in theory. It's easy for all of us to say, but not so easy when you're the one who has to do it. Years ago there was a challenge against *Gilly Hopkins* in Salinas, Kansas. I can't remember exactly what year, but I know my kids were still in high school. They had a swimming meet the day the school board was going to vote. I was sitting there at that swimming meet, wondering what was going on in Salinas. I wrote about that two or three years ago in an article on censorship in the *New Advocate*. I called the librarian who had stood up to keep the book available. I had never met her, but she was one of my heros because she was alone in the whole school. There were some teachers who suggested that the book be hidden under the desk, or perhaps sequestered so that only the teachers could read it. But this librarian took the lead in convincing her supervisor and the other librarians to pursue the issue with the school board or carry it to the courts if necessary. They were terrific. The librarian wrote me to say how grateful she was for the article. She said I might not have regarded her as a hero if I had known how frightened she was. She said she was the only black on the staff and had gotten along very happily until that moment. Then suddenly things became very difficult. Even though the book was reinstated by the school board, she couldn't go back to work the next year. Things were so uncomfortable for her that she moved on to another job. She's now a university librarian at Lincoln University. My heart goes out to such people in these bookbanning situations."

I asked Paterson if she had difficulty getting her works included in textbooks. "Textbooks are a different world. They are notorious for sanitizing literature, which is why you will seldom ever find anything written by me in a textbook. Because the minute they get hold of my material, they try to cleanse it of all personality. When a textbook publisher wants to publish excerpts from one of my books, they try to take out the words they don't like. I just tell them, 'I'm sorry, you can't use this.' Now I simply have a blanket policy that I do not write for textbooks. I have had a complete chapter put in a textbook, but even there they wanted to remove the word *damn*. It was not even used as an oath. It was used as a verb. I said, 'If you can't publish the chapter without that word, then you can't use it at all.' They decided to go ahead and use the word. Another time, a popular school magazine wanted to use a short story of mine in which a mother is nursing a baby. That wanted to eliminate that. I said, 'I'm sorry, I don't care if you use the story or not, but if you do, the mother will nurse the baby.' I want children to know that women's breasts are used for something besides pornography. For them to call nursing a baby dirty was beyond my belief. They ended up using the story with the mother nursing the baby."

When asked whether school and public library censorship was a First Amendment issue or simply a problem of administrative authority, Paterson answered: "It's both. I think it's a First Amendment problem, because I don't think children should have fewer rights than other human beings." But what about the right of parents in a community to determine what their children read? "In every case that I know of," Paterson said, "when a parent objects to a book used in the classroom, there is no problem in assigning a different book for that child. But the parent often claims that the child would feel strange reading a different book. In other words, the parent obtains control over the entire classroom because one child would feel uncomfortable. It's like saying my child is uncomfortable with mathematics, so there should be no math in the classroom. Perhaps, though I might argue otherwise, a parent has the right to tell his or her child what to read, but that parent may not prevent my child from reading the book. A parent has the right to object to a book but not the authority to prevent anyone in the school from reading it.

"I was raised by very conservative parents who were very careful about what movies we saw. There was no television, so that was not a problem. But they never censored our reading. I considered that a great vote of trust and confidence in me, and it encouraged a sense of responsibility in me. Every time my parents trusted me, and I could see that many other parents were not trusting their children, it made me feel more responsible. We cannot protect our children from this world, which is a scary place. The only thing we can do is to help them develop an inner strength to meet the inevitable challenges they will face."

I mentioned that one of the hot topics among the bookbanners today was satanism. "I've been accused of that, too," said Paterson. "In *Bridge to Terabithia,* the children play an imaginative game where they enter the 'Sacred Grove' and invoke the spirits of the Grove. Some critics have charged that this is an example of 'New Age religion.' When I was told that, I said, 'Please, don't accuse me of New Age religion, when I haven't even figured out what secular humanism is.' In addition, *Bridge to Terabithia* was published in 1977, before the notion of New Age religion was conceived. I guess I'm so avant-garde that I knew about it before anyone else did."

I asked Paterson if she had any advice for teachers and librarians when dealing with censorship. "Schools and libraries need to have a procedure in place to deal with book challenges, so that one parent's objection is not going to result in a book immediately being removed from the library shelf. At the same time, full respect must be shown to those people who object to books. Frequently, these are people who are desperate to be heard. If they know that their objections are given a full hearing, the problem can often be defused. We should be less defensive and more sympathetic to these people, because all of us want to protect our children, don't we? We may not agree on how that is best done, but to despise someone for trying to protect his children is wrongheaded."

But Paterson was quick to add, "I think eternal vigilance is the price of liberty. If you think it won't happen here, you may be sadly surprised. It can happen anywhere, and it won't always be the fundamentalist lunatic fringe that you expect. It may be the doctor's wife who dresses impeccably. It may be the wealthy or the well educated. The challenges may come from unexpected sources and may be directed against unlikely books. You have to be ready. Get in touch with the American Library Association, the Freedom to Read Foundation, and the National Council of Teachers of English for advice and up-to-date information on what is happening throughout the country. The Cooperative Children's Book Center at the University of Wisconsin has a wonderful system for helping people all over the country involved in bookbanning incidents. They are concerned that as these incidents proliferate, authors are going to begin to exercise self-censorship. They may be afraid to write what they really want and need to write. That certainly is a real danger, because it's easy to begin weighing every word to avoid offending anyone. This can cripple an author's work.

"I can't imagine Gilly Hopkins being Gilly Hopkins without the language she uses. You don't have a child who is so angry at the world, and who lies and steals and bullies, whose mouth doesn't somehow reflect that anger. She would not be a believable character otherwise. In the case of Jesse Aarons, that's the way those people talk. If you want him to be a country boy from the rural part of northern Virginia, that's part of the package. On the other hand, some amount of discretion is not altogether a bad thing. If a word or phrase is not fundamental to the book, and if it is going to be a gratuitous offense, then I might question it."

I asked Paterson if the various acts of censorship against her books had been brought to her attention by school officials. "No, no, never," she said. "I've never had a call directly from a school board. It's usually a teacher or a librarian or a reporter. It's haphazard notification. Somebody may call me up and ask if I know what's going on in our school systems. I say no, and they tell me. Apparently, the school officials think that authors are the last people on earth who could shed light on a conflict over their books. When it reaches that point, there is such heated feeling about the author that the author becomes a dangerous commodity. For example, the protester in Connecticut was calling Jan Slepian and me 'perverts.' "

What is the basis for most objections to Paterson's books? "It used to be language entirely," said Paterson. "Now it's become more broadly rationalized. I've been accused of anti-Christian bias. Actually, I'm very pro-Christian. In fact, it would be much more reasonable to accuse me of a pro-Christian bias. I regard *Gilly Hopkins,* the book that was challenged in Cheshire for being anti-Christian, as my rewriting of the parable of the prodigal son. I thought it was so Christian that a secular publisher might not want to publish it."

Jan Slepian

Jan Slepian says, "I'm a writer by chance. I didn't go from the cradle to the typewriter. I set out to be a clinical psychologist, turned to speech therapy and because of that work began writing picture books when my own children were young."[22] But Slepian soon joined the ranks of the premier writers for young adults. *The Alfred Summer* was selected as one of *School Library Journal's* Best Books of the Year for 1980, and it was a finalist for the American Book Award. It won the *Boston Globe/Horn Book* Award Honor Book for Fiction in 1981. *Lester's Turn* was selected as one of the *New York Times'* Best Books for Children, one of *School Library Journal's* Notable Children's Books, and one of *Social Education's* Notable Children's Trade Books in Social Studies. *The Night of the Bozos* was selected as one of the American Library Association's Best Books for Young Adults, one of the Child Study Association of America's Children's Books of the Year, and one of Library of Congress' Books of the Year.

Yet her work has been banned in a number of schools and libraries around the country.

Jan Slepian believes that language is the focus of most of the objections to her books. For example, several challenges have identified the words *Christ* and *shit* as offensive. But as with most banned works, there may be more subtle social irritants as well. Slepian says, "I think Lester, the handicapped boy in *The Alfred Summer,* may be seen by some of the censors as having a bad attitude, of being irreverent, saying things like, 'I don't appreciate God's sense of humor.' Lester, a fourteen-year-old cerebral palsy victim, has the same kinds of private sexual fantasies that any fourteen-year-old would have. I tried to make clear that these unfortunate people have the same dreams and the same hormones as any other boy or girl."[23]

Like most of the other "banned" authors interviewed for this book, Slepian has never been contacted by school or library officials when her books were banned. She says, "In Cheshire, Connecticut, I wasn't contacted at all by the officials involved. A newspaper reporter called me and said he had heard that there was a complaint about one of my books. He wanted to know what I thought about the incident, and I told him. I asked him to send me a copy of the article, but I never received it. Perhaps it was never published. That's the only time anyone has contacted me about the censorship of my books. No one else ever tried. Actually, there was a very nice outcome in Cheshire, and I was quite pleased with the board. There was a wonderful meeting at which the parents demonstrated that they were too knowledgeable and sophisticated to allow this sort of censorship to occur.

The Cheshire incident was very interesting because the censors focused their anger on two important books that are acknowledged as illustrious in children's literature. Katherine Paterson's *Great Gilly Hopkins* won the Newbery Award, and my book, *The Alfred Summer,* was a nominee for the American Book Award. These are not like most of the 'hazerei' [junk] that parents might think is all right for their children. Ultimately, Cheshire parents recognized these books as the kind of literature that they should be proud to have their children read.

Parents and librarians really have to stand fast. Librarians should not buckle under to fear and intimidation. There are organizations that are willing to come to our help, organizations like the American Civil Liberties Union, the American Library Association, People for the American Way. Librarians are our conduit. They are our best friends. They're the channel through which our books are funneled. We depend on them to help us tell the truth as we know it."

Like Judy Blume, Jan Slepian seldom participates directly in the local censorship battles involving her books. "I've followed Judy Blume's advice. I believe she recommended that rather than trying to fight the critics personally, authors should refer challenges or complaints about their work to those organizations designed to deal with such matters, organizations like the American Library Association or the National Coalition against Censorship."

However, Slepian has occasionally written letters to those who attempt to ban her books. In 1983 she was informed by Scholastic Press, the publishers of the paperback edition of *The Alfred Summer,* that the book might be removed from the school library shelves in Charlotte, Virginia. In a letter to Otis Lovelace, library supervisor in the Charlotte County Public Schools, Slepian spoke of the book, its purpose, and point of view. "The book largely deals with the growing friendship between two afflicted young people, Alfred and Lester. My intention was to get to know the person behind the damaged body. I wanted to show that such a person shares the same fears, the same need for love and friendship, that he yearns for and responds to much the same things as we all do. . . . In *The Alfred Summer,* my spokesman for these sentiments is Lester, a 14 year old cerebral palsy victim. . . . It was important to the book that Lester be shown as having natural internal language, one that any other kid that age would have. To have left this point out, to not allow him to express himself naturally would not have been true or faithful to what he is. Actually, only once does he openly use what could be thought of as an objectionable word, but that once was necessary to make the point. . . . The book affirms the wonder and the joy of life despite affliction. It seems to me that this is a timeless message that I sincerely hope will remain open to the children of Charlotte. . . . The Alfred in this book is based on my own brother Alfred, and the observations based on my experience with growing up with a damaged boy. . . . Finally, I feel the book is its own best spokesman and will speak for itself in the hearing."[24]

Did the letter convince the school officials in Charlotte? "I don't think so, said Slepian." "If all it took were letters, we probably would have convinced all these people long ago. Perhaps if I could speak one-on-one with a complaining parent, I might be able to reach some understanding. But the motivation behind these well-organized censorship campaigns is beyond my ken and beyond my control."

I asked Slepian if she had received many letters from her readers. "I've heard from a lot of kids," she said, "and most of the letters are very positive. Their letters are enough to bring tears to your eyes. Even when a child's letter is critical of my books, it never expresses shock at the language. I may have bored a child, but I don't seem to have offended them. I have never heard anything from a child suggesting that my readership has been affronted in any way. It would be a weird child who would write me and complain that I had said a bad word. I've never received such comments from children, yet some parents seem compelled to protect their children from such harmless language."

"In my generation, my parents hardly knew what I was doing in school. This may be in part because I was a good girl, but they were also busy making a living. I was reading all the time, and they wouldn't question what I was reading. I never thought much about my parents' influence on my reading habits, or about censorship generally. My parents never attempted to tell me what I should or shouldn't read. There were always lots of books around the house, and reading and learning were always encouraged. I remember reading Voltaire's *Candide* when I was twelve years old, and there were things in it that I had never thought about. Of course, I didn't understand the book's irony, but I've always been entranced by the music of words, and I remember thinking that some of those words were dancing around the page."

Was she embarrassed or offended by the "adult" portions of *Candide*? "Offended? I would have been thrilled to think I was old enough to be offended by something. I was too innocent to be offended."

When I asked if she thought the attempts to ban her books were First Amendment violations, Slepian responded: "It depends on the individual case. For instance, in Charlotte, Virginia, there were just a few vocal Moral Majority people who wanted the book removed from the library shelf, and they intimidated the school principal and the librarians. I have the impression that it's not the teachers, educators, or even the school officials or board members who initiate these censorship incidents. It's usually a group of citizens within the community who exploit local politics to impose their taste upon others. There is a disturbing climate in this country which allows a few noisy people to frighten school officials into removing books. These officials simply want to avoid trouble, and they will do anything to make it go away. In the case of Cheshire, where the book was being read in the classroom, the school board apparently decided that they would raise the grade level for the book from fourth grade to fifth grade. If parents feel that their children would benefit more by reading the book next year rather than this year, that seems perfectly all right to me. But when a book is removed from a library shelf, denying all children the right to read it, that is certainly interfering with First Amendment freedom. What we're awakening to is the threat of book burning. It has echoes for us all, because the looney few are able to put their imprint on the rest of us by making enough of a stir. This problem has a different face each generation. The religious groups today are much more aggressive, and the fundamentalists are gaining ground, forcing many publishers to withdraw certain textbooks."

Has Slepian ever felt pressure from her publisher to soften her writing? "Never," she answered. "Never have I felt the hint of pressure from my publishers or editors. I've been very lucky. No one has told me not to use certain words or not to address certain topics to avoid trouble. It was always up to me. I don't think about the effect of what I say, or what my characters say, on my audience. That's not the way to write a true book. Rather, one inhabits the skin of a character, say, an eleven-year-old girl, ensuring that she is saying something true and in character. Would this character say that? Regardless of what it is, whether she's saying a string of curses or a string of novenas. I don't think about whether this would offend someone. I simply consider whether it's true. If it isn't, I would take it out. But the recent furor has made me more conscious of what I put on paper.

"My friend Barbara Cohen had an interesting run-in with her editor. Barbara wrote *Molly's Pilgrim*, which was made into an Academy Award–winning short subject. *Molly's Pilgrim* is a storybook for six-, seven-, eight-year-olds. When the book was about to be reprinted in a textbook, Barbara was called by the textbook editor, who wanted her to delete a section about God. She simply mentions God. There was nothing blasphemous about it, but the publisher was frightened. Barbara considered that section to be critical to the book, and she absolutely refused to remove it. The section remained in the book, but the incident demonstrates how frightened, how sensitive, publishers have become. They respond to any hint that a book might offend someone on the Right, on the Left, in the middle, someone up, someone down."

Have any of her works been excerpted in textbooks or anthologies? "I know my picture books have been reprinted here and there. Many of my books have been reprinted in braille for the blind. By the way, I've never had a blind person say he was offended by my books."

I told Slepian of the travails of the most censored book series in the country, the *Impressions* textbook set by Holt, Rinehart and Winston. Interestingly, three of the five authors interviewed in this chapter were excerpted in *Impressions*. Jan Slepian's *The Hungry Thing*, a harmless rhymed tale for small children, was among the selections, and I asked Slepian if she could imagine any basis on which it could be considered offensive. She was incredulous, but I pointed out that excerpts from *Winnie the Pooh* and the *Wizard of Oz* had already been attacked by critics of *Impressions*. Why not *The Hungry Thing*? "If they are banning that," she said, "it's pathetic. That's scraping the bottom of the barrel."

I asked Slepian if she was currently working on a new book. "Of course," she answered. "That's like asking if I'm breathing. I'm working on a book for eleven- or twelve-year-olds, a book about beginning again, about renewal. It's called *Back to Before,* and it should be out in 1993. It's about children who go back in time, giving them a second chance at things, a chance to make them right."

Was there anything in this new book that could conceivably offend the censors? Slepian's first response, as always, was to call that an absurd impossibility, but she told me, "There is a section of the book that puritans might object to. The father in the book is going out with a woman, whom he describes as an 'associate,' but the reader knows the father is really fooling around. It's conceivable that someone might be offended, but there is more to object to in Grimm's fairytales than there is here."

I expressed hope that the new Clinton administration would improve the climate for free expression in this country. Slepian responded, "Well, it certainly couldn't get worse. I admire your optimism. We should all be so hopeful."

NOTES

1. *Contemporary Authors. New Revision Series,* vol. 13 (Detroit, Mich.: Gale Research Co., 1984), p. 60. (Hereafter references to various volumes of *Contemporary Authors* are cited by title and volume.)

2. Ibid., pp. 60–61.

3. Telephone interviews with Judy Blume during spring 1992. Unless separately endnoted, all subsequent Blume quotes are from these interviews.

4. Mark I. West, *Trust Your Children: Voices against Censorship in Children's Literature* (New York: Neal-Schuman, 1988), pp. 4–5.

5. Ibid., p. 4.

6. *Contemporary Authors. New Revision Series,* vol. 13, p. 60.

7. Judy Mann, "The Witching Hour," *Washington Post,* September 16, 1992, p. E19.

8. "Witches, Devils and Demons: Legitimate Resources or a Satanic Force?" American Library Association, 1992 Conference, cassette ALA-222.

9. Ibid.

10. Ibid.

11. Ibid.

12. Telephone interviews with Daniel Cohen during spring 1992. Unless separately endnoted, all subsequent Cohen quotes are from these interviews.

13. *Contemporary Authors. New Revision Series,* vol. 23, p. 88.

14. Telephone interview with Robert Cormier, February 1992. Unless separately endnoted, all other Cormier quotes are from this interview.

15. West, *Trust Your Children,* p. 33.

16. *Contemporary Authors. New Revision Series,* vol. 23, p. 89.

17. West, *Trust Your Children,* p. 37.

18. Cormier recently sent me a note indicating that *I Am the Cheese* had finally been returned to the library.

19. "Some Thoughts on Censorship," a page of comments prepared by Robert Cormier and distributed to authors, journalists, and other interested parties.

20. *Contemporary Authors. New Revision Series,* vol. 28, p. 363.

21. Telephone interviews with Katherine Paterson during spring 1992. Unless separately endnoted, all subsequent Paterson quotes are from these interviews.

22. *Something about the Author: Facts and Pictures about Authors and Illustrators of Books for Young People,* vol. 51 (Detroit, Mich.: Gale Research Co., 1988), p. 156.

23. Telephone interview with Jan Slepian in spring 1992. Unless separately endnoted, all subsequent Slepian quotes are from this interview.

24. Letter from Jan Slepian to Otis Lovelace, library supervisor, Charlotte County Public Schools, May 11, 1983.

| 4 |

The Most Frequently Banned Books in the 1990s

Ranking the most banned or challenged books is an inexact and some-what arbitrary process, but the two most extensive annual listings of banned books, produced by People for the American Way and the American Library Association's Office for Intellectual Freedom, are a reliable sample. Combining the reports of these two organizations, I have calculated the fifty most banned/challenged books from January 1990 through December 1992, listing them, in descending order, by frequency of challenge and analyzing their content and the basis for their controversy. Of course, not all challenges against these titles have been reported, and of those that have, only a selected number have been described in this chapter. The number of challenges described for each title is roughly proportional to the number of challenges re-ported. The distribution of publication dates for the fifty most banned books in the early 1990s suggests that the censors will not yearn for the good old days. Only two of the fifty titles were published in the 1990s, sixteen in the 1980s, eighteen in the 1970s, six in the 1960s, three in the 1950s, two in the 1930s, and three in the nineteenth century.

1. **Impressions,** edited by Jack Booth et al. Holt, Rinehart and Win-ston, 1984–1987.

The *Impressions* language arts textbook series is a literature-based reading series for kindergarten through sixth grade. It is in use in thirty-four states and 1,500 schools nationwide. It teaches reading, speaking, and writing through exposure to poetry, folklore, myth, songs, and fictional and factual narrative. *Impressions* contains works by many award-winning authors, including C. S. Lewis, Laura Ingalls Wilder, Martin Luther King, Jr., Rudyard Kipling, A. A. Milne, and Dr. Seuss. Nonetheless, the PAW and the ALA's Office for Intellectual Freedom reported over a hundred challenges to the series. Some of those reports are duplicated between the two organizations, but the total number of incidents makes *Impressions* far and away the most challenged book in the nation.

The *Impressions* series has been the subject of nationwide attacks reaching back to 1987, and it is now the subject of a lawsuit in Woodland, California (see Chapter 2) by parents represented by Reverend Donald Wildmon's American Family Association Law Center. The AFA also recently filed, and then withdrew, a similar suit against the school district of Willard, Ohio. The controversy over *Impressions* first surfaced during the 1987–1988 school year in several small communities in Washington and Oregon, where some parents claimed the books had "overtones" of witchcraft, mysticism, and fantasy and presented themes of rebellion against parents and authority figures. One parent argued that the books can serve no purpose except to introduce children to witchcraft. Others objected to the occasional Canadian spelling in the texts. But teachers and students were enthusiastic about the series, which had been chosen after years of evaluation and community involvement.

The schools in Oak Harbor and Gig Harbor, Washington, attempted to appease complaining parents by offering alternative assignments, but some parents persisted in demanding total removal of the series. Only after protracted and costly battles was the series retained in the Washington schools. In Troutdale, Oregon, the series never made it into the schools, as a besieged school board decided not to adopt the books. In an attempt to accommodate the demands of a small minority of parents, the publisher produced a new version of the series that eliminated the most controversial selections, but still the attacks escalated.

During the 1990–1991 school year, *Impressions* was challenged in forty-five school districts around the country, up from about two dozen challenges in 1989–1990. In most of these cases, the school districts reviewed the series and voted to keep the books, but the time, energy, and money spent fighting these battles is having a chilling effect. In addition to the AFA, which brought suit against *Impressions* in California, other organizations like the Christian Educators Association International (CEAI), Citizens for Excellence in Education (CEE), and the Traditional Values Coalition (TVC) have joined the attack. Robert Simonds, head of CEE, has publicly declared war on the series, and Reverend Lou Sheldon of TVC has urged parents to fight *Impressions* by trying to "disgrace" school officials. Reverend James Dobson, head of Focus on the Family, has published an article instructing parents on how to challenge the series.

In the Willard, Ohio, lawsuit, the complainant claimed that the series promoted "occult religions," including the religion of witchcraft. Complainants in other suits have accused the books of being amoral and an indoctrination in "relativism." Children's rhymes were equated with chanting, thus constituting devil worship. The word *gay* in the traditional folksong "Lavender's Blue" was interpreted as a reference to homosexuality. Illustrations of rainbows were considered objectionable because the rainbow is a symbol associated with the New Age movement. One Willard parent complained that the series taught an inordinate affection for animals, while another labeled the books evil and blasphemous.

In Yucaipa, California, some parents complained that the face of the devil could be seen in illustrations in *Impressions*. When a school official was unable to detect the devil's face, he was instructed to photocopy the illustration, turn it upside down, and hold it up to a mirror. He did as instructed but still was unable to see the devil that was tormenting these parents.

In October 1992, another of the proliferating court challenges to *Impressions* was decided in Illinois by Judge James B. Moran. In dismissing the complaints against *Impressions,* Judge Moran wrote:

> The *Impressions* series has, apparently, generated a certain amount of controversy around the country, with parents having views similar to the plaintiffs complaining to other school boards about the contents. . . . [T]he publishers have apparently reduced the number of stories relating to witches and goblins, perhaps as a marketing response to that controversy, and plaintiffs wanted to be sure that the court was aware that defendant was using the prior edition. The court is so aware. . . . The series does contain a few scary stories, with spooks of one sort or another—the kind of stories often told around an after-dark fire at camp, but that is a far cry from fostering some pagan cult. [1]

Despite the continuing attacks on *Impressions* by fundamentalist organizations, most parents, students, and teachers continue to respond to the series with enthusiasm. Teachers have observed increased reading activity among students, especially those who previously had reading difficulties. School librarians report that students are requesting more books by authors who are excerpted in *Impressions*.

The following editorial from the Whidbey *News-Times* summarizes the conflict:

> There is in this controversy a struggle for power, not morality and decency. Armed with rhetoric developed by national political organizations,

some of the critics seek to convince us that teachers we once knew as wholesome and reasonable are suddenly part of a plot to undermine the moral character of our youth. The people who spread these lies are the true censors and the book burners. Their narrow perspectives hold innocent exploration to be dangerous. They are afraid of uncontrolled ideas and are threatened by the thought that the world can be a changing mosaic of wonderful contrasts, of differing viewpoints, of diverse beliefs systems, cultures and experiences. . . . They point out our public schools are supposed to be free from sectarian control. But make no mistake. Sectarian control is what they seek.[2]

Selected Challenges in the 1990s: The Office for Intellectual Freedom and People for the American Way together reported 200 challenges to *Impressions* from 1990 through 1992, and though there is some duplication between the reports of the two organizations, the total number of separate censorship incidents far exceeds that of any other book in the country. From New York to California, from Alaska to Hawaii, the sheer numerical weight of these challenges defies detailed documentation in this book. For the other banned titles analyzed in this chapter, we will document a number of censorship incidents approximately proportional to the total number of challenges against the title. We have insufficient space here to do the same for *Impressions.* The best we can do is itemize a number of challenges to demonstrate the broader geographical and political pattern, and examine a particular case to reveal the flavor and intensity of this dispute.

During the 1990s, *Impressions* has been removed, after first being approved, in the following cases.

1. Castro Valley, California. March 1990.
2. Coeur d'Alene, Idaho. April 1990.
3. Frederick, Maryland. The board reversed itself on October 26, 1992, voting to place the *Impressions* teaching guides into the public review process.
4. North Marion, Oregon. Challenged and retained in 1989, but a new challenge led to its removal.

Lawsuits were filed over the use of *Impressions* in the following districts, after they had responded to challenges by retaining the series.

1. Dixon, California. Suit over procedural issues filed in 1990.
2. Willard City, Ohio. Suit filed December 1990 alleged that the use of *Impressions* established the religion of witchcraft and violated

parents' rights to free exercise of their own religion. Suit was dropped January 1991.

3. Woodland, California. Suit filed January 1991 alleged that *Impressions* unconstitutionally establishes the religion of witchcraft. (See Chapter 2 for legal details.)

4. Wheaton, Illinois. Suit filed in 1992 claiming *Impressions* violated the establishment clause of the U.S. Constitution and the due process rights of parents.

5. Washoe County, Nevada. Suit filed in 1992 alleging that the public funds used to purchase the series were illegally spent. A second suit has been threatened by a new objector.

Among the districts in which *Impressions* was challenged before being retained are the following:

1. Fairbanks, Alaska. Series retained, February 1991.
2. Amador County, California. Series retained, May 1990.
3. Ballard, California. Series retained, December 1990.
4. Bella Vista, California. Series retained, November 1990.
5. Black Butte, California. Series retained, September 1990.
6. Buckeye, California. Series retained, December 1990.
7. Campbell, California. Series retained, July 1991.
8. Dixon, California. Series retained, April 1990. Lawsuit pending.
9. Enterprise, California. Series retained, January 1991.
10. French Gulch, California. Series retained, November 1990.
11. Grant, California. Use of series upheld, May 1991.
12. Grass Valley, California. Series retained, April 1991.
13. Happy Valley, California. Series retained, January 1991.
14. Hayward, California. Series retained, April 1990.
15. Lawndale, California. Series retained, July 1990.
16. Lincoln, California. Series retained, April 1990.
17. Los Banos, California. Series retained, April 1990.
18. Napa, California. Series retained, March 1991.
19. Nevada City, California. Series retained, June 1991.
20. New Haven, California. Series retained, June 1990.
21. Pleasant Ridge, California. Series retained, March 1991.
22. Redding, California. Series adopted for supplemental use, December 1990.

23. Redondo Beach, California. Series retained, February 1990.

24. Ripon, California. Series retained, April 1990.

25. Saratoga Union, California. Series retained, September 1990.

26. Willits, California. Use of series confirmed, April 1990.

27. Winters, California. Series adopted, July 1990.

28. Woodland, California. Series retained, June 1990. Lawsuit filed, January 1991.

29. Yucaipa, California. Series retained, January 1990.

30. Arlington Heights, Illinois. Series retained, April 1991.

31. Barrington, Illinois. Use of series confirmed, May 1991.

32. Palatine and Rolling Meadows, Illinois. Series retained, February 1991.

33. Wheaton–Warrensville, Illinois. Series retained, March 1991.

34. Dexter, Maine. Series retained, December 1990.

35. East Holden, Maine. Series confirmed for use, June 1991.

36. Gardiner, Maine. Series retained, July 1991.

37. Frederick, Maryland. Series approved, October 1992.

38. Washoe County, Nevada. Teachers anthologies challenged and retained, March 1991.

39. Dansville, New York. Series retained, March 1991.

40. Hilton, New York. Series retained, January 1991.

41. Willard, Ohio. Lawsuit filed, then dropped, January 1991.

42. Klamath County, Oregon. Series retained, February 1991.

43. Lincoln County, Oregon. Series retained, February 1991.

44. Redland, Oregon. Series retained, June 1991.

45. Reedville, Oregon. Complaint dropped after review, July 1991.

46. Douglas, South Dakota. Series retained, December 1990.

47. Sioux Falls, South Dakota. Series retained, March 1991.

48. Anacortes, Washington. Series retained, May 1990.

49. Finley, Washington. Series retained, April 1991.

50. Pasco, Washington. Series retained, July 1991.

51. Walla Walla, Washington. Series adopted, June 1990. Challenged again after adoption, September 1990, with threat of lawsuit. Series retained, July 1991.

An examination of one of the recent success stories associated with the *Impressions* controversy may give a sense of perspective to this struggle. In fall 1989, the Curriculum Steering Committee in California's Winters School District recommended *Impressions* as the new language arts curriculum for grades 1 through 3, and in April 1990 they made the same recommendation for grades 4 through 6. The following month, the Winters School Board heard the first formal presentation of *Impressions,* along with speeches of support and opposition from the audience. By this time, allegations had begun to surface that the series emphasized witchcraft and the occult, promoted disrespect for parents and other authorities, and had a Canadian bias. The source for most of these complaints appears to have been material circulated by several ultraconservative religious groups, including Educational Research Analysts (ERA) and the CEE. ERA is the Texas textbook "review" organization formed by the infamous Mel and Norma Gabler. CEE was founded by Robert L. Simonds, who claims to be God's spokesperson and whose stated goal is to reclaim Christian morality for the public schools and elect Christians to public school boards. Among his enemies, Simonds cites "atheist groups" like the National Education Association.

The Winters school district made the *Impressions* series available for public review for two months. After reading a story about trolls under a toll bridge, one local parent said she and her children could never again cross a toll bridge. Other parents complained of the frequent appearance of rainbows among the illustrations, a symbol supposedly associated with New Age religion.

Many parents, teachers, and scholars in the area were roused to rebut the strident and often misinformed attacks on *Impressions.* Dr. John Boe, who teaches children's literature at the University of California at Davis and has served as a consultant for various hospitals on the therapeutic use of children's literature, wrote to the superintendent and board of trustees, saying that *Impressions* represented an admirable trend in recent education, that of giving children "real literature" rather than "hack work" written for specially produced textbooks. Dr. Boe subsequently testified before the school board and has written of that experience.

> I'd always thought Mark Twain had it right: "First God made idiots. That was for practice. Then he made school boards." But after a recent school board meeting in Winters, I'm not so sure. The issue was whether to adopt a textbook series, Holt's *Impressions.* Some townsfolk, spurred on by national Christian organizations, had protested that this series was literally the work of the devil and was as well a foreign product (that is, Canadian). There were three TV cameras in the crowded auditorium, one of them from CBS' *48 Hours.* . . .
>
> My turn came early. I talked of my experience with a project at St. Mary's Hospital in San Francisco, where the kind of fantasy literature

people were objecting to in *Impressions* was actually used as part of the *treatment* for disturbed children, including children abused by real Satanists!

Having read one of the texts in question, I simply couldn't understand the bizarre allegations: the books supposedly promoted drug and alcohol abuse (the troll princess in *Beauty and the Beast* puts a sleeping tablet in the prince's wine), cannibalism (the story of the *Gingerbread Man*), satanic ritual (encouraging the children to "chant" rhymes), black magic (in one story musical instruments control the colors of the sunset), New Age religion (references to rainbows), the practice of witchcraft (various fictional witches, including the one from *The Lion, the Witch and the Wardrobe*, by C. S. Lewis, one of modern literature's most passionate Christians), and the Wicca religion (this is not the worship of furniture, as I first thought). I also couldn't understand the fear that the texts promoted Canadian culture. Is there some International Canadian Conspiracy I'm simply not aware of? . . .

Finally, the vote. We anxiously awaited the words of Michael Roberts, the Superintendent of Schools. . . . He recommended *Impressions* be adopted. To the surprise of most in the audience, the rest of the board unanimously voted to adopt the books. It turned out they weren't really convinced by the various speakers, many of whom, on both sides of the issue, were intelligent, passionate, and eloquent. The crucial factor was that most of the board members had test marketed the books, simply trying them out on their own kids. Their kids had all loved *Impressions* and hadn't turned into either Satanists or Canadians.[3]

2. **Of Mice and Men,** by John Steinbeck. Viking Penguin, 1937.

Synopsis and Background: Of Mice and Men, published in 1937, has earned a host of awards while leaving a trail of controversy within the public school curriculum. In making it the second-most banned book in the 1990s, the censors claim to be protecting the young and impressionable from this tragic tale of crude heroes speaking vulgar language within a setting that implies criticism of our social system. The story focuses on two vagrant workers, Lennie, big and simpleminded, and George, small and clever, who take jobs at a large ranch. The childishly naive Lennie is tormented by the boss's arrogant son Curley. Simultaneously, Lennie forms a friendship with Curley's young wife, which eventually leads to her accidental death at his hands. George's act of self-sacrifice to protect Lennie from a vengeful mob forms the tragic conclusion to the story.

Despite the controversy surrounding its use in the classroom, *Of Mice and Men* remains an extremely popular choice of teachers and educators. Thomas Scarseth, of the University of Wisconsin at LaCrosse, says, "There is one good reason for reading John Steinbeck's short novel *Of Mice and Men*—it is a very good book. There is one good reason for teaching it—it is a teachable good book: simple and clear, yet profound and beautiful." Scarseth says that *Of Mice and Men* treats the great themes of dreams and death and love with simple power and clarity. "It does so with a classically elegant structure—another reason for using the book as a teaching tool: it allows a reader—especially an untrained or beginning reader of literature—to see (or be shown) how structure supports and presents content."[4] *Of Mice and Men* has plot structure uncluttered by diversions, distractions, or subplots, and its stark inevitability makes the point of the story unavoidable. The style is simple, using clear, direct sentences of description and action and the unadorned speech of simple people.

Scarseth describes *Of Mice and Men* as a book to show beginning readers the paths to great books that might initially be too difficult for them. It is a tragedy in the classic Aristotelian/Shakespearean sense, showing humanity's ability to achieve nobility through and in spite of defeat. Steinbeck democratizes the tragic world, extending the realm of tragedy beyond the royal or God-like figures to the lowly of the earth. In the modern tradition of *The Hairy Ape* and *Death of a Salesman*, *Of Mice and Men* shows that even the least of us has the human potential for tragic nobility.

Scarseth says,

> Some people seem to believe that the function of literature is to provide vicarious "happy endings," to provide in words a sugary sweetness we would like to have but cannot always get in real life. To such people, true literary tragedy is distasteful. But the greatest writers and the best readers know that literature is not always only mere sugar candy; it can sometimes be a strong medicine: sour perhaps—at least to the untrained taste—but necessary for continued health.[5]

There are no purely good or purely bad people in *Of Mice and Men*. The characters are a complex mixture of good and bad, of bad results from good intentions. They occupy subordinate positions in a gross and dirty world in which they do the best they can. But, as the poet Robert Burns wrote long ago, "The best laid schemes o' mice and men gang aft a-gley." Lennie and George are good friends who share a good dream. They are too inarticulate to express their love for each other, but it is revealed through Steinbeck's moving narrative.

The simple desire of Lennie and George to have a small place of their own is doomed by their own limitations and the tragic chain of circumstance and coincidence that destroys them.

Selected Challenges in the 1990s: In 1990, a parent in Salina, Kansas, objected to *Of Mice and Men,* used in a tenth-grade English class, for profanity and taking the Lord's name in vain. The school board accepted the recommendation of a review committee to retain the book, though it advised that the book not be read aloud.

A parent in Lexington, North Carolina, objected to the use of *Of Mice and Men*, citing profanity and taking the Lord's name in vain. A review committee report to the principal recommended that the book be retained, although the student was given an alternative assignment.

In December 1990, a parent in Riviera, Texas, requested the removal of *Of Mice and Men* from eleventh-grade English classes, citing profanity and the use of God's name in vain. About fifty teachers and administrators and ten high school students attended the board meeting that considered the request. Several people, including students and the school librarian, spoke in favor of the book. Only one person spoke against it. The objector went through three levels of appeal before the school board voted 3 to 2 to continue using the book in high school English classes.

In 1991, a parent in Fresno, California, objected to the use of *Of Mice and Men* in tenth-grade college preparatory English classes, alleging profanity and racial slurs. The objector's child was provided an alternative reading assignment, but the book was retained in the curriculum. A school official said, "I feel sorry for the [student] who did not get a chance to read a masterpiece of literature by a great American author."[6]

A parent in Iowa City, Iowa, objected to the use of *Of Mice and Men* in seventh-grade literature courses, alleging profanity such as the word *Goddamn*. "I feel my daughter was subjected to psychological and emotional abuse when the book was read aloud," said the objector. "I hope when my daughter completes school, she will not talk like a migrant worker." A review committee decided that the book was appropriate for use in the classroom.[7]

A student and a local pastor in Michigantown, Indiana, objected to the use of *Of Mice and Men* in an eleventh-grade English class, alleging filthy language and disrespectful use of religious names. The objectors threatened a full-page ad in the local newspaper, demanding removal of the book. Nevertheless, the objectors declined to pursue the district's formal complaint procedures, and the book was retained.

A parent in Branford, Florida, objected to *Of Mice and Men* in the high school library, alleging vulgar language and taking the Lord's name in vain. The objector, who had not read the book, said that if the language was as bad in any of Steinbeck's other novels, they, too, should be banned. The book was removed from the library, pending a final decision on the complaint. A review committee subsequently voted to retain the book.

Parents in Buckingham, Virginia, objected to *Of Mice and Men*, used in a tenth-grade English class, citing profanity and the use of the Lord's name in vain. The school board upheld a review committee's recommendation to retain the book but decided that in the future parents would be notified of all required reading in advance of each semester.

Parents in Jacksboro, Tennessee, objected to the use of *Of Mice and Men* in a tenth-grade English class, citing blasphemous language, profanity, and sexual overtones. The objectors presented a petition at a school board meeting, demanding that the book be removed. The board voted 6 to 1 to retain the book.

In August 1991, *Of Mice and Men* and another book were removed from a high school reading list in Suwannee, Florida, after a local resident, Zeke Townsend, informally complained that they were indecent. A school review committee returned both books to the reading list, causing the objector to file a formal complaint calling for the removal of the book from district classrooms and libraries. Townsend told the board, "We go to church and we teach our children right on Sunday morning for a couple of hours and we send them to school five days a week and they put trash in their minds." In October 1991, the school board voted unanimously to return *Of Mice and Men* to the shelves of the high school library, confirming a recommendation of the Appellate Material Review Committee. Melissa Woodrum, chairperson of the high school's English Department, told the appellate committee: "John Steinbeck was a deeply Christian man, he was a brilliant Bible student, his books are full of Christian imagery and Christian theology. He purposefully used Christian themes in his book because part of his desire was that people love each other." [8]

In 1992, community members and clergy in Mobile, Alabama, proposed to local school officials the creation of a special textbook screening committee "to weed out objectionable things" from the schools. In particular, *Of Mice and Men,* used in an eighth-grade writing class, was attacked for containing profanity and morbid, mystical, and depressing themes. District officials rejected the proposal, and because no formal complaint against the book was lodged, the book remained in use.

In May 1992, Bob Barnett, vice-president of a Parents Coalition at the high school in Hamilton, Ohio, complained that *Of Mice and Men* contained anti-Christian content, profanity, vulgarity, and racial slurs. Barnett claimed that the book contained 108 profanities, 12 racial slurs, and used God's name in vain 45 times. Offers of alternative reading assignments were refused, and, in violation of the district's procedures, the novel was removed from the school's optional reading list, pending a recommendation by a review committee. The review committee's deliberations were attended by about 150 parents, students, and teachers, who overwhelmingly supported the book. A student who submitted a petition containing 333 signatures in favor of keeping the book told the committee that *Of Mice and Men* provoked the reader to explore his or her own values and reflect personally on what is right or wrong. Speaking against the book, the Reverend Oscar Hughes said, "Anybody that's got a child shouldn't want them to read this book. It should be burned up, put in a fire. . . . It's not fit for a heathen to read."[9] The review committee voted 8 to 0 to reinstate the book to the curriculum, and the board of education unanimously upheld the committee's recommendation. One of the objectors subsequently appeared on television, where he tore a copy of *Of Mice and Men* to shreds and raked it off of the stage with a hoe, claiming he was clearing a garden of weeds.

In October 1992, a school board member in Alexandria, Louisiana, attempted to remove *Of Mice and Men* from the school system's approved reading list after a minister complained to him about its use. "I know it's a classic and all that stuff, but my constituents don't like it, I don't like it," said the board member. "The ones I've heard from, they are ministers, and I can appreciate their feelings."[10] A school librarian and two English teachers defended the book before the board, and the full board voted 7 to 2 to retain *Of Mice and Men*.

3. **The Catcher in the Rye,** by J. D. Salinger. Little, Brown, 1951.

Synopsis and Background: When *The Catcher in the Rye* was first published in July 1951, it was simultaneously made available as a Book-of-the-Month Club selection. The book quickly reached number four on the *New York Times* list of best-sellers, and when subsequently released in paperback, it reappeared on the best-sellers list in fifth place among all paperback books. *The Catcher in the Rye* aroused controversy from the beginning, but its sales and curricular appeal continued to climb. The earliest recorded attempts at censorship were in 1954 in Marin County and Los Angeles County, California. In 1955–1956 eight more attempts to ban the book occurred nationwide. A 1961–1962 survey of New York high school librarians and 1963 and 1965 surveys of English teachers in Utah and Arizona found *The Catcher in the Rye* to be their most frequently censored title. Yet a 1962 survey of California English professors showed the book to be their number-one choice to teach to college students.

By 1981 the original edition of the book had been reprinted thirty-five times and the paperback edition fifty-two times, with a total number of copies in excess of 10 million. Indeed, during 1981, *The Catcher in the Rye* had the unusual distinction of being the nation's most frequently censored book and, at the same time, the second-most frequently taught novel in the public schools. What is it about *The Catcher in the Rye* that makes schools and libraries so ambivalent about it? Most of the objections to the book have centered on its profane or vulgar language. A complaining parent in California counted 295 occasions in which God's name was taken in vain, while another complainant in Kansas noted 860 obscenities. A parent in Washington counted 785 profanities, including 22 *hells*, 27 *Chrissakes*, 7 *horneys*, as well as numerous *bastards*, *damns*, *craps*, and so on. All of this language comes from the adolescent hero of the book, Holden Caulfield. Yet Holden spends much of his time at school trying to wash obscene graffiti off the walls, because he feels younger children should not be exposed to such language.

Academic critic Edward Corbett claims:

> As a matter of fact, Holden's patois is remarkably restrained in comparison with the blue streak vernacular of his real-life counterparts. Holden's profanity becomes most pronounced in moments of emotional tension; at other times his language is notably tempered—slangy, ungrammatical, rambling, yes, but almost boyishly pure.[11]

The book's theme is the difficulty and ambiguity of transition from the world of childhood to adult society. In Holden Caulfield's eyes, childhood is idealistic and innocent, while adult society is "phony" and perverted. Not surprisingly, such a portrayal is disturbing to educators, clergy, and parents, who seek to chart the adolescents' path to adulthood. Perhaps a broader, more political offense is involved here. In 1978, the parent in Washington who counted 785 profanities in *The Catcher in the Rye* claimed that such language was brainwashing students as part of an overall communist plot. The same explanation had been given by the 1960–1961 California protesters, who claimed that the book could weaken the moral fiber of students, making them susceptible to communism.

Holden Caulfield is a prep school kid who leaves school in anticipation of expulsion, explaining that his nerves were shot. He then takes a train to New York City, where he spends the next forty-eight hours. The book chronicles his aimless activity as he kills time at some local bars, encounters a prostitute, visits his sister, and contacts his favorite teacher from earlier school days. Throughout his meanderings there is a lot of anxious adolescent musing on sex and society, and a lot of doubt expressed about American values. This troubled teenager has grand dreams and idealistic values that overwhelm him. The reader sees Holden as a crazy, mixed-up kid (indeed, the book suggests that he ends up in a mental institution), but we respond favorably to him, perhaps seeing ourselves in him. Adult readers seem to appreciate this novel of adolescence as an accurate, even typical, narrative of transition to adulthood, yet they consider it too mature and negative for student readers. Rather than shielding adolescent readers from themselves, the adult censors seem to be protecting them from the social reality that the American character may have difficulty developing in any meaningful sense beyond adolescence.

The comparison of Holden Caulfield to Huckleberry Finn is inescapable. Both characters hope to escape from a venal and hypocritical society. Holden dreams of hitchhiking west, while Huck plans to light out for the "territories." Huck is an alienated fourteen-year-old, and that characterization is surely true of Holden. Both are in idealistic rebellion against and flight from mature society. Huck is thrust into the expansionist nineteenth century, while Holden is the prisoner of a contracting twentieth century. The censorship difficulties of *The Catcher in the Rye* and *Huckleberry Finn* are also strikingly similar, ranking third and fourth overall in the number of bookbanning incidents in my survey.

Selected Challenges in the 1990s: In 1990, a parent and a local minister in Aberdeen, Maryland, objected to the inclusion of *The Catcher in the Rye* on the ninth-grade supplemental reading list, alleging profanity. A committee consisting of a school official, librarian, and staff member voted to retain the book. The minister threatened to campaign against the book on his religious radio show.

Parents for Integrity in Education (PIE), a conservative group in Grayslake, Illinois, objected to the use of *The Catcher in the Rye* in an eleventh-grade English class. In response, a student group was formed to support academic freedom. The school board heard from both groups, as well as teachers and community members, and decided to retain the book. They wrote: "The board steadfastly refuses to censor the materials offered to students, believing the shadows of book banning often imperceptibly become the early morning hues of book burning."[12]

A minister in Latta, South Carolina, objected to *The Catcher in the Rye* on an optional reading list for ninth-grade English classes, claiming that it contained profanity and had no literary value. After meeting with the minister, the principal decided to leave the book on the list. The minister appealed the decision to a teacher review committee, which upheld the principal's decision, but another appeal to the school board produced a decision to restrict the use of the book to eleventh and twelfth grades only.

A parent in Middleton, Idaho, objected to *The Catcher in the Rye* for use in a tenth-grade English class because the characters used profanity and questioned religion. School officials stopped the teacher on her way to class and told her to collect all copies of the book immediately, to cancel the quiz she had planned for that day, and to begin teaching something new. The book was removed with no formal procedure, despite the fact that alternative assignments were offered to those who objected to the book. The teacher chose to leave the school system at the end of the semester.

A parent in Sherwood, Oregon, objected to the use of *The Catcher in the Rye* in a tenth-grade English class, alleging profanity. The objector did not pursue the school's complaint process, and the book was retained.

A student's guardian in Palm Springs, California, objected to *The Catcher in the Rye* being read aloud by and to eighth-grade English students, though all profanity was omitted in the reading. The book was removed from class without following the school's formal process, and school staff decided to cease using the book in the future.

In 1991, a group calling itself Concerned Citizens of Florida objected to the availability of *The Catcher in the Rye* in a Leesburg, Florida, high school library. Citing "profanity, reference to suicide, vulgarity, disrespect, and anti-Christian sentiments," the objectors contended that the book would lead to "rebellion," "despair," and "low self-esteem." The objectors noted twenty-nine uses of profanity and references to death mockery, consumption of alcohol, dope, and nicotine. "The particular book espouses no values," said the objector. "Every page is filled with pessimism, profanity, poor attitudes and vulgarism." A review committee voted unanimously to retain the book.[13]

A parent in St. Edwards, Nebraska, objected to the use of *The Catcher in the Rye* in an eleventh-grade English class, citing profanity. The school board upheld a review committee's decision to retain the book.

Parents in Greeley, Colorado, objected to *The Catcher in the Rye* and two other books used in tenth- to twelfth-grade English classes, alleging violence, profanity, and sexual overtones. Some objectors requested removal of the books, while others requested a restrictive labeling system. In response to the complaints, the English Department agreed to prepare an analysis of the books and a portfolio of reviews, making them available to parents or students. Parents who do not want their children to read a particular book may ask a teacher to help them choose an alternative title.

In January 1992, a student and several parents in Sidell, Illinois, objected to the use of *The Catcher in the Rye* in a twelfth-grade English class, for alleged obscenity, profanity, immorality, and references to premarital sex, alcohol abuse, and prostitution. The student was given an alternative assignment, but the student's parents insisted that the book be removed from classroom use. The teacher of the English class said that one student had already opted out, and if two or three more followed suit, the book could no longer effectively be taught. A community member joined the complaint, claiming that respect for God's name overrides the separation of church and state. After a review committee said it was not within its purview to decide on the complaint, the school board voted to retain the book for the balance of the school year but asked the English Department to select a less controversial title for the next year.

In March 1992, a parent in Waterloo, Iowa, objected to the use of *The Catcher in the Rye* as optional reading in twelfth-grade advanced English classes. The objector said she was too offended to read the entire book but alleged that it contained "too much swearing, repeated [use of] God's name in vain, and remarks about Jesus Christ." She charged that reading the book would result in "increased use of bad language . . . , turn kids off to religion . . . [and] encourage kids to think about sex." A school committee was formed to reconsider the book.[14]

In October 1992, a parent in Carlisle, Pennsylvania, challenged the inclusion of *The Catcher in the Rye* in the high school curriculum, claiming that the book contained profanity and was immoral. A review committee recommended that the district retain the book in its honors English class for sophomores, and the school board subsequently voted to accept the committee's recommendation.

4. **The Adventures of Huckleberry Finn,** by Mark Twain (Samuel Clemens). Harper and Row, Centennial Edition, 1978.

Synopsis and Background: The Adventures of Huckleberry Finn, a narrative written in the idiom of a shiftless, unlettered boy from the lowest class of the antebellum South, was considered objectionable by America's genteel society almost immediately after its publication in 1885. Huck, the outcast son of the town drunkard, was the hero and narrator of a tale that ridiculed America's work ethic, polite manners, prayer, and piety.

Before its publication as a book, *Huckleberry Finn* was excerpted in a magazine, but only after references to such things as nakedness and dead cats were deleted. In order to have the book published in unexpurgated form, Mark Twain was forced to set up his own publishing house. Immediately upon its publication, it was banned by the Concord Public Library in Massachusetts, which described the book as follows:

> It deals with a series of adventures of a very low grade of morality; it is couched in the language of a rough dialect, and all through its pages there is a systematic use of bad grammar and an employment of rough, coarse, inelegant expressions. It is also very irreverent. To sum up, the book is flippant and irreverent in its style. It deals with a series of experiences that are certainly not elevating. The whole book is of a class that is more profitable for the slums than it is for respectable people, and it is trash of the veriest sort.

Twain's response was:

> That will sell 25,000 copies for us sure. For instance, it will deter other libraries from buying the book and you are doubtless aware that one

book in a public library prevents the sale of a sure ten and a possible hundred of its mates. And secondly it will cause the purchasers of the book to read it, out of curiosity, instead of merely intending to do so after the usual way of the world and library committees; and then they will discover, to my great advantage and their own indignant disappointment, that there is nothing objectionable in the book, after all.[15]

During Twain's lifetime, *Huckleberry Finn* was banned from numerous other libraries, including the Denver Public Library, the Omaha Public Library, the Brooklyn Public Library, and even the New York State Reformatory. Upon hearing that his books had been banned in Brooklyn, Twain provided the library with the following straight-faced defense:

> I wrote *Tom Sawyer* and *Huck Finn* for adults exclusively, & it always distresses me when I find that boys & girls have been allowed access to them. The mind that becomes soiled in youth can never again be washed clean. I know this by my own experience, & to this day I cherish an unappeasable bitterness against the unfaithful guardians of my young life, who not only permitted but compelled me to read an unexpurgated Bible through before I was 15 years old. None can do that and draw a clean, sweet breath again this side of the grave. . . . Most honestly do I wish that I could say a softening word or two in defense of Huck's character since you wish it, but really, in my opinion, it is no better than those of Solomon, David, and the rest of the sacred brotherhood. If there is an unexpurgated [Bible] in the Children's Department, won't you please . . . remove *Tom & Huck* from that questionable companionship?[16]

In 1907, *Library Journal* printed an article entitled "The Children's Librarian versus *Huckleberry Finn*" in which it was claimed that Twain's book had been banned somewhere in the United States each year since its publication. Yet the book has been translated into virtually every language spoken on earth and is widely regarded as America's greatest novel. Ernest Hemingway proclaimed, "All modern American literature comes from one book by Mark Twain called *Huckleberry Finn* . . . the best book we've had." H. L. Mencken said his discovery of *Huckleberry Finn* in 1889, when he was nine years old and the book only four, was "probably the most stupendous event of my whole life. . . . If I undertook to tell you the effect it had upon me my whole talk would sound frantic, and even delerious." He proclaimed Mark Twain as "the true father of our national literature, the first genuinely American artist of the royal blood." T. S. Eliot said that in *Huckleberry Finn* Twain had proved himself to be one of those few writers "who have brought their language up to date" and "who have discovered a new way of writing, valid not only for themselves, but for others."[17]

In the face of such universal acclaim, how can schools and libraries in the 1990s make this the fourth most banned book in the nation? Lionel Trilling has characterized *Huckleberry Finn* as a subversive book. Huck's agonizing struggles with right and wrong, freedom and slavery, humanity and racism suggest that society's moral pronouncements are often nothing more than the engrained customary beliefs of a particular time and place. Together, Huck and Jim ruthlessly examine the social contract upon which the stability of modern society rests, and in the process, they reject public opinion as a basis for human conduct. Huck's heart and conscience showed him the evil of slavery and led him to help Jim run away from his legal owner, an act that society regarded as both a sin and a crime. Huck was happy to live as a pariah, rejecting what he considered unjust and immoral laws. Even today, Huck and Jim are an affront to polite society. In *Born to Trouble*, Justin Kaplan wrote, "They are simply too good for us, too truthful, too loyal, too passionate, and, in a profounder sense than the one we feel easy with, too moral." [18]

A more recent twist in the continuing controversy over *Huckleberry Finn* is the allegation that it is racist. This bitter irony was dramatized in 1982, when an administrator at the Mark Twain Intermediate School in Fairfax County, Virginia, called the book a grotesque example of racism. The major basis for such charges is that some of the book's characters use the racial epithets common to the Mississippi Valley thirty years before Emancipation. But Mark Twain and Herman Melville may have been the least "racist" of all the major writers of their time. In particular, *Huckleberry Finn* is a devastating satire on racism, bigotry, and property rights in American society. Huck and Jim seek escape on their raft from a nightmare society torn by bigotry, violence, exploitation, greed, ignorance, and depravity.

Selected Challenges in the 1990s: In 1990, a teacher in Bourg, Louisiana, objected to the use of *Huckleberry Finn* in an eleventh-grade English class because of the use of the word *nigger*. School officials ordered that the book not be used, though it had been taught in the school for more than twelve years without complaint. There are no plans to reinstate the book in the curriculum.

A parent in Loudon County, Virginia, objected to the use of *Huckleberry Finn* in a tenth-grade honors English class for containing objectionable language and presenting African-Americans in a demeaning fashion. A school committee, the principal, the superintendent, and the school board all decided that the book was suitable for the class and should be retained. Alternative assignments were offered to those requesting it.

In September 1990, a school director in Erie, Pennsylvania, asked that *Huckleberry Finn* be removed from the high school English reading list because of the use of the word *nigger*. Superintendent Joseph Rodriguez said that a curriculum committee of teachers and administrators would review literature by minority authors and add some of their works to the reading list.

In January 1991, a parent in Mesa, Arizona, objected to *Huckleberry Finn,* taught in eleventh- and twelfth-grade English classes, for containing the word *nigger*. Despite the availability of alternative assignments, the removal of the book from the reading list was requested. The school board voted unanimously to retain the book, and a review committee recommended that *Huckleberry Finn* be taught in conjunction with the writings of Frederick Douglas, Soujourner Truth, and other black authors from that period.

A city council member in Plano, Texas, objected to the use of *Huckleberry Finn* and *Tom Sawyer* in the eleventh grade because of the use of the word *nigger* and degrading portrayals of black people. A school district committee voted to remove the books, but after 500 students signed a petition in support of the books, the school board voted unanimously to retain them.

A guardian in Elmira, Oregon, objected to the use of *Huckleberry Finn* in a tenth-grade honors English class because of the word *nigger* and degrading depiction of African-Americans. The principal, teacher, and objector discussed the book and agreed to continue its use but to discuss the period in which it was written and invite African-American guest speakers. The matter was resolved without reaching the school board.

Parents in Portage, Michigan, objected to the use of *Huckleberry Finn* in a tenth-grade English class because of the use of the word *nigger* and the poor role model that the character Jim represented to black youth. Pending a formal review, school officials removed the book from the classroom. When teachers protested the temporary ban and supported the book, it was returned to the classroom. Administrators and teachers developed new lesson plans to more clearly present the book's antiracism themes.

In March 1992, Harold Fleming, the interim superintendent of schools in Kinston, North Carolina, said that students at the predominantly black middle school were too young to read *Huckleberry Finn* because of its use of the word *nigger*. Fleming, who is African-American, told a teacher that the book could not be assigned in the middle school, though it remained in the school's library and was still taught in the high school. The principal of the middle school agreed with Fleming, though he had never read the book. The local school board then decided that an error in judgment had been committed, and they returned *Huckleberry Finn* to the middle school curriculum.

In May 1992, a parent in Modesto, California, along with the high school's Black Student Union, objected to the inclusion of *Huckleberry Finn* on the reading lists in eleventh-grade classes because of the use of the word *nigger*. The objector stated, "The word not only offends the sensibilities of black Americans, but all Americans and people who respect the heritages, cultures and ethnicities of people in this country." On the recommendation of the district's language arts chair, school officials denied the request to remove the book while affirming the right of students to request alternative assignments. The district's director of secondary education noted:

> Our position is that the eleventh-grade literature is American literature, and [*Huckleberry Finn*] has long been considered by many to be a great, if not the greatest, American novel. . . . A lot of things may be offensive, but we teach kids how to deal with the issues, look critically at them from several angles and to make informal decisions about the literature.

The board voted to retain the book and to add a guide that discusses racial issues.[19]

5. **The Chocolate War,** by Robert Cormier. Pantheon, 1974.
Synopsis and Background: In *The Chocolate War*, the leader of a secret society, the Vigils, in a Catholic high school manipulates and intimidates most students to follow the gang's dictates. One student, Jerry Renault, tries to stand up to the gang when it bullies the students into selling chocolates at the school, but he finds that the struggle against conformity has unfortunate consequences. He shows courage in facing the combined forces of the secret society and school officials, some of whom act in complicity with the gang. Like so many of the heroes of banned young adult novels, Jerry Renault bucks the system, making decisions for himself in an attempt to gain control over his life. Jerry did not set out to be rebellious, but the repressive control of the school over the students' lives causes him to refuse to participate in the annual chocolate sale. For this act of rebellion, he receives personal punishment on the football field, telephone threats, the silent treatment from the student body, and a final brutal beating on stage before the entire school. This assault by the Vigils is perpetrated with the encouragement of the assistant headmaster, who supports "school spirit" over individuality.

The *New York Times* called *The Chocolate War* "masterfully structured and rich in theme." Kenneth Donelson and Alleen Pace Nilsen's *Literature for Today's Young Adults* proclaims: "The book that we have chosen as an example of the best of modern realism for young adults is Robert Cormier's *The Chocolate War*."[20] Why would this textbook example of literary excellence be the source of repeated controversy and censorship? All of Cormier's young adult novels focus on the struggle between individuals and dehumanizing institutions, and in *The Chocolate War*, the institution is a combination of church and school. W. Geiger Ellis of the University of Georgia tells us:

> School, church, hospital, government—surely these are people-serving, individual-enhancing institutions. Look more closely, as Cormier guides us, for unsettling views are waiting. Such a negative portrayal of established institutions is bound to be unpopular in some circles and will make some individuals uncomfortable, especially when they themselves are a part of and subject to such an institution. Specifically, many teachers feel that they dare not disturb the universe, and as Cormier has made perfectly clear, there is danger in doing so.[21]

Selected Challenges in the 1990s: In February 1990, R. Lee Smith, a Methodist minister in Haverhill, New Hampshire, demanded that *The Chocolate War* be removed from the required reading list for ninth-graders at Woodsville High School. In response, Superintendent Douglas McDonald suspended the use of the book until a district committee could examine the issue. At a school board meeting, Smith submitted a list of objectionable passages containing expletives, references to masturbation and sexual fantasies, and derogatory characterizations of a teacher and of religious ceremonies. A test on *The Chocolate War* had been scheduled in the ninth-grade English class, but Smith convinced Superintendent McDonald to cancel it. "I said, 'No, there's not going to be a test,' " recalled Smith. "Mr. McDonald said he'd allow my child to be excused. I said, 'No, there's not going to be a test for any student' and he said OK." Superintendent McDonald released a formal statement saying, "The book has been on the required reading list for 13 years. There will be a temporary suspension in use of the book."[22]

In 1991, a parent in Paola, Kansas, supported by a minister, objected to the use of *The Chocolate War* in a ninth-grade English class for being disrespectful of religion, containing curse words, and depicting sexual desires. The school board voted 4 to 3 to accept a review committee's recommendation to retain the book and reaffirmed its policy of offering an alternative assignment to anyone who objected.

A seventh-grade language arts teacher in Augusta, Maine, objected to the availability of *The Chocolate War* in the middle school library, alleging a lack of positive role models, a negative view of the Catholic church, and an unhappy ending to the story. The teacher requested that the book be removed from the middle school and placed instead in the high school. The district superintendent upheld a review committee's recommendation to retain the book in the middle school library.

A parent in Vista, California, objected to the availability of *The Chocolate War* in a middle school library, alleging that the book contained sexual references. After repeated discussions with a librarian, the objector withdrew her complaint.

In January 1992, parents in New Milford, Connecticut, challenged the inclusion of *The Chocolate War* on an eighth-grade reading list. Parent Nancy Mowrey told a school board review committee that the book contained "crude and blasphemous" language and unnecessary "sexual activities" and that it should therefore be removed from the school system. "Why do we find it necessary to fill our children's heads full of this?" she asked. Another parent complained, "Students are exposed to enough negativism every day. It doesn't mean they have to read about it." Assistant Superintendent Karen McCarthy disagreed. "I think it's a fine book," she said. "It's extremely well written and I do not take exception to the language or sexual references. They are not that explicit or out of the ordinary. . . . This is the kind of book students want to read. They can identify with it." Language arts coordinator Judy Goeler said, "I think it's a very good book with some important, hard-hitting themes. It gets across the point that sometimes when you fight for something, you're absolutely all alone. That's important for eighth graders who are constantly surrounded by peer pressure."[23]

The review committee subsequently recommended the book's retention but suggested that the board might want to reconsider the grade level at which it is taught. When the board of education met to consider the recommendation, about 150 people attended, with equal numbers supporting and opposing the bookban. An eleven-year-old student told the board that he had read the book and enjoyed it. He acknowledged the occasionally strong language but said that in comparison with the language on the school bus "that's a Little Bo Peep story." A high school teacher and mother of a seventh-grader said she was thankful that the book was actually addressing some of the things that make her son's life almost intolerable in the middle school. "I don't think this book goes too far," she said. "In fact, I don't think this book goes far enough." She claimed that the eighth grade was too late for the book to be used, since her son had been victimized by such acts in the sixth grade. After two hours of discussion, the board of education voted 9 to 1 to maintain *The Chocolate War* on the featured reading list for eighth-graders.[24]

A parent in Maumee, Ohio, objected to the inclusion of *The Chocolate War* on middle and high school reading lists, alleging that the book contained vulgar and profane language. Although a review committee voted to retain the book at the high school level, citing its literary value, the book is no longer used by nor recommended to middle school students.

A parent in Maiden, North Carolina, objected to *The Chocolate War,* available in a middle school library and used in an eighth-grade class, alleging bad language, discussion of homosexuality, and descriptions of obscene gestures. A review committee decided to retain the book in the library and class, explaining that it was a student's right to read books that challenge them to think about the complex issues they must face in our society.

6. **Bridge to Terabithia,** by Katherine Paterson. HarperCollins Pubs., Inc., 1977.

Synopsis and Background: This Newbery Award–winning novel tells the story of a ten-year-old farm boy who finds an important new friend and then loses her in a tragic accident. Young Jesse Aarons loves to draw and loves to run. His two goals are to be the fastest runner in the fifth grade and to find a friend. Leslie Burke, the new girl in his school class, becomes that friend. Leslie's parents, seeking to escape city life, have moved onto the farm next to the Aarons's. Leslie is not like the other girls Jesse knows. She wears blue jeans and sneakers, and she shares Jesse's interest in running. In fact, she proves to be the fastest runner in the fifth grade. Leslie, whose parents are writers, shares her own lively imagination and knowledge of literature with Jesse. The two children create a secret hiding place and an imaginary world they called Terabithia, where the shy Jesse slowly gains confidence and sophistication. As Easter vacation approaches, Jesse and Leslie agree to meet in Terabithia on Easter Monday. Early Monday morning Jesse follows the path to Terabithia, reaching the bridge of tree branches they had built to cross the creek. When Jesse finds the creek dangerously swollen from heavy rains, he turns back and decides instead to spend the day at the art museum. When he returns home, he is told that Leslie was found drowned in the creek. Jesse's anger and guilt cause him to run away from home, but he is quickly brought home by his father.

When spring arrives and the creek subsides, Jesse crosses the bridge to Terabithia once more, this time with his seven-year-old sister May Belle. When May Belle finds herself caught in crossing the fragile bridge, Jesse rescues her in an act of bravery. He subsequently builds a real bridge over the creek, using lumber donated by Leslie's parents. As the novel concludes, Jesse decides to introduce May Belle to the magic of Terabithia, as Leslie had done for him.

Selected Challenges in the 1990s: In 1990, a parent in Burlington, North Carolina, objected to *Bridge to Terabithia,* used in a fifth-grade academically excelled class, for allegedly containing profanity, violence, disrespect for authority, New Age religion, and inappropriate use of

God's name. Despite an offer to provide an alternate assignment, the objector requested removal of the book, stating, "We care about not only what our daughter reads, but what other children read as well." Several parents in Burlington also requested that all teachers be trained to root out New Age influence in the curriculum. A review committee was to be created to review every book at the school in order to "systematically eliminate any book and piece of literature which can be identified with New Age practices—anything that in any way seeks to erode traditional, moral values." The school did not agree to the request.[25]

A parent in Harwinton, Connecticut, objected to *Bridge to Terabithia* and several other books for profanity, rebellion, and prejudice. The school system accepted the recommendation of a review committee that all of the books be retained.

In 1991, a parent in El Cajon, California, objected to *Bridge to Terabithia*, available in the junior high school library and used in some fifth-grade classes, citing a portrayal of a preacher, treatment of death on a theological level, and encouraging students to have contempt for the church. A review committee voted to retain the book, and the decision was not appealed.

A parent in Santa Ana, California, objected to *Bridge to Terabithia*, used in the fifth-grade curriculum and available in the elementary school library, for taking the Lord's name in vain. The objector requested that the book be removed from the library and curriculum, but a review committee voted unanimously to retain the book.

In December 1991, a parent in Apple Valley, California, attempted to ban *Bridge to Terabithia* from local schools, complaining that the book contained vulgar language and scriptural inaccuracies. A passage in which a father tells his daughter that God would never send a little girl to hell offended the parents, because it suggested that no one under the age of eleven could go to hell. The book was required reading in some fifth-grade classes, though parents were able to request that their children not participate. The district board of trustees voted unanimously to continue using the novel, following the recommendation of a review committee, which cited the novel's literary value and the strong interest in it among parents and students. Trustee Bill McDaniel told the complaining parent that he would not support banning the book because students had the option of using an alternative book.

In May 1992, parents and church members in Mechanicsburg, Pennsylvania, objected to *Bridge to Terabithia*, available in the elementary school library, for offensive language and negative images of the church and Christianity. One objector cited forty examples of the word *Lord* used as curse word, four instances of *damn*, two of *hell*, and one of *bitched*. Another objector said the book could encourage a morbid fascination with death and spirits. Another claimed that there should be no material in the libraries that did not reflect the parents' opinions. A review committee recommended that the book be retained, saying the language was not meant to be disrespectful and was incidental to the purpose of the story. The superintendent upheld the review committee's unanimous decision to retain the book.

A parent in Walled Lake, Michigan, objected to the use of *Bridge to Terabithia* in fifth-grade literature and reading classes, alleging profanity such as *hell, damn,* and *hellhole.* A review committee voted unanimously to retain the book, stating: "After reading and studying *Bridge to Terabithia,* students will have gained a further understanding of their own fears and joys. Their appreciation of literature will be enhanced by the quality of this piece."[26]

7. **Scary Stories to Tell in the Dark,** by Alvin Schwartz. Lippincott, 1981.

Synopsis and Background: This folklore collection presents ghostly stories suitable for telling or reading at home, around a campfire, at Halloween, but particularly in the dark. The stories are both scary and funny but are not so macabre as to be inappropriate for even the lower elementary grades. Most of the stories are old, but some have contemporary settings. For example, a young babysitter has a frightening experience as she drives home. The usual symbols of fear abound, including witches, graveyards, and wolves. The book includes rhymes, songs, and prose tales and is broken into sections covering things like traditional ghost tales, contemporary folklore, and chilling tales with surprising endings. The text is accompanied by eerie illustrations of staring eye sockets, gory hands, and wild-eyed animals. All of the tales are carefully documented as to source and background, and there is a surprising degree of scholarship reflected in the source notes and bibliography.

Selected Challenges in the 1990s: In June 1990, an elementary school teacher in Lavonia, Michigan, objected to the use of *Scary Stories to Tell in the Dark* and another book after her daughter was frightened by one of the stories. The Livonia Board of Education subsequently voted against placing restrictions on the two books, stating, "If we restrict it, we will take away the teacher's ability to use it at all. To remove it is unfair to the kids who want it. If these books are not included, then there will be other books which will offend someone else." However, the board urged teachers to be sensitive to the emotional effects of such books on young children, warning that caution should be exercised in using materials for whole group instruction.[27]

In 1991, a parent in Dallas, Oregon, objected to *Scary Stories to Tell in the Dark,* available in the elementary school library, on the grounds that reading the book could cause children to experience a lack of appetite, nightmares, sickness, and an unhealthy curiosity about death. A review committee was split in its recommendation, but the school board unanimously voted to retain the book.

In January 1992, parents in Kirkland, Washington, objected to the inclusion of three books by Alvin Schwartz in the elementary school libraries. *Scary Stories to Tell in the Dark, More Scary Stories to Tell in the Dark,* and *Scary Stories 3: More Tales to Chill Your Bones* were cited as unacceptably violent for children. A nine-member volunteer committee of parents and school officials decided unanimously to retain the books but recommended that teachers and librarians use discretion and consider alternative selections. One parent said that after her son read the books, he compared them to what he called "a really scary book," a biography of Supreme Court Justice Thurgood Marshall in which a fourteen-year-old black boy was beaten and shot for talking to a white woman. The parent said her son thought that the Schwartz books were just silly in comparison. Another parent said, "You have to take out the emotionalism and look at the basic issues, which are censorship and control. Who is going to control what you read, what you think, what you wear and what you eat."[28]

A parent in Gilbert, Arizona, objected to nine books, including *Scary Stories to Tell in the Dark* and *More Scary Stories to Tell in the Dark,* all available in the elementary school library. The objector claimed that the books promoted satanism and the occult. The parent rejected the option of noting on her child's library file those books that her child was not allowed to read, insisting that no other child be allowed to read them either. A school-level committee reviewed the books and recommended that they be retained. After the objector appealed that decision to the superintendent, another review committee was appointed and upheld the initial decision. The board then voted to retain all the books. A supporter of the books stated, "When that parent begins deciding what my children can or cannot read, I draw the line. . . . [W]e must respect the opinions and beliefs of everyone and their right to choose for themselves."[29]

A fourth-grade student in Riverside, California, objected to *Scary Stories to Tell in the Dark* and two other Alvin Schwartz books in the elementary school libraries, saying they were frightening and could cause bad dreams. The student said, "The books are more than gory and the stories aren't anything the other kids need to read. . . . I just would enjoy it if the books were off the school grounds." A district review committee decided to retain the books, saying they were well written, had received favorable reviews, form a unique collection, and were very popular with children in the district schools. The committee pointed out, "Notes and sources for the tales were well-documented and it was also felt that those children to whom these stories appeal are well able to distinguish them as fantasy and that they are appropriate for recreational reading."[30]

A teacher in Jacksonville, Florida, objected to the inclusion of *Scary Stories to Tell in the Dark* in an elementary school library, alleging that it encouraged violence, cruelty, brutality, cannibalism, and aberrant behavior. In a formal complaint, the objector asked the school official to "be not wise in thine own eyes; fear the Lord and depart from evil." A review committee voted to retain the book but required parental permission for students in kindergarten through third grade. One committee member wrote, "I found the book valuable in its reference to the 'scary story' as part of our cultural heritage. . . . For children, scaring one another in a 'safe' manner, i.e. telling or reading stories, may allow them to deal with the fear of the unknown." Another committee member explained, "The book is exactly what the title says. . . . This book seems mild compared to the modern stories kids watch at the movies or on T.V."[31]

In October 1992, a request was made to remove *Scary Stories to Tell in the Dark* from a school library in Liberty, Indiana. The county superintendent told the school board that the district's Library Censorship Committee had reviewed the book and found it appropriate for the library. The superintendent agreed with the committee's conclusion that children reading the book could separate reality from folklore. The school board voted to accept the committee's recommendation.

8. More Scary Stories to Tell in the Dark, by Alvin Schwartz. Lippincott, 1984.

Synopsis and Background: This sequel to Alvin Schwartz's 1981 *Scary Stories to Tell in the Dark* has been banned with much the same frequency and motivation as the original. Like the first book, it is a collection of horror stories suitable for children, written as children might tell them, rather than as literary tales. It has been labeled a children's book but frequently finds its way into junior high school collections. Each story is short, some just one or two pages, and the print is large for easy reading. The stories involve bloodcurdling ghosts, murders, graveyards, and other horrors. One story describes a butcher who makes tasty sausages from his friends and neighbors. Also included are what are called "jump stories," where the teller concludes by unexpectedly jumping up and shrieking at the audience. There are also some funny stories, such as the one about two baseball fans, Todd and Leon, who wonder whether baseball is played in heaven. When Todd dies and goes to heaven, he comes back to tell Leon the good news that there is a heavenly baseball team—and the bad news that Leon is scheduled to pitch the next day. The stories lend themselves to being read aloud in the classroom, and some are structured to encourage discussion. They are suspenseful, full of enjoyment, and soundly rooted in traditional folklore, representing the best storytelling traditions. The stories are enhanced by eerie drawings of dismembered bodies, hideous creatures, and mysterious lights, providing realistic images that create a scary mood.

Selected Challenges in the 1990s: In 1991, parents in Wake County, North Carolina, objected to *More Scary Stories to Tell in the Dark,* available in the elementary school library, on the grounds that the book "promotes murder, death, tragedy, and anti-religious sentiment," could cause "irreparable psychological damage and [a] lifetime of fears," "actually [condones] the types of behavior portrayed," encourages "violence through the pro-death themes promulgated throughout the book," and is "anti-religious" and "anti-parent." The objectors said they hoped to "ensure [that] our children and other parents' children are not exposed to this book and other books like it in the future." Objectors demanded a written apology from the first-grade teacher who read the stories aloud and "a written statement from the school board assuring us parents that the book . . . and other books of this genre be removed from the shelves . . . in addition to being withdrawn from any reading list." A review committee voted to retain the book but to restrict its availability to fourth- and fifth-graders. Although the committee noted that the book was "representative of American folklore" and "lends itself well toward learning the art of storytelling," it urged primary school teachers not to read aloud from the book to any students. The objectors were not satisfied and appealed the decision, but the board voted unanimously to accept the recommendation of the review committee.[32]

A parent in Beavercreek, Ohio, objected to the inclusion of *More Scary Stories* in an elementary school library, charging that it promoted suicide and "death and destruction." The objector said the book's illustrations were "gross, contain a high degree of occult/Satanic symbolism and indicate that death rather than life is the primary focus." He said the book should "not [be] required in the education of any civilized individual" and requested that it be removed from all district libraries. A school-level review committee unanimously decided to limit the book's availability to middle grade students, while noting that the stories were collected from American and English folklore and that the book was highly recommended by all the major review sources for grades 4 through 6. A district-level committee then voted unanimously to retain the book, stating that it was one of the most widely circulated in the school system, had positive reviews, and was a Buckeye Children's Book Award winner.[33]

A parent in Rock Springs, Wyoming, objected to the inclusion of *More Scary Stories* in the elementary school library, claiming the book was too violent and frightening. The school board upheld a review committee's unanimous recommendation to retain the book, but district librarians were asked to suggest alternative titles to primary grade students. One school official noted that numerous students had checked out the book throughout the district and that there had never been a complaint before.

A parent in Tacoma, Washington, objected to the inclusion of *More Scary Stories* in the elementary school library, claiming that the book had caused a fourth-grader to have nightmares. A school review committee voted to retain the book but to restrict its availability to third-through fifth-grade students. The committee also directed teachers not to read stories from the book aloud in class.

Parents in Prairie du Sac, Wisconsin, objected to *More Scary Stories,* available in the elementary school library, for allegedly containing gruesome material and violence and lacking respect for life. Specific objections were raised over the story of a butcher who makes sausages out of his enemies. The school board took statements from teachers, librarians, a school psychologist, and committee members, after which the board voted to retain the book. The superintendent expressed concern about the precedent that would be set if the board removed the book from the library.

In 1992, a parent in Goldsboro, North Carolina, objected to *More Scary Stories* and *Scary Stories,* both available in the elementary school library, claiming that they were too graphic. A review committee recommended that the books be removed from the library, stating that they were not suitable for kindergarten through fourth-grade students.

9. **The Witches,** by Roald Dahl. Farrar, Straus & Giroux, 1983.

Synopsis and Background: When a seven-year-old boy, presumably Dahl himself, is orphaned in an automobile accident, he goes to live with his cigar-smoking grandmother, a longtime witch-lover, who teaches the boy all about witches. The boy learns that witches all look like nice ladies, but you can spot them if you look closely. For one thing, they all wear wigs to cover their bald heads, and they have itchy scalps. When the boy and his grandmother visit a hotel, he notices that the lady delegates to a conference are all scratching their heads. He soon discovers that this is a coven of witches and that the Grand High Witch is planning to destroy every child in England. The witch then turns the boy into a mouse, using her Formula 86 Delayed Action Mouse-Maker, but the boy's grandmother helps him turn the tables on the coven, turning them into mice. In this fast-paced adventure, Dahl presents the witches as purely evil creatures intent on exterminating children. Some adults may consider this frightening, but they will approve of the special relationship between the grandmother and grandson, a relationship that persists even when the boy is a mouse-person. The message of love and acceptance is unmistakable.

Selected Challenges in the 1990s: In January 1990, a book reconsideration committee at an elementary school in Maquoketa, Iowa, met in closed session to consider a complaint about *The Witches* and another book. A parent had asked the principal of the elementary school to remove the book from the school libraries and classrooms, complaining that the boy in *The Witches* is turned into a mouse and will have to stay a mouse for the rest of his life. The committee considered the criteria for selection and then voted to retain both books without restriction.

Two opposing challenges were lodged in LaGrange, Kentucky, against *The Witches,* contained in the local elementary school library. One of the complaints came from members of the Wiccan religion who claimed that the book portrayed witches negatively. The other came from parents who said the book was occultic, nightmarish, and unfit for young children. The first complaint did not result in any change in the status of the book, but the school board responded to the second complaint by reassigning the book from the elementary to the middle school.

In 1991, a parent in Dallas, Oregon, objected to the inclusion of *The Witches* in the elementary school library. The objector requested the removal of all copies of the book, saying that it devalues the life of children, stereotypes women, and fails to distinguish between witches and "nice" people. The school board voted to uphold a review committee's recommendation to retain the book, which had been removed from the shelves during the reconsideration process. One parent said, "If we keep protecting our children from certain ideas, there won't be any ideas left. The more creativity and wonder I see in my children, the happier it makes me." [34]

A parent in Burnsville, Minnesota, objected to the use of *The Witches* in a sixth-grade class and its inclusion in the elementary school library, claiming that the book would lead children to take witchcraft and satanism lightly. The superintendent upheld a review committee's decision to retain the book. The committee said the book was enjoyable, imaginative, well written, and the perfect humor for a sixth-grader.

Parents in Elverta, California, objected to the inclusion of *The Witches* in an elementary school library, claiming that it was scary, encouraged an unhealthy interest in the occult, and promoted the religious practice of witchcraft. Objectors complained that *The Witches* was too realistic, would lead children to distrust their parents, and would cause a breakdown in a child's self-esteem. A review committee recommended that the book be retained without restriction, but the assistant superintendent, describing the book as offensive, imposed access restrictions requiring students in kindergarten through fifth grade to have parental permission before borrowing the book.

In February 1992, four parents in Escondido, California, filed complaints against the use of *The Witches* in the elementary schools, alleging that it promoted the occult. One complaint said, "We object to the introduction to the occult, to the teaching about witchcraft that this book claims to be fact, to the parts about cutting kids up, destroying them and making them disappear." Another complaint said the book would result in "confusion from mixing truth with fiction, unhealthy interest in the occult, [and] seeds of unhealthy fear and mistrust placed in children, especially concerning women." A review committee voted 3 to 1 in support of the book, but the superintendent and assistant superintendent decided to place the book on a restricted list, the first time any book in the district had been so restricted. In making the decision to restrict the book, the assistant superintendent said it was "offensive in terms of common decency standards" and would frighten children at the elementary level. But Stan Reid, principal of the local elementary school and a member of the review committee, found the book to be quite the opposite. "It was a tongue-in-cheek approach and the bottom line was that good will overcome evil. In talking with kids out in the playground and in the lunch lines, for the most part the kids thought it was hilarious. They understood that it was a fairy tale and it was make believe."[35]

10. **Daddy's Roommate,** by Michael Willhoite. Alyson Pubs., 1990.

Synopsis and Background: One of the earliest books aimed at children with homosexual parents, *Daddy's Roommate* addresses the subject in a straightforward manner. After his parents' divorce, the young son must adjust to his father's new male companion. The boy describes his father's relationship with his roommate, Frank, and his own relationship with the two men. We are told of the normal family activities, shopping, gardening, trips to the zoo, the ball game, the beach, movies, and the like, and the healthy, affectionate bonds that develop between the boy and the adults in his life. The boy concludes that being gay is just one more kind of love. The book delivers the message that alternative life-styles can be as nurturing as traditional ones. Watercolor illustrations provide a light and attractive tone.

Selected Challenges in the 1990s: In February 1992, a library patron in

Olympia, Washington, requested that *Daddy's Roommate* be transferred to an adult section of the Timberland Regional Libraries or removed altogether. She charged that the book promoted homosexuality and was offensive. At a subsequent library board meeting, most of the forty patrons who spoke favored keeping the book, and the board voted to retain the book without restrictions. The acting library director said the board's decision was based on the library's policies on diversity and parental responsibility.

In May 1992, the wife of a minister in Roswell, New Mexico, asked the board of trustees of the Roswell Public Library to remove *Daddy's Roommate* from the children's section of the library. At the board meeting, Reverend Kerry Holton, his wife, and about 150 supporters addressed the trustees. The Holtons presented a petition calling for the relocation of the book. Mrs. Holton said she wanted the library to respect the rights of parents to determine what their children should read and when they should read it. But board president Robert Belles said the board does not decide where books are shelved, nor does it pass judgment on library purchases. He said the board's policy was to allow free access to everything in the library.

In May 1992, parents in Harrisburg, Pennsylvania, gathered nearly 2,000 signatures urging the library system to remove *Daddy's Roommate* from its shelves. The protestors said the book's intent was indoctrination into a gay life-style. Library officials said the book would remain in the library and accessible to all patrons. Library director Richard Bowra said the protestors appeared to want the library to reject any books that touch on homosexuality. "What is important is that the library's role is to have material on any number of issues," said Bowra, who noted that *Daddy's Roommate* had been charged out twenty-one times without incident. He said, "There is nothing in the book which says this is the best lifestyle there is." Bowra admitted that the protesters would not be pleased that the book will remain on the shelves. "What we may have to do is agree to disagree. They have to realize we are here to serve over 200,000 residents of Dauphin County. If the library were to remove and relocate all items that people might object to, there would be vast open spaces."[36]

In June 1992, *Daddy's Roommate* and another book relating to homosexuality were donated to the public library in Springfield, Oregon. In deciding whether to accept the books, children's librarian Judy Harold had to consider a recent city charter amendment prohibiting the city from "promoting, encouraging or facilitating" homosexuality. The amendment had been sponsored by the Oregon Citizens Alliance (OCA), which said of the donated books, "We're not going to do anything unilaterally, but if some Springfield parent decides to challenge these books, we will give support and assistance to that effort." Previously, OCA had taken the position that voter approval of the amendment meant that the community opposed the public availability of books promoting homosexuality. The director of the local chapter of the ACLU said that if the librarian rejected the books because they violate the terms of the charter amendment, he would file suit to challenge that decision.[37] The librarian decided to apply the same selection criteria to the donated books as she would to any other books.

In October 1992, about twenty-five people in Tillamook County, Oregon, lodged complaints against the inclusion of *Daddy's Roommate* in the local public library. The complaints were filed during a heated statewide ballot initiative that would have declared homosexuality "abnormal, wrong, unnatural and perverse." The statewide initiative was defeated, and the Tillamook library board was to review *Daddy's Roommate* for appropriateness.

In October 1992, complaints were received at a public library in Gwinnett County, Georgia, concerning *Daddy's Roommate.* The objectors were well organized and the complaints increasingly orchestrated. The five or six requests to remove the book were supplemented by a 150-name petition followed by a 200-name petition. After the library staff recommended keeping *Daddy's Roommate* in the collection, the patron then requested a board review. The library board then voted to take *Daddy's Roommate* off the shelves and place it behind a circulation desk, allowing it to be used only on request. Board President Kay Dickinson said:

> The majority felt it should be read as or by an adult, or it might be damaging to a three- to seven-year-old who might get the wrong idea. It might be confusing for them. . . . Homosexuality is something we have to deal with in our lifetime, and we don't want to be censors, but maybe a little restriction.[38]

11. **Curses, Hexes, and Spells,** by Daniel Cohen. Lippincott, 1974.

Synopsis and Background: Ironically, although *Curses, Hexes, and Spells* has frequently been banned for encouraging occult ideas, the book is almost entirely devoted to debunking and discrediting *all* supernatural explanations for such things as family curses, the disappearance of ships and planes in the Bermuda Triangle, the curse on the ship *Mary Celeste,* and the legend of the Wandering Jew. Cohen nonetheless maintains enough mystery to keep the youthful reader's rapt attention. Cohen has fully researched the historical evidence on the origins of many allegedly magical practices and supernatural events. He describes and analyzes a wide variety of curses, spells, and magical powers while speculating on how and why they occurred. Black and white reproductions and photographs illustrate these strange images, complementing a text that attempts to bring light and reason to the subject while maintaining the excitement befitting Lippincott's *Weird and Horrible* Library series.

Selected Challenges in the 1990s: In September 1990, a parent in Howard County, Maryland, filed a complaint against *Curses, Hexes, and Spells,* telling a school committee that her ten-year-old son was given the book by a school librarian when "he asked for a book about Halloween to do research for costumes." The parent said her son followed the book's instruction on how to cast a spell, drawing a circle in the driveway and placing candles inside the circle. "Children are influenced by these things, and the occult is as much a threat as alcohol and drugs," she said. "I felt the book teaches how to go about demonic worship. It is a very dangerous thing to have in the hands of young children." In response to the complaint, the associate superintendent of schools agreed to remove *Curses, Hexes, and Spells* from the county's elementary school libraries.[39]

Curses, Hexes, and Spells and several other books were removed from school libraries in Detroit, Michigan, in violation of existing reconsideration procedures. The books were removed in response to complaints that they contained material on witchcraft and the supernatural. After learning of the order to remove the books, the elementary school book-selection committee, acting on its own initiative, evaluated the books and recommended that all but one be reinstated in the library collections. That recommendation was neither acknowledged nor followed by the school district, but growing criticism caused the district to appoint a review committee. That committee met in March 1991 and recommended that *Curses, Hexes, and Spells* and all but one of the other books be reinstated.

A grandparent in Salina, Kansas, objected to *Curses, Hexes, and Spells,* available in the elementary school library, claiming that it was a misrepresentation of Christianity; endangered children physically, mentally, and spiritually; and encouraged experimentation with witchcraft. A review committee unanimously recommended that the book be moved from the elementary to the junior high school level, citing two reviews that recommended the book for a higher grade level.

In 1991, a parent in Kansas City, Missouri, objected to *Curses, Hexes, and Spells* and three other books in the middle school library. The objector claimed that *Curses, Hexes, and Spells* promoted witchcraft. A district review committee recommended that the books be retained, and no appeal was filed.

A parent in Carlton, Oregon, objected to *Curses, Hexes, and Spells* in the middle school library, alleging that the book contained profanity and exposed children to witchcraft. The objector said no child of any age should be allowed to read the book because a student could use it to put hexes on other students. A school review committee decided to retain the book but to place it on a reserve shelf where students may use it only under the supervision of a librarian or teacher.

12. **A Wrinkle in Time,** by Madeleine L'Engle. Dell, 1962.

Synopsis and Background: This Newbery Award–winning novel is a thought-provoking tale enjoyed by children in schools around the country. The main character, twelve-year-old Meg Murray, has an unusual family. Her father is a physicist who has disappeared mysteriously on a secret space mission. Her five-year-old brother Charles is a clairvoyant. One stormy night, Meg gets out of bed and goes down to the kitchen to get a cup of hot cocoa. She is joined by her brother Charles, her mother, and finally by an old lady seeking shelter from the storm. This is Mrs. Whatsit, who lives in a haunted house nearby. The following day, Meg, along with her brother and a friend, visit Mrs. Whatsit and meet her two companions, Mrs. Who and Mrs. Which. Using their supernatural powers, these three ladies take the children on a space ride through a "wrinkle in time." The children soon discover that their father is being held prisoner on a distant planet, Camazatz, which is controlled by the Power of Darkness. They travel alone to Camazatz and enter the Central Intelligence Building, where they are confronted by the Prime Coordinator who captures Meg's brother. Meg then locates her father trapped behind a glass wall, and by using Mrs. Who's magic glasses, she is able to pass through the wall and free him. She then proceeds to free her brother from the Prime Coordinator by repeating the words "I Love You" to him, thus releasing him from the Power of Darkness. Meg, her father, and brother then return safely to earth. *A Wrinkle in Time* is more than an exciting science fiction adventure. It teaches the importance of individuality, respect for others, and the power of love.

Selected Challenges in the 1990s: In November 1990, Tom Price, a parent in Anniston, Alabama, asked the board of education to order that *A Wrinkle in Time* not be read by or sold to elementary school children. Price also asked that parents be informed before teachers read from any book other than an approved text. Price claimed that the novel dealt with New Age religion and sent a mixed signal to children about good and evil, since witches are among the fantasy creatures that help a child. He also objected to placing the name of Jesus Christ alongside the names of great artists, philosophers, scientists, and religious leaders in a list of defenders of the earth against evil. School officials responded that the book appealed to most students and that many, including Price's son, had purchased the book on their own. Price told the board that he had withdrawn his son from the school because the book had been read to him and he had been allowed to purchase it. In December 1990, the Anniston Board of Education informed Price that his request to ban the book had been denied.

In 1991, a parent and a pastor in El Paso, Texas, objected to the use of *A Wrinkle in Time* in sixth-grade classes because it represented New Age religion that would produce "confusion, anti-family units, and anti-Christian values." The objector concluded that the book "has no valuable contribution and the only possible point of this book is to undermind [*sic*] and confuse the children who are Christians." A review committee noted the book's high acclaim, its overall theme of love for one's family, and the fact that New Age religion had not even been conceived when this book was written.[40]

Parents in Rialto, California, objected to the inclusion of *A Wrinkle in Time* in the sixth-grade reading curriculum for being a frightening book that encourages one to believe in make-believe. A review committee voted to retain the book, noting the book's universal values and literary merit.

A parent in Snellville, Georgia, objected to *A Wrinkle in Time,* available in the elementary school media center and read aloud in fifth-grade class, charging, "The overall mystical theme of the book raises concerns about impressionable children being exposed to mysticism and Far Eastern religious practice." The objector claimed that much of the book was based on Hindu and Buddhist culture and that it represented the "New Age movement," which "consists of individuals and organizations that interpret reality mystically and strive to enhance their spirituality through the use of occult practices." A review committee voted to retain the book in both the classroom and media center.[41]

Parents in Waterloo, Iowa, in conjunction with the conservative organization Citizens for Excellence in Education, challenged *A Wrinkle in Time,* available in the middle school media center and read aloud in sixth grade, alleging "cult implications," "sadism," "Satanic suggestions," and "indoctrination of the Occult." The objectors also claimed that "the book associates Jesus together with other great artists . . . not distinguished as being any different or acknowledging that he is the son of God." A school review committee voted to retain the book in the classroom and media center.[42]

13. **How to Eat Fried Worms,** by Thomas Rockwell. Watts, 1973.

Synopsis and Background: Two school boys, Billy and Alan, make a $50 bet that Billy will eat fifteen worms in fifteen days. Billy begins his one-worm-a-day process, while a concerned and disgusted Alan wonders how he will get the $50 from his father. Billy tries fried worms with ketchup, mustard, and horseradish sauce and baked "Alsatian Smothered Worm" with onions and sour cream, as prepared by his supportive mother. Billy's mother had called the family doctor to check on the safety of this unusual diet, but once assured that fried worms represented no danger, she accepted the plan with equanimity. Alan tries every means imaginable to sabotage Billy's plan or talk him into quitting, but Billy proceeds worm by worm, each day's dish more bizarre than the previous day, as the book moves to a tense and hilarious conclusion.

Selected Challenges in the 1990s: In 1990, a parent in North East, Pennsylvania, objected to the use of *How to Eat Fried Worms* in the third-grade reading program because the story contains profanity and the father in it drinks beer. The objector claimed the story did not portray normal family life. The school board accepted a review committee's recommendation to remove the book from the assigned reading list but retain it in the library.

A parent in Clinton, Connecticut, objected to the use of *How to Eat Fried Worms* in a fourth-grade language arts class, claiming it contained profanity and encouraged peer pressure. The book was removed from class until the complaint was resolved, but the superintendent eventually upheld a review committee's recommendation to retain the book.

In 1991, a parent in Antigo, Wisconsin, objected to the inclusion of *How to Eat Fried Worms* on the reading list for grades 3 and 4 because the book contained the word *bastard*. The librarian, a member of the school-appointed review committee, distributed a packet of book reviews, author information, and related articles to the committee members and to the objector. After reviewing the packet, the objector dropped the complaint.

How to Eat Fried Worms has been published in two versions, one containing the word *bastard* and the other expurgating the word. In LaPaz, Indiana, the elementary school had originally acquired the expurgated version, but when replacement editions were ordered, copies containing *bastard* found their way into the school. When a student reported the offending word to her mother, the parent went to the school library and removed the book without charging it out. The school first billed her $12 for the stolen book but eventually agreed to replace the offending copies with expurgated editions only. Still, the parent refused to return the stolen book or pay the fine. "I think the immoral majority may have had their way long enough," she said. The school principal agreed with the objector and said a review committee did as well. "We are not going to have that particular book with that particular word in it," he said. The principal claimed that censorship has its good and bad points. "Many sources of media aren't suitable for kids, and censorship is certainly one option that the people do have."[43]

In 1992, parents in Columbia, Maryland, objected to *How to Eat Fried*

Worms, used in a third-grade language arts class and available in an elementary school library, for offensive language, including the phrase *enormous pigeon-breasted middle-age woman* and the word *bastard.* The objector requested the removal of the book, but a school review committee recommended that it be retained in the library and the school curriculum.

14. **Blubber,** by Judy Blume. Bradbury, 1974.
   Synopsis and Background: Blubber provides an inside look at how insensitive some wealthy, fifth-grade children can be to each other, and to adults. Blubber is the nickname given to Linda Fischer, an overweight fifth-grader, by her mean-spirited classmates who, like a pack of dogs, follow the directions of Wendy, the class troublemaker. In addition to the name-calling, the class has tormented Linda in a variety of ways, stripping her in the girls' room, locking her in the storage closet, and forcing her to eat "chocolate ants." Blubber takes her punishment docilely. The story's narrator, Jill Brenner, goes along with this organized harassment, but she eventually crosses Wendy by standing up for Blubber at a mock trial. This, predictably, makes Jill the next target for harassment. Though Jill eventually gains an understanding of the pain of ostracism when she becomes a victim, she never really learns that it is wrong to persecute someone. This warts-and-all view of adolescent social dynamics is realistic and entertaining.
   Selected Challenges in the 1990s: In 1990, a parent in Louisville, Kentucky, objected to the inclusion of *Blubber* in the elementary school, claiming that the book contained characters who use racial slurs and behave unkindly. The parent did not follow up the initial letter of complaint with a formal request to remove the book, and *Blubber* was retained in the curriculum.
   In 1991, a parent in Lugoff, South Carolina, requested that *Blubber* be removed from the elementary school library because of profanity and the use of the word *bitch.* The parent, who was also a teacher in the local elementary school, complained to both the school principal and the librarian but declined to file a formal complaint. The book was retained in the library.
   A parent in Kansas City, Kansas, requested removal of *Blubber* from the elementary school library because of objectionable language. The parent, who admitted to not having read the book, noted the word *bitch* in the complaint. A school district review committee voted to retain the book, and the objector did not appeal that decision.
   In November 1991, Brent Burner, a parent in Perry Township, Ohio, asked the school board to remove *Blubber* from the elementary school libraries, claiming that the book taught stealing, cheating, and

lying, and twice used curse words. The book was removed from the library shelves, pending resolution of the complaint. The parent said, "There are so many uplifting, positive things they could be reading. Why choose to dwell on something entirely negative? . . . [B]ad is never punished. Good never comes to the fore. Evil is triumphant. . . . There's no use hoping the teachers can save you; they can't. They're fools." In December 1991, a district review committee recommended that *Blubber* be retained, but the objector appealed to the school board. Board President Chuck Stewart said, "I think the book should be trashed. I don't think there's a thing redeeming about the book." Stewart eventually agreed that the book might be retained, but with restricted circulation and parental permission required. "I think we can legally do that," he said.[44]

In 1992, a parent in Williston, Florida, objected to the inclusion of *Blubber* in an elementary school library, citing inappropriate language. After the informal objection, the parent was advised to file a formal complaint, as required by school policy. Although the parent did not submit the complaint form, the school administration arbitrarily removed the book from the library shelves, and the book remains banned today.

15. **Revolting Rhymes,** by Roald Dahl. Knopf, 1982.

Synopsis and Background: Dahl takes familiar nursery rhymes and changes them into "revolting rhymes," using the kind of crude humor common to adolescents. In "Cinderella," the prince chops off the head of her stepsisters, and when Cinderella refuses to marry him, he cries, "Who's the dirty slut?/ Off with her nut!" Snow White takes up residence with seven little bearded men who are addicted to gambling. Snow White uses the magic mirror to help them, saying, "Gambling's not a sin/ Provided you always win." In "Jack and the Beanstalk," Jack's mother refers to him as a "little creep," until the beanstalk grows to the sky, at which time she declares, "I'll sell the Mini, buy a Rolls!" But in the end, the giant eats her and Jack becomes the millionaire. Goldilocks notices that on her shoes "Was something that a dog had done." Little Red Riding Hood pulls a pistol from her knickers and shoots the wolf. She is later seen wearing a wolfskin coat. Needless to say, the satirical treatment leaves these traditional childhood tales in tatters.

Selected Challenges in the 1990s: In January 1990, a Reconsideration Committee at the elementary school in Maquoketa, Iowa, met in closed session to consider a parent's complaint against *Revolting Rhymes* and *Witches,* both by Roald Dahl. The parent had requested that the books be removed from elementary school libraries and classrooms on the basis of alleged violence, the use of the word *slut,* and the fact that a boy is turned into a mouse. The school principal was quoted as saying, "I'm against censorship, but I don't consider removing these two books censorship." After examining the school's selection policy and letters from interested persons, the Reconsideration Committee voted to keep both books in the elementary school libraries and curriculum without restriction.[45]

In 1991, parents in New Richmond, Wisconsin, objected to the inclusion of *Revolting Rhymes* in an elementary school library, alleging that it contained violence. Objectors pointed out that references were made to beheading and that Jack of "Jack and the Beanstalk" was beaten with a vacuum cleaner wand. A review committee voted 5 to 0 to retain the book, and no appeal was filed.

A parent in Pasco, Washington, objected to *Revolting Rhymes* in an elementary school library for containing morbid themes and the words *slut* and *hell*. The objector filed a formal complaint, which should have initiated the district's regular reconsideration process, but the school librarian chose to remove the book from the library without a review. The book remains off the library shelves.

A parent in Norridgewock, Maine, objected to *Revolting Rhymes,* available in an elementary school library and read aloud in a third-grade class, for alleged violence and the use of the word *slut*. A review committee voted unanimously to retain the book in the library but recommended parental notice before using the book in the classroom.

In October 1992, a parent in Rockland, Massachusetts, complained that *Revolting Rhymes* was offensive and inappropriate and should be removed from local schools. The parent charged that the book promotes violence and encourages disrespect toward women, parents, and teachers. The school superintendent announced that the book was not to be used in the K through 4 curriculum and would not be available in elementary school libraries. The book was also removed from the curriculum for grades 5 through 7, but will be retained in the middle school library and in the high school library and curriculum.

16. **Halloween ABC,** by Eve Merriam. Macmillan, 1987.

Synopsis and Background: Halloween ABC is a laughably ghoulish run through the alphabet, using twenty-six poems to send chills up the spine of the reader. For example, *A* is for Apple, which is "Delicious/malicious/one bite and you're dead." *C* is for Crawler, with all the associated grisley images. *I* is for Icicle, the classic murder mystery weapon. *P* is for an unusual Pet, which "finds the neighbors quite nutritious." The mystical and surrealistic illustrations have a dark, nightmare quality. The sophisticated language of the text, for example, "abhorrent torrent" and "virulent villain," make the book less of an ABC primer than a set of fun-filled, scary poems for intermediate readers.

Selected Challenges in the 1990s: In May 1991, parents in Howard County, Maryland, asked that *Halloween ABC* and another book be removed from county school libraries. The objectors complained particularly about two of Merriam's poems, "Demon" and "Icicle," and concluded, "There should be an effort to tone down Halloween and there should not be books about it in the schools." A review committee, made up of parents, teachers, administrators, and students recommended that the books be retained in the libraries, and that decision was upheld by the associate superintendent for curriculum.[46]

Parents in Wichita, Kansas, objected to *Halloween ABC* and another book available in an elementary school library for allegedly being satanic. The objectors wrote to the school, demanding the removal of the two books and all literature that "promotes, endorses and exposes our children to the religion of Satanism," including "witches, goblins, evil spirits, ghosts, demons, ghouls, vampires, ogres, monsters, Halloween and related subjects." They alleged that such material "is destroying our children's minds." The school board upheld the review committee's recommendation that the books stay on the shelves but restricted their availability to students in the third grade or above.[47]

In January 1992, a parent in Castle Rock, Colorado, challenged the inclusion of *Halloween ABC* in the elementary school library after her first-grader brought the book home from school. The parent said the book's verses were dark and sinister and would heighten the children's awareness of the macabre and pique their curiosity about the occult. The complaint was communicated to the district's Challenged Resource Committee, made up of four parents, three teachers, and a high school student. The committee determined that the book met all selection requirements and recommended that it be retained but shelved with the poetry rather than picture books. Librarians were advised to suggest its use by students in the third grade or above. The school board voted 4 to 3 to accept the committee's recommendation.

A parent in Glendale, Arizona, objected to the inclusion of *Halloween ABC* in the elementary school library because of its depiction of devils and demons. In response to the complaint, the school principal ordered the librarian to remove the book, in disregard of existing procedures that require submission of a formal complaint and review by a committee. The book remains banned from the library.

17. **A Day No Pigs Would Die,** by Robert Peck. Knopf, 1972.

Synopsis and Background: The autobiographical novel *A Day No Pigs Would Die* takes place in rural Vermont in the late 1920s. The novel provides a tender picture of a close father–son relationship and a glimpse of the stark realities of farm life in a Shaker community. The story is told by a young Shaker farm boy, Rob, who describes how he passed from childhood to adult responsibility in a single year. Rob tells us of the good and bad times during this period, the happiest coming when he receives a pet piglet as a birthday present. Rob spends most of his spare time with his pet, named Pinky. But after a bad apple crop that fall and a poor hunting season, there was no food for the family, and Rob's father was forced to slaughter Rob's pig. Though his heart is breaking, Rob helps his father kill and dress his pet. Late the following spring, Rob's father dies quietly in his sleep, and Rob automatically becomes the head of the household. He makes the funeral arrangements and digs his father's grave in the valley. Late that night, Rob returns alone to the valley to say his last farewell. Because Rob's father was the area's hog butcher, this is "a day no pigs would die."

Selected Challenges in the 1990s: In 1991, a parent in Harwinton, Connecticut, objected to *A Day No Pigs Would Die* and four other books, all in use in the local school. The parent said the books contained profanity and discussion of prejudice, rebellion, and death. The school system accepted the recommendation of a review committee that all of the books be retained.

A parent in Tilton, New Hampshire, objected to the use of *A Day No Pigs Would Die* in eighth-grade reading classes for describing the birth of a cow in an explicit manner. The teacher and principal decided to retain the book, but the objector's child was provided an alternative assignment.

A parent in Carbondale, Illinois, objected to *A Day No Pigs Would Die,* taught in a ninth-grade English class and available in the high school library, citing profanity. A review committee was convened, but when the objector failed to appear at the hearing, the complaint was dropped. The book remains in the library and curriculum.

In 1992, parents in Califon, New Jersey, objected to *A Day No Pigs Would Die,* used in a sixth-grade reading class, claiming the book contained violence to animals and a depiction of animals mating. The school board voted unanimously to uphold a review committee's recommendation to retain the book.

18. Heather Has Two Mommies, by Leslea Newman. In Other Words, 1989.

Synopsis and Background: Three-year-old Heather is the child of a lesbian couple. She thinks having two mommies is perfectly normal until she joins a play group and meets children who have a mommie and a daddy. The understanding adult who is in charge of the play group leads the children in a discussion of their different family structures, telling them that the most important thing about a family is that all the people in it love each other. The first part of the book deals with the events leading to Heather's conception and birth, while the latter half takes a positive approach to the issue of homosexual families. As more lesbian couples are choosing to have children through alternative insemination, *Heather Has Two Mommies* has become an important title in many libraries serving both conventional and alternative families.

Selected Challenges in the 1990s: In February 1992, members of the Bay Ridge School Board in Brooklyn, New York, voted to remove *Heather Has Two Mommies* and two other books from the district's curriculum. *Heather Has Two Mommies* had been on the optional reading list for the city's first-grade students. The board president said the board objected to words in the books that were age inappropriate.

In June 1992, *Heather Has Two Mommies* and *Daddy's Roommate* were donated to the public library in Springfield, Oregon, forcing the librarian to decide whether the books violated a recent city charter amendment prohibiting the city from "promoting, encouraging or facilitating" homosexuality. The charter amendment had been sponsored by the Oregon Citizens Alliance (OCA), whose communications director said, "If we find a book about homosexual lifestyle like *Heather Has Two Mommies* is in a library, we will do everything we can to get it out of there." Dave Fidanque, director of the local chapter of the ACLU, said they would monitor the librarian's book selection process, and if the books were rejected simply because of the charter amendment, they would file suit. Fidanque said, "Frankly, we expect the city to accept the books. If they don't we expect they will use some other reason not tied to the OCA measure." Indeed, the city librarian said she would use the same selection guidelines she uses for all other books.

In October 1992, a Right to Life group in Fayetteville, North Carolina, objected to the inclusion of *Heather Has Two Mommies* and *Daddy's Roommate* in the county library. After the library received six written complaints and a petition to ban the books, a heated public hearing was held at which protesters said the books promoted a dangerous and ungodly life-style from which children must be protected. One of the objectors admitted that she had never seen the books, but said "anything that promotes or teaches homosexuality is decaying the minds of children." The library's director said:

> The library thinks it is important for parents to exercise their legal and moral responsibilities to monitor what their children read, see, and do. We don't encourage and we don't force people to believe what they don't want to believe. We just provide information for people to make up their own minds on the issues of our times.

The library's board of trustees voted unanimously to keep the two books in the children's reading section of the library. Trustee Jim Scurry said banning the books would have "satisfied some small faction of the community, probably infuriated many and violated the rights of all." In response to the board's decision, the protesters organized a movement to defeat a bond issue to finance the library system, urging voters to reject "expansion of a library system that encourages young children to affirm and endorse conduct or a 'life style' that leads . . . to untimely death and serves no biological utility."[48] The bond issue passed by a narrow margin.

In November 1992, members of the Bladen Coalition of Christians in Elizabethtown, North Carolina, asked the County Commission to remove *Heather Has Two Mommies* and *Daddy's Roommate* from the Bladen County Library. The books had been recently purchased but not yet shelved in the library, and the librarian told the commissioners that she had not yet decided how to handle them. The objectors called the books wicked, seditious, and dangerous. In addition to the removal of the two books, they asked the commissioners to appoint a committee, including a representative from the Coalition of Christians, to prepare new guidelines for library book selection.

19. **Christine,** by Stephen King. Viking, 1983.

Synopsis and Background: In this comic and macabre tale of teenage love and tragedy, Stephen King invests the ordinary automobile with a diabolical power. A teenage misfit named Arnie Cunningham is devoted to his 1958 Plymouth Fury, considered a real wreck by Arnie's friend Dennis, who narrates the story. Arnie is a scrawny, pimply-faced kid who feels a kinship with his car, named Christine, because, like himself, it is ugly on the outside but has something special inside. Dennis is wary of the hateful old man LeBay, who sells the car to Arnie and then dies soon afterward, but the boys have no way of knowing the consequences of the purchase. Christine mysteriously takes on supernatural powers, going on homicidal rampages under a spell cast by LeBay from his grave. This breathtaking horror story leans heavily on King's knowledge of teenage culture, their music, their language, and their cars. It mixes terror with humor, producing realism out of the absurd.

Selected Challenges in the 1990s: In the fall of 1990, the librarian at the Livingston, Montana, middle school removed a number of books from the library's collections, including *Christine* and *The Shining* by Stephen King. The King books were removed because they were deemed unsuitable for the intended audience, owing to violence, explicit sex, and inappropriate language. In commenting on the removals, the school principal said the librarian was using "good judgment."

A grandparent in South Saline, Kansas, requested the removal of *Christine* from the school library, claiming the book was not appropriate for seventh-grade readers. The school board unanimously accepted the recommendation of a review committee that the book be retained without restriction in the library. A local newspaper editorial praised the decision, saying, "[E]ducation is not accomplished by hiding things from our children. It is accomplished by giving them the tools to read and hear and see any number of things and place them in proper perspective."[49]

In 1991, parents in Hazel Park, Michigan, objected to the use of *Christine* in a high school American novel class because of alleged profanity. In response to the verbal complaints, a school official removed the book from the curriculum.

In February 1992, a parent in Peru, Indiana, asked the school board to remove twelve Stephen King books from the high school library, saying they contained violence and obscenity. The board voted 5 to 1 to ban *Christine, Cujo,* and *The Dead Zone.* The sole dissenting member on the board said:

> If there are books in a library—public or school—that I do not approve of for literacy, style or content, then I have the choice not to read such a book. But if other individuals want to read it, they also have the choice to do so. As a parent, I monitor the choice of material the children read, whether it's age or content appropriate. Other parents also have this responsibility.[50]

20. **I Know Why the Caged Bird Sings,** by Maya Angelou. Random House, 1969.

Synopsis and Background: In this first of her four-volume autobiographical series, Maya Angelou, the famous black writer, dancer, singer, director, and civil rights activist, recounts her childhood and adolescence. The book describes the divorce of her parents and her subsequent difficulties as she moves about the country, living with various relatives and bearing an illegitimate son when she was just sixteen years of age. The censors have complained of sexually explicit scenes, foul language, and irreverent religious descriptions. Some have accused Angelou of blasphemy simply because she rejects the fatalism that religion brought to many southern blacks who gave all credit to God for whatever meager pleasures they enjoyed but did not blame God for their many misfortunes. *I Know Why the Caged Bird Sings* offers a message of survival and hope. The author is a real-life role model who overcame low self-esteem, economic deprivation, and societal barriers to reach artistic success. Reading of Angelou's troubled beginnings and knowing of her later triumphs instill confidence and motivation in adolescent students. Since Maya Angelou wrote and delivered the inaugural poem for President Bill Clinton, *I Know Why the Caged Bird Sings* has reached number eight on the Ingram's paperback bestseller list.

Selected Challenges in the 1990s: In 1990, a parent in Bremerton, Washington, objected to the "graphic" description of child molestation in *I Know Why the Caged Bird Sings* and requested that the book be removed from the required reading list for gifted ninth-graders. The parent also said that the book raised sexual issues without giving them moral resolution. Teacher Jan Chapuis said the passages about molestation were a small part of the book, and the main focus was the oppression that Maya Angelou struggled against to become a fulfilled woman. On a 4-to-1 vote, the school board chose to remove the book from the required reading list, with Board President Larry Littlefield explaining that his constituents expected him to uphold a level of moral standards that were not met by the book.

In 1991, *I Know Why the Caged Bird Sings* was removed from the Benning, California, eighth-grade curriculum after several parents complained about sexually explicit passages. The school superintendent said the book had been bought on the recommendation of a teachers' committee, which drew from a state list of recommended literature. The teacher and the junior high school principal agreed to stop using the book until the controversy was resolved. One parent said her thirteen-year-old son didn't want to go back to class because the book was "gross." She characterized the book as morally and religiously offensive smut.

A parent in Charles County, Maryland, complained about the use of *I Know Why the Caged Bird Sings* in a middle school honors English class, claiming that the book contained sexually explicit material. In response to the complaint, the student was given an alternative reading assignment, but the objector filled out another complaint, demanding that the book be removed from classroom and library use. A review committee rejected that demand, and the school board agreed that the book would be retained.

In April 1992, a parent in Pleasanton, California, asked that *I Know Why the Caged Bird Sings* be pulled from the high school's required reading list for sophomores. The parent, who complained of sexually explicit language, said, "I would like it out of the school system. I don't feel that it has any purpose. We don't want anybody to think we're on a witch hunt, but this is wrong." The high school English teacher responded, "I don't think we can hide negatives from the students.

They live those negatives every day. Reading any newspaper has a much more explicit language than what will be found in that novel."[51]

21. **Fallen Angels,** by Walter Myers. Scholastic, 1988.

Synopsis and Background: In one of the few teenage novels about the Vietnam War, Walter Myers tells the painful story of seventeen-year-old Richie Perry. Though the newspapers are filled with stories on the peace talks, Richie, like many others around him, decides to enlist in the army, not so much to defend his country as to escape the Harlem ghetto. He has no idea of what awaits him overseas, where the war will quickly dissolve his youth and test his sanity. Later he will write from Vietnam, "We're all dead over here. . . . We're all dead and just hoping we come back to life." The novel shows how the tension and tedium of war breed violence even among comrades, black against white, black against black, white against white. The eventual terror of battle reveals heroism and cowardice, causing young soldiers to question their ideals, their religious beliefs, and their morality. The descriptions of the action are shocking and explicit, and the language is realistic. The social issues of the day—antiwar sentiment, draft dodgers, drug abuse—are also woven into the plot.

Selected Challenges in the 1990s: In September 1990, four parents in Bluffton, Ohio, attended the monthly school board meeting to protest the use of *Fallen Angels* in a sophomore English class. The parents complained of profane language, pointing out that the book violated school rules prohibiting the use of obscene language by students. Although board member Phil Liginbuhl acknowledged that "a lot of students are used to that kind of language at their own home," he concluded, "I could see using this book in big cities, but not in Bluffton."[52] The parents were allowed to choose alternative books for their children, but they continued a letter-writing campaign to the board, protesting *Fallen Angels* and other books.

A parent in Cheshire County, New Hampshire, requested the removal of *Fallen Angels* from the middle school library because of alleged profanity. The objector refused to file a formal complaint because she didn't believe in the process, but she threatened to file a petition and cause controversy in the community. The school officials said they would consider her request only if she followed the existing complaint process. In the meantime, the book would remain in use.

In 1992, a parent in Waterloo, Iowa, objected to *Fallen Angels* and three other novels on the optional reading list for twelfth-grade advanced English classes. The objector had previously attempted to prevent the acquisition of these titles, and after their purchase, she filed formal complaints. She complained that *Fallen Angels* contained minority bashing and vulgar language and that the book might encourage children to use obscene language. She said she had heard that *Fallen Angels* was a good book that portrays Vietnam in a true light, but she said it was not for minors.

In May 1992, the parents of a high school student in Jefferson, Georgia, challenged *Fallen Angels* after their daughter Emily read the book in her English class. The parents asked the school board to withdraw the book from all use at the school, stating, "I think you can tell Emily how sorry you are that she was subjected to this for three weeks by voting unanimously to take this book out of the school system."[53] The school board voted unanimously to keep the book but restricted its use to supplemental classroom reading. The board also required that parents of students in classes where the book was made available be notified that it may contain sensitive material and undesirable language and that a list of alternative books was available.

22. **The New Teenage Body Book,** by Kathy McCoy and Charles Wibbelsman. HP Books, 1987.

Synopsis and Background: As in the original edition, *The New Teenage Body Book* uses personal questions to lead into informal but informative discussions and advice on topics of interest to young men and women. Much of the material in this new edition remains essentially the same as in the earlier volume, including sections on nutrition, pregnancy and parenthood, and physical and emotional development. All topics are treated sensitively, providing commonsense answers to questions. Among the vital additions to the book's coverage are discussions of acquired immunodeficiency syndrome (AIDS) and sexually transmitted diseases, a discussion of safe sex, and an evaluation of birth control methods. The authors take a cautionary view of the personal decision to have sex, and they take a strong stance against the use of alcohol, drugs, and tobacco.

Selected Challenges in the 1990s: In 1990, a group in the Silver Lake, Massachusetts, School District calling itself the Ninth Grade Parent Task Force objected to *The New Teenage Body Book* for its discussions of sex, homosexuality, and masturbation. The objectors described the book as a "how-to sex manual" that "gives them the green light." A passage stating that some people "will find that they always prefer their own sex and for them, this too is normal" drew the complaint: "It's not the norm and they're making these kids think it is."[54] When the school committee voted to retain the book, the objectors organized a boycott of the course using the book, but despite such efforts, only 6 of the 441 students involved requested waivers from the class. The assistant superintendent decided to allow the text to remain as a curricular and library resource but decreed that it could no longer be distributed to students or taken home by them.

In late 1990, a couple in Pembroke, Massachusetts, withdrew their fourteen-year-old daughter from her health class in order to prevent her from reading *The New Teenage Body Book*. Nearly a thousand parents signed a petition calling the textbook "a pompous, thinly disguised how-to manual masquerading as the final scientific word on adolescent sexual behavior." Reverend Donald Anderson, a member of the parent task force, said, "What we're talking about is postponing sexual activity until adulthood." [55]

In January 1991, a group of ten parents in nearby Kingston, Massachusetts formed a parent task force objecting to the use of *The New Teenage Body Book* in the high school's health curriculum. They asked a regional school committee to substitute a text that teaches sexual abstinence until marriage and offers the possibility for "secondary virginity" for teenagers who tried sex but didn't like it.

Robert Hayes, leader of the Pembroke, Massachusetts, John Birch Society, charged that the use of *The New Teenage Body Book* in the local school system violated the law. The text, which was used as a supplemental guide in the ninth-grade health curriculum, aroused protests over its descriptions of various sexual practices. Hayes, who had earlier withdrawn his daughter from the high school health class to protest the book, said the book was obscene, and he demanded its removal from the curriculum. School officials assured parents that if they chose to remove their children from the offending class, it would not prevent their graduation. A school committee then reviewed the book and decided to retain it. But in September 1991, school administrators decided not to distribute the text to students, limiting it to use as a classroom resource while retaining it in the school library. Mr. Hayes was still not satisfied. He demanded that school officials be indicted for distributing obscene materials to minors, corrupting the morals of minors, and violating a statute calling for teachers to instruct students in sexual abstinence. He asked to go before the grand jury with evidence of a school conspiracy to violate the laws.

23. **Little Red Riding Hood,** by Jacob and Wilhelm Grimm. German edition, 1812. A recent translation is included in *The Complete Fairy Tales of the Brothers Grimm,* Bantam Books, 1987.

Synopsis and Background: What can one say about *Little Red Riding Hood?* The earliest recorded European version of this beloved fairytale was the stylized literary retelling by Charles Perrault in 1697. But its best-known version came from the Brothers Grimm in their 1812 volume of folktales and legends. The familiar tale involves a sweet little maiden who goes to visit her loving grandmother, carrying with her a basket of food and wine. As Little Red Riding Hood is on her way through the woods to her grandmother's house, she meets the wolf, who asks her where she is going. When she tells him, the wolf runs off to grandmother's house, where he eats up the grandmother, dresses up in her clothing, and awaits Little Red Riding Hood. When the young girl sees the wolf in her grandmother's clothing, she questions the grandmother's odd appearance, concluding with: "Oh, Grandmother, what a terribly big mouth you have." The wolf then shouts, "The better to eat you with," and gobbles up the young girl. After the wolf falls asleep, a hunter finds him and cuts open the sleeping wolf's belly, from which Little Red Riding Hood and her grandmother emerge, alive and well. Little Red Riding Hood then fetches some stones to put in the wolf's belly, causing him later to die.

Selected Challenges in the 1990s: In 1990, two California school districts banned the 1989 version of the Grimm Brothers' *Little Red Riding Hood,* saying the presence of a bottle of wine in the young girl's basket condoned the use of alcohol. The banned edition, published by Houghton Mifflin, had won a Caldecott Honor Book Award. The curriculum director in Empire, California, expressed additional concern about the end of the tale, where the huntsman cuts the wolf open and Little Red Riding Hood jumps out. The Empire school district decided that such descriptions were inappropriate for first-graders.

A similar ban was imposed on the book in Culver City, California, where Assistant Superintendent Vera Jashni said the story gives children the wrong impression about alcohol. Jashni said the final paragraph of the story really convinced her to ban the book. It tells how after the huntsman killed the wolf, the grandmother drank some of the wine, and after a while, she felt quite strong and healthy and began to clean up the mess that the wolf had left in the cottage.

Parents in Clay County, Florida, challenged *Little Red Riding Hood* because the title character brings wine to her grandmother. The objector requested that *Little Red Riding Hood* and two other children's books be removed from use in the fifth and sixth grades. As a result of the complaint, the books were removed from use for three weeks while a review committee deliberated. The school board subsequently accepted the committee's recommendation that the books be retained.

In 1991, *Little Red Riding Hood* was pulled from a school in Bradford County, Florida, after teachers questioned passages where the young girl brings wine to her grandmother. The school district chose to switch to a "nonalcoholic" version of the tale. During the same year, another challenge to the tale was placed by teachers in Florida's Levy County, but the storybook was retained in the schools after a review by a committee of educators and parents.

24. **The Headless Cupid,** by Zilpha Snyder. Atheneum, 1971.

Synopsis and Background: Eleven-year-old David Stanley is the oldest of four children, and he has been looking after his younger brother and sisters since his mother's death. When his father remarries, David is happy to pass these responsibilities to his new stepmother, but he is unprepared for his twelve-year-old stepsister, Amanda, a student of witchcraft who dresses in weird ceremonial costume. Amanda, who carries with her a snake, a horny toad, and a crow, is haughty and patronizing with David and the other children, but when she offers to make them neophytes in the occult, they are too fascinated to refuse. She subjects the children to a series of initiation rites, and David begins to suspect that Amanda is less a witch than a spoiled troublemaker. But when the house is invaded by a poltergeist, even Amanda loses her cool, and soon the whole family is terrorized by a series of mysterious disturbances. The tale is concluded with just enough left unexplained to maintain the sense of mystery.

Selected Challenges in the 1990s: In 1990, a parent in Grand Haven, Michigan, asked that *The Headless Cupid* and another book be removed from local school libraries, claiming that the books would introduce children to the occult and immoral fantasy. School officials denied the request, affirming the obligation of a public school library to be open to a wide variety of ideas.

In July 1991, a parent in Waldorf, Maryland, asked that *The Headless Cupid* be removed from the approved reading list at the local middle school because of its references to witchcraft. "I believe the book gives them an introduction to the world of the occult because of the terms they use," said the parent who filed a petition against the book with the school board. "We had an incident in Charles County of cemetery desecration which was cult-related. . . . I would hate to think that some sixth-grade teacher was the one to get one of those children involved with the occult from offering a book about it in reading class." The book had been previously challenged by another parent in the school district who wrote: "This book can easily stir up a child's curiosity to experiment in witchcraft." A school committee reviewed the complaint and recommended that the book be retained on the reading list, and the school board upheld the committee's decision.[56]

In January 1992, a couple in Escondido, California, submitted a complaint about the inclusion of *The Headless Cupid* in the elementary school libraries. They charged that children who read the book may develop an unhealthy interest in the occult, thinking its practices are acceptable behavior. The complaint listed thirty objectionable references in the book, including a sentence referring to a trance. The school superintendent attempted to unilaterally restrict access to *The Headless Cupid* and another book, but the board decided that only they had the authority to make such a decision. On April 30, the board voted 5 to 0 to keep *The Headless Cupid* in the school libraries.

25. **Night Chills,** by Dean Koontz. Atheneum, 1976.

Synopsis and Background: In this horror tale, a sadistic scientist, an evil tycoon, and a wicked general conspire to control the world through the use of drugs and hypnotic suggestion conveyed on the television screen. The evil experiments are begun in a small company town in Maine, where they infect virtually the entire population. A veterinarian and his family turn out to be the "good guys" who save the town, and thus the world, from the horrible conspiracy. In the process, the reader follows the adventures and romance of our heroes.

Selected Challenges in the 1990s: In 1990, a parent in Somerset, Kentucky, objected to the inclusion of *Night Chills* in the high school library, alleging pornographic language and content. In addition to the removal of *Night Chills,* the objector demanded a review of all other library books that might be "pornographic." *Night Chills* disappeared from the library shelves, and a school official claimed that the complaining parent simply checked the book out and never returned it. Others involved have disputed this explanation, saying that a review committee had judged the book to be objectionable and removed it from the shelf.

In 1991, a parent in Fort Kent, Maine, requested that *Night Chills* be removed from a high school library, alleging "sexual imagery." A review committee voted 6 to 2 to remove the book, claiming that the selection policy had not been followed when choosing the book.

In October 1992, a parent in Bend, Oregon, asked that *Night Chills* be removed from the high school library, alleging that it contained explicit sexual references. The parent, who saw the book when her son brought it home for a book report, said she did not belong to any organization that bans books but simply felt that *Night Chills* was inappropriate for the high school library. A school review committee recommended that the book be removed from the high school and given to the county library, but the school board was unable to reach agreement on final action. One board member proposed that the book be retained in the school, where students could read it under supervision. Another board member proposed that the book be removed. Another board member proposed that the book be restricted to juniors or seniors or to those obtaining parental permission.

26. **Lord of the Flies,** by William Golding. Faber & Faber, 1954.

Synopsis and Background: Lord of the Flies has been interpreted as a parable of life in the second half of the twentieth century, the nuclear age, where technology has overwhelmed morality. The setting for this tale is in the tradition of *Robinson Crusoe* or *The Swiss Family Robinson,* as a group of boys is stranded on a tropical island. In this dark tale of the future, a plane fleeing Australia, with whom England is engaged in a nuclear war, crashes, and all are lost except a group of English schoolboys. Left to fend for themselves in a tropical paradise, these proper young men begin a slow retreat from civilized behavior. Eventually, the boys descend into savagery, indulging in ritual killing within their own group, including a manhunt to kill their original leader, Ralph, who had tried to convince them of the need for restraint. Quite by coincidence, a British man-of-war discovers the boys on the island, and a naval officer interrupts the boys' manhunt, not realizing that he has prevented premeditated murder. Golding suggests the further irony that the naval officer will soon resume his own deadly manhunt in the adult game of war. Golding's pessimistic view of "human nature" and human society has caused some to regard *Lord of the Flies* as inappropriate reading for young students, but the book remains a popular choice in schools and libraries because its parable encourages the reader to confront the major question haunting the world today: How can civilized society elude the barbarism that pursues it?

Selected Challenges in the 1990s: In 1990, a parent in Rocklin, California, initiated a complaint against a number of books on the junior high reading list, including *Lord of the Flies.* The complaining parent said the books did not reflect the social standards and good citizenship that are expected from students on campus. As the result of the complaint, the school board removed one book and a short story from the suggested reading list, but *Lord of the Flies* was retained.

A parent in Gloucester County, New Jersey, objected to *Lord of the Flies* because of the author's notes included with the novel. The parent requested the removal of the book from use in eighth-grade honors English. Though no formal complaint was ever filed and the school followed no formal process, the book was removed from use during the 1990 school year, pending receipt of copies of the novel without the author's notes.

In April 1992, the Waterloo, Iowa, Board of Education voted 6 to 1 to purchase textbooks, including *Lord of the Flies* and three other novels that some protesters had called indecent. The one board member who voted against the purchase claimed that the books contained profanity; lurid sexual passages; and statements defaming minorities, God, women, and the disabled.

27. **A Separate Peace,** by John Knowles. Dell Publishing Co., 1959.

Synopsis and Background: A Separate Peace is a novel of maturation in the tradition of *Huckleberry Finn* and *The Catcher in the Rye.* Set in a small New England prep school during World War II, the novel reveals the pressures exerted by the impending war on young students. Knowles examines the war within the human breast and how it divides even the best of friends. The book's universal message is that while war may take on form in France or Germany or Vietnam, we must find its causes within ourselves. *A Separate Peace* encourages the reader to pass through the sufferings of war to achieve a peace based on understanding. At the end of the novel, its narrator, Gene, concludes: "I never killed anybody and I never developed an intense level of hatred for the enemy. Because my war ended before I ever put on a uniform; I was on active duty all my time at school; I killed my enemy there."[57] Some critics believe *A Separate Peace* embodies the same philosophy as *Lord of the Flies,* depicting human nature as depraved without the restraints imposed by social institutions. But Gene's discovery of a "separate peace" through personal growth provides an optimistic ending quite different from the cynicism of *Lord of the Flies.* Knowles ascribes the war within to ignorance, not evil. David G. Holborn of the University of Wisconsin says:

> *A Separate Peace* is a novel that should be read by adolescents and adults alike, and it should be discussed openly. Jealousy, misunderstanding, and fear do indeed breed violence when they are kept within. Or they can be liberated, not once and for all perhaps, but over and over again if they are seen for what they are in the light of day. This is all we know of peace in this world.[58]

Selected Challenges in the 1990s: In May 1990, three parents in Champaign, Illinois, challenged the use of *A Separate Peace* in high school English classes, claiming that the book contained unsuitable language. The parents objected specifically to the use of *damn* and *goddamn.* The book had been used in the local schools for more than twenty-two years and had never been challenged before. A curriculum review committee recommended that the book be retained and asked the school board to reaffirm its use.

In February 1991, a parent in Troy, Illinois, objected to profanity and negative attitudes in *A Separate Peace,* used in the local high school. Appearing before the school board, the objector claimed to have counted forty-five profane references in the book, including *God damn it, Shut up,* and *I swear to God.* Superintendent William Hyten said the board would take the complaint under advisement.

A parent in Jacksonville, Florida, objected to *A Separate Peace* in the high school library, alleging that it contained material unsuitable for youth, including vulgar language; controversial religious dialogue; and depictions of students skipping class, breaking school rules, and trespassing on school property. Among the objectionable language was *for God's sake, Oh God, Christ, damn,* and *hell.* A district review committee decided to retain the book, calling it "truly a well-written piece of art." One committee member said, "To ban or restrict this book reflects the paranoia existing in today's society. Reasons conjured for the banning of the book are unjustifiable."[59]

28. **Slaughterhouse-Five,** by Kurt Vonnegut. Dell, 1969.

Synopsis and Background: Kurt Vonnegut served with the U.S. infantry in World War II, and after being captured by the Germans in the Battle of the Bulge, he was held as a prisoner of war in Dresden while the city war firebombed by Allied aircraft. After the war, he felt compelled to write about his traumatic experience. *Slaughterhouse-Five* therefore has a foundation in history and fact, but it is not a typical "realistic" novel. It mixes reality and science fiction, tragedy and slapstick, in describing the adventures of Billy Pilgrim, an American soldier lost behind enemy lines in 1944. Pilgrim is taken prisoner, and during the subsequent shock and privation, his mind wanders, "unstuck in time," revealing his postwar life, fantastic space travels, even his death, before we are transported back to the Dresden firebombing. Vonnegut describes the horror of the fire storm, connecting it with historical or mythical events like the destruction of Sodom and Hiroshima. *Slaughterhouse-Five* is a provocative war novel that cuts through nationalistic and jingoistic stereotypes to emphasize the common bonds of humanity. Vonnegut focuses on the helpless victims of modern aerial warfare, which has shifted the battlefield to civilian cities. Peter J. Reed of the University of Minnesota says:

[T]his novel seems important not just in its ideas, or in its morality, or as an example of modern fiction, or for what it might teach about how to write, but for its lesson in thinking. It is provocative, even maddening to some, because of its irreverence. It challenges sacred cows, set ideas, merely traditional ways of thinking. And it does not do so irresponsibly, but from the foundation of a moral human decency. This kind of invitation to openness is surely the essence of education.[60]

Selected Challenges in the 1990s: In 1990, the parent of a high school student in Jackson Township, Ohio, called the school principal, Tom Chain, to complain about *Slaughterhouse-Five* and several other books used in the college-level English class. Principal Chain formed a review committee and stated, "At this point there has been a lot of discussion. I wouldn't say any [books] have been actually banned. I would say we've put at least one on hold at this point." That one book was *Slaughterhouse-Five*. Chain said all the books were being examined for "profanity, sexual content and innuendos." When a high school senior discovered what was being done, he distributed a leaflet charging that the committee was secretly meeting to decide which books to ban. He was suspended for one day for distributing unauthorized printed material.[61]

In 1991, parents in Plummer, Idaho, objected to the use of *Slaughterhouse-Five* in an eleventh-grade English class. Citing the use of profanity, the parent said it was wrong for the public schools to have the book. Because the school district had no formal policy for dealing with challenges, a school official was able to unilaterally order that the book be removed. The teacher of the class using *Slaughterhouse-Five* said she was now obliged to throw the books away and not to use them again.

A parent in Waterloo, Iowa, objected to *Slaughterhouse-Five* and three other books selected as optional reading in twelfth-grade advanced English classes. The objector admitted that she had read only portions of *Slaughterhouse-Five* but claimed that certain passages might cause students to be embarrassed or insulted.

29. **The Color Purple,** by Alice Walker. Harcourt Brace Jovanovich, 1982.

Synopsis and Background: In a story told almost exclusively through the letters of the main character, Celie, and her sister Nettie, *The Color Purple* documents the agonizing struggle and triumph of a black woman over sexist abuse and racist oppression in the Deep South of the 1930s. Fourteen-year-old Celie is raped and twice made pregnant by her stepfather, who warns her to tell no one except God. This begins a series of letters from Celie to God, documenting her pain and struggle. The two sisters, Celie and Nettie, are separated when Nettie is taken from their small southern town to serve as a missionary in Africa. Celie then becomes the child bride of a local widower, beginning a harsh and poverty-stricken marriage. She is sustained only by her continuing letters to God and to her sister Nettie. Nettie, in turn, writes back of the brutal colonialism she finds in Africa, providing the reader with another perspective on the racism and violence Celie endures in the American South. Despite the dreadful circumstances of their youth, Celie and Nettie find joy and beauty that sustain them until their emotional reunion.

Selected Challenges in the 1990s: In February 1990, a parent in Ten Sleep, Wyoming, complained about the inclusion of *The Color Purple* on a high school reading list for sophomore English. Superintendent Les Stencel reminded the objector that the book was not required reading, and students had the option of reading another book if their parents objected to it.

Also in 1990, parents in Tyrone, Pennsylvania, objected to several books on the high school's supplementary reading lists, including *The Color Purple*. A local minister commented, "I know people are going to look at us like a bunch of fanatics, but I blush to read this out loud." The school board agreed to form a committee to review guidelines for reading lists and material not on approved curriculum lists.[62]

In May 1992, a mother and father in New Bern, North Carolina, leafed through their son Kenny's tenth-grade reading assignment, *The Color Purple*, and noticed the passage where Celie tells God that she was raped by her stepfather. The complaining father insisted that the book be removed from the school, stating, "I plan on pushing it until it's out of our system. What it says is what they [children] see. They aren't able to interpret what they read."[63] The high school principal appointed a review committee and allowed the complaining parents to select a different book for their child. In addition, there were restrictions placed on how *The Color Purple* could be taught to other students, but the parents were unsatisfied and vowed to continue efforts to ban the book.

30. James and the Giant Peach, by Roald Dahl. Knopf, 1961.

Synopsis and Background: This classic child's tale concerns a boy's adventures after he spills magic crystals onto a peach tree, causing it to produce a peach of gigantic proportions. James goes through a variety of adventures with the giant peach. After it has fallen in the water, where it is attacked by sharks, James has the Silkworm and the Spider spin thread, which 502 seagulls use to lift the peach out of the water. As the gulls are carrying the peach through the air over New York City, an airplane accidently cuts the threads supporting the peach, sending it plummeting toward the city. Dahl's imaginative style almost makes the absurd event seem real:

[P]eople who had not yet reached the underground shelters looked up and saw it coming, and they stopped running and stood there staring in a sort of stupor at what they thought was the biggest bomb in all the world falling out of the sky and onto their heads. A few women screamed. Others knelt down on the sidewalks and began praying aloud. Strong men turned to one another and said things like, "I guess this is it, Joe."[64]

The bizarre conclusion will delight young readers.

Selected Challenges in the 1990s: In April 1991, the mother of a fourth-grade student in Charlotte Harbor, Florida, complained that *James and the Giant Peach,* being read in class at the elementary school, was not appropriate material for young children. The mother, who leafed through the book when her daughter brought it home, complained about references to witchcraft, saying, "The whole book is strange if you ask me." She then wrote a letter to the local newspaper, encouraging parents to complain to the school. However, no formal complaint was ever made to the school, other than a letter from the child to the teacher, saying she was not allowed to read the book. The child was given an alternative assignment. The school's principal said the book was a classic, and the director of special projects said, "Literature exposes students to a variety of ideas. The purpose of education is not only to communicate factual information, but to develop in the young the ability to discriminate and choose."[65]

In November 1991, a parent in Altoona, Wisconsin, asked that *James and the Giant Peach* be removed from an elementary school reading list after her nine-year-old son brought the book home. The parent objected to the use of the word *ass* and to other words, as well as parts of the book that dealt with wine, tobacco, and snuff. "I couldn't believe my son was reading this to me," said the parent. "He looked at me and told me that if he used words like this around the house, I'd send him to his room." The parent's request was reviewed by the district's reconsideration committee, which voted unanimously to retain the book. The school board then unanimously upheld the committee's recommendation. School Superintendent Jon Lamberson said, "According to board policy no parent has the right to exclude material from other students in the district and I think that's a very fair standard."[66]

In November 1992, a parent in Brooksville, Florida, protested the inclusion of *James and the Giant Peach* in a local elementary school library, complaining that the book contained a foul word and promoted drugs and whiskey. The county school board voted unanimously to retain the book, concurring with the recommendations of two review committees and Superintendent Dan McIntyre, who said the book was merely a fantasy about good triumphing over evil.

31. **The Learning Tree,** by Gordon Parks. Harper & Row, 1963.

Synopsis and Background: The Learning Tree is a novel based on the author's youth, recounting his education and the formation of his character from his childhood to his premature independence upon the death of his mother. Through his alter ego, Newt Winger, Gordon Parks tells us of his confrontation with love, death, sex, race, hatred, religion, law, friendship, loneliness, and unhappiness. Twelve-year-old Newt is a black child in Cherokee Flats, Kansas, in the 1920s. The reader comes to understand Newt's special feeling of responsibility for his behavior in a community where one individual may be regarded as representing an entire group. *The Learning Tree* has been frequently challenged and banned since its publication in 1963, with censors complaining of vulgar language, racial epithets, and sexually explicit passages. The comic characterization of Pastor Broadnap and Newt's skepticism about religion may offend religious fundamentalists, and the images of a hypocritical school board and foolish teachers may disturb those who revere authority figures.

Selected Challenges in the 1990s: In 1990, Kansas City, Missouri, parents objected to the inclusion of *The Learning Tree* on the recommended reading list of an eighth-grade English class. The complaint cited profanity and a sex scene and requested removal of the book. Though no written complaint was filed, the area superintendent removed the book from the reading list and from the class. A review committee later recommended that the book be retained but that students be allowed to opt out of using it and that objectionable parts not be read aloud in class.

In August 1991, *The Learning Tree* and another book were removed from a suggested reading list at a Florida high school after a local resident complained that the books were indecent. After a two-month review procedure, the books were reinstated to the reading list.

In Tallahassee, Florida, a parent objected to *The Learning Tree* and another book used in a tenth-grade English class, alleging profanity and sexual references. The objector requested removal of the books, but the principal accepted the recommendation of a review committee that the books be retained. Upon appeal, the school board also voted to retain the books.

32. **The Witches of Worm,** by Zilpha Snyder. Atheneum, 1972.

Synopsis and Background: Jessica Porter, a twelve-year-old fatherless child, is frequently left alone at home to take care of herself. She is a voracious reader, currently reading *The Witches of Salem Town*. She finds a blind, newborn kitten and names it Worm. As Jessica learns to care for the kitten, she comes to believe that it has the power to suggest frightening ideas to her. Influenced by these imagined suggestions from Worm, she causes trouble between her friend Diane and the girl's mother, ruins her own mother's expensive dress, and throws her friend Brandon's trumpet out of the window. Jessica is horrified at her misdeeds and convinced that she is possessed. She overcomes her delusions with the help of an old lady who lives in her building. The lady advises Jessica, "We all invite our own devils, and we must exorcise our own." The book's conclusion leaves the reader guessing whether witchcraft or imagination has been at play.

Selected Challenges in the 1990s: In February 1990, a parent in Grand Haven, Michigan, requested that *The Witches of Worm* and another book be removed from the local school libraries. The parent claimed that the books introduce children to the occult. Assistant Superintendent for Instruction Rich Kent denied the request, citing the *Pico* Supreme Court decision and "our obligation to be, as a public school system, open to a whole range of ideas. We had to take a stand."[67]

In 1991, a teacher in Jacksonville, Florida, objected to the inclusion of *The Witches of Worm* in elementary and middle school libraries, alleging "occult" content. In a page-by-page analysis of the book, the objector cited such things as a magical cat controlling a girl. A review committee voted to retain the book at the middle school level but to remove it from the elementary schools.

In 1992, a parent in Clute, Texas, requested the removal of *The Witches of Worm* from a middle school library on the grounds that it promotes witchcraft and satanism. The objector complained informally to the school principal, who, in apparent violation of the district's reconsideration policy, unilaterally removed the book from the library. Indeed, the book will remain banned from the middle school library until the objector's child graduates.

33. **My Brother Sam Is Dead,** by James Lincoln Collier and Christopher Collier. Scholastic, 1974.

Synopsis and Background: James Collier is a professional writer with many juvenile titles to his credit, while his brother Christopher is a professor of history specializing in the American Revolution. The authors state that the Meeker family depicted in the book is fictitious, but most of the other events and characters are real. The setting for this Newbery Honor Award–winning novel is Redding, Pennsylvania, during the tense period preceding the bloody American Revolution. Eleven-year-old Tim Meeker has confused loyalties. Although his parents feel no strong loyalty to England's King George III, they are strongly opposed to revolutionary violence. On the other hand, Tim's sixteen-year-old brother Sam is caught up in the clamor for liberation and independence, and he joins the rebel army to serve under Captain Benedict Arnold. Sam later returns to the Meeker home to steal his father's musket, and Tim tries unsuccessfully to talk him out of it. As the violence of the war grows, Tim's father is taken prisoner, and he subsequently dies on a prison ship. Tim becomes sickened by the wanton destruction and death of war. In late 1778, Sam's regiment encamps near Redding, and he steals away from his post to visit his family. Sam is subsequently court-martialed and sentenced to death, and despite pleas for leniency from Tim and his mother, Sam is executed by firing squad. Years later, Tim looks back on the revolution and the way it destroyed his family. We share his doubts about whether the same ends could have been achieved without war.

Selected Challenges in the 1990s: In 1990, the Richmond, Ohio, Board of Education removed *My Brother Sam Is Dead* from the curriculum of fifth-grade classes after a parent complained that the book contained words such as *bastard, goddamn,* and *hell.* The school board president said the books were removed from the curriculum because the board heard from no supporters of the book, but a fifth-grade teacher said she had been advised to express her support through the school principal. The elementary school librarian who had recommended the book to teachers asked, "Is the next step going to be that they want me to take the book from the library? That frightens me."[68]

In 1991, a parent in Greenville, South Carolina, objected to *My Brother Sam Is Dead* and four other books being taught in the district schools. In January 1991, a petition signed by 864 people asked the school board to take the five books off the district's approved reading list. However, a materials review committee recommended that the books be maintained on the list, and the board accepted that recommendation, stating that approving or disapproving of individual books was not the board's function. The policy upheld by the board allowed parents to request that alternative books be assigned to their children.

In 1992, parents in Cheshire, Connecticut, objected to *My Brother Sam Is Dead,* used in fifth- and sixth-grade classrooms and available in the school library, alleging that the book contained graphic violence and an inaccurate depiction of the Revolutionary War—this despite the fact that the author is Connecticut's state historian and an authority on the Revolutionary War. Objectors claimed that the book's violent passages were inappropriate for elementary school students and described the book as inflammatory propaganda. The objectors complained about the book at several school board meetings and circulated a petition against it at a local church. However, they failed to follow the district's reconsideration procedure and never filed a formal complaint. The book therefore remained on the library shelf and in use in the classroom.

34. **The Grapes of Wrath,** by John Steinbeck. Viking, 1939.

Synopsis and Background: The Grapes of Wrath, published in 1939, won a Pulitzer Prize in 1940, and its author won the Nobel Prize in 1962. Yet from the moment of its publication, the book was attacked and banned in schools and libraries across the country. Copies of the book were actually burned in St. Louis. The censorship of *The Grapes of Wrath* has continued to this day, but its appeal has persisted through the decades. Its power derives in part from its stirring depiction of a major period of American history, the depression and drought years of the 1930s. Steinbeck depicts the personal tragedies of this period in the struggles of the Joad family to survive together and farm the land. Throughout their tribulations, the Joads display traditional American values and Christian virtues, and many critics have described characters like Tom Joad or Jim Casey as Christ figures, illustrative of Christ's life of self-sacrifice. Even the structure of *The Grapes of Wrath* is tied to the Bible, with the Joad's journey westward compared with the biblical exodus. Interspersed with the narrative are interludes describing the broader social and political context in which the Joad family finds itself. These interludes draw on Steinbeck's general views on the depression and his observations during visits to migrant worker camps. Such images, along with Steinbeck's clear sympathy for the family farmer in his struggle with depersonalized institutions, have led some censors to call the book "collectivist" communist propaganda.

Selected Challenges in the 1990s: In the spring of 1990, elementary school officials in San Diego, California, ordered a children's mural to be painted over because it showed banned books, including *The Grapes of Wrath,* used as a stairway to the wonders of the universe. A few teachers and parents claimed that such books were not appropriate for elementary school students to see. The artist who had supervised the children who painted the mural said:

> I knew the vice principal was upset because she called me to tell me that the book titles were not appropriate, but I never knew they had painted them over because I never gave them permission to do that. My feeling was that, if the kids can read that well, they ought to be able to read the books if they want.[69]

In 1991, a parent in the Greenville County, South Carolina, School District objected to *The Grapes of Wrath* and two other books on the high school reading lists. The complaint said the books contained profanity and sexual innuendo and used God's name in vain. Despite the long-standing policy of offering alternative reading to objectors, the removal of the books was demanded. The school board of trustees accepted a review committee's decision to retain the three novels. One of the school trustees who had voted to remove the books explained, "I know you all are looking at this from an educational viewpoint but I have to look at it from whether it's right or wrong." A county legislator called another trustee and threatened to oppose tax revenues for the school district if she did not vote to remove the books. The controversy spread when the objector circulated lists of other allegedly profane books in the community and succeeded in getting over 2,000 signatures on a petition to ban the books. Nonetheless, the majority of parents, students, and teachers supported the continued use of the books.[70]

In 1992, a parent in Midland, Michigan, objected to the use of *The Grapes of Wrath* in an eleventh-grade English class because of "references to sexual adventures," "581 curse words," and "283 cases of taking the Lord's name in vain." The school provided an alternative reading assignment to the student, but the parent said no student should be allowed to read it. Because the objector declined to file a formal written complaint, the school board did not act on her request to ban the book.

35. **Cujo,** by Stephen King. Viking, 1981.

Synopsis and Background: Once more, Stephen King brings credibility to outrageous characters and events by setting them in Middle America. This bizarre embodiment of horror is Cujo, a placid, 200-pound Saint Bernard pet, a typical "good dog." After Cujo is bitten by a rabid bat one summer night in Castle Rock, Maine, the dog goes berserk, attacking his owner, auto mechanic Joe Cambers, and an advertising man, Vic Trenton. As if that's not bad enough, we are led to believe that Cujo is possessed by the ghost of local mass murderer Frank Dodd. There are terrifying scenes, such as when people are caught in stalled automobiles, awaiting deadly assault by Cujo. The many acts of terror are woven effortlessly into the everyday life of a small town, revealing the potential for savagery in the ordinary world around us.

Selected Challenges in the 1990s: In 1991, the school superintendent in Peru, Indiana, recommended to the school board that three Stephen King novels, *Cujo, The Dead Zone,* and *Christine,* be available only to students who get parental permission, but the motion died for lack of a second. The school board then voted 5 to 1 to ban the books entirely from the high school library.

In 1992, a middle school library in South Portland, Maine, received complaints from parents about Stephen King's *Cujo*. Removal of the book from the library was requested because of its alleged profanity and sexual content, including references to adultery and rape. A review committee subsequently recommended that the book be retained in the library's collections, and that recommendation was approved by the superintendent of schools.

In April 1992, the board of education in Sparta, Illinois, heard a request to remove *all* books by Stephen King from the school libraries. The complaining parent said she prohibited her son from reading the King books after reading portions of *Cujo*. The parent objected to the violence, sex, and explicit language in the books. The board did not take immediate action on the request to ban the books, but it did honor the parent's request that her own children be barred from using them. The parent vowed to continue challenging the board on this matter.

36. **The Great Gilly Hopkins,** by Katherine Paterson. Crowell, 1978.

Synopsis and Background: Gilly, the central character in *The Great Gilly Hopkins,* is an eleven-year-old foster child who has difficulty adjusting to an endless succession of foster homes, three in the last three years. Gilly, whose real name is Galadriel, does her best to assert her identity and dignity, sometimes abrasively. Her longings and fears lead her to distrust anyone who is friendly toward her. Gilly cannot remember her real mother, but she retains a photograph of her and a letter, all that was left with her when she was placed in a foster home as a very young child. Gilly has constructed a fantasy image of her mother, the beautiful, wealthy Courtney Rutherford Hopkins, who will someday rescue her from the "undesirable" foster homes. Gilly pictures her mother living in splendor in the enchanting land of California, where Gilly claims the sun always shines. When Gilly tries to run away to California, using stolen money to buy a bus ticket, she is turned away by the ticket clerk. In the emotional conclusion, Gilly finds an adult she can love.

Selected Challenges in the 1990s: In 1991, complaints were lodged in Maiden, North Carolina, against the use of *The Great Gilly Hopkins* in the elementary school curriculum and in the school library. The complaints alleged that the book contained fifty profane words, and its removal was requested on the grounds that it was derogatory to the Christian faith. A review committee recommended that the book be retained but that parental permission be required before student use.

In 1992, *The Great Gilly Hopkins* and another book were challenged in Cheshire, Connecticut (see Chapter 1) for profanity, blasphemy, obscenities, and derogatory remarks toward God. One objector alleged that the book referred to *Bible* readers as religious fanatics. Fifth-graders who had read *The Great Gilly Hopkins* sent a letter to Cheshire officials, stating: "We are critical readers who know the difference between a character's language and our own. We would understand your banning the books for lower grades, but we feel that fifth graders . . . are mature enough to read these books."[71] After a three-month controversy during which objectors collected 1,000 signatures on a petition to ban the book, the school board upheld a review committee's decision to retain the book for the fifth grade. The school district allows alternative assignments for children whose parents object to the book.

In October 1992, a petition was circulated by a group of parents in Alamo Heights, Texas, requesting the removal of any books in the elementary schools that contain vulgar or profane words. In particular, the parents objected to the words *hell, damn,* and *frigging* in *The Great Gilly Hopkins* and *On My Honor.*

37. **The Figure in the Shadows,** by John Bellairs. Dial, 1975.

Synopsis and Background: In this suspenseful occult novel, the orphaned Lewis Barnavelt struggles with the mysterious powers emanating from an amulet that once belonged to his grandfather. Lewis is fat and timid, but he believes that the power of the amulet will allow him to stand up to a sixth-grade bully who taunts him. Indeed, wearing the amulet around his neck, Lewis beats him in a fight. But when the ghost of the amulet's original owner returns to retrieve it, Lewis becomes increasingly frightened as the word *venio*—meaning "I come"—turns up in unexpected places. The phantom figure seems to stalk him in the shadows. His friend Rose Rita tries to help him by locking the amulet away, but Lewis feels compelled to recover it. Eventually, Lewis finds himself captive to the phantom's growing power, until his Uncle Jonathan, a wizard, and Mrs. Zimmerman, his witch friend, decipher the mysterious forces and rescue Lewis.

Selected Challenges in the 1990s: In the spring of 1990, a parent in El Mirage, Arizona, complained about two occurrences of profanity in *The Figure in the Shadows.* In one case, a boy says "Goddamn" when he is unable to defend a friend against a bully. In another passage, a man who rescues a boy from a storm says "hell." The complaining parent also expressed concern that there was a friendly witch and wizard in the book. A review committee recommended that the book be retained, but the school board voted to restrict the circulation of the book to those children who have parental permission. The elementary school librarian said the book was the first to be placed on such a restricted status.

In 1991, parents in Nashua, New Hampshire, objected to *The Figure in the Shadows,* available in the elementary school library and used in fourth-grade class, because of the book's references to witchcraft. A school review committee decided that the book would be retained.

In Joliet, Illinois, a parent objected to the use of *The Figure in the Shadows* in a sixth-grade advanced reading class, alleging that the book endorsed witchcraft. A review committee voted to retain the book, but the objector's child was given an alternative assignment.

38. **On My Honor,** by Marion Dane Bauer. Clarion/Houghton Mifflin, 1986.

Synopsis and Background: Twelve-year-old Joel Bates is goaded by his best friend, Tony, into going with him on a twelve-mile bike trip to the state park. Joel's father gives him permission but only after cautioning that Joel is on his honor to go only to the park. But on the way to the park, Tony talks Joel into trying to swim across the treacherous Vermillion River. Tony's taunts and dares lead to a race to the sandbar, during which Tony is dragged under by the strong current. Joel tries desperately to find Tony, but to no avail. Torn by guilt and fear, Joel returns home alone and lies to his parents, telling them that Tony went to the park without him. Finally, confronted by the police and Tony's parents, Joel tells the truth but shouts at his father, "It's all your fault. You should never have let me go!" His father's love and understanding eventually help Joel to realize that all people must live with their choices, and they will have to live with theirs.

Selected Challenges in the 1990s: In 1990, the parents of a fourth-grader in Cedar Falls, Iowa, told the board of education that the Newbery Award–winning book *On My Honor* should be removed from the class reading list because it contained offensive material, two swear words and one vulgarity. The parents said the book undermined their value system. The elementary school recommended that the book remain on the fourth-grade reading list, and the Cedar Falls Board of Education, in a unanimous vote, upheld that decision. Superintendent James Robinson said parents have the right to keep their children from reading any book they find objectionable but not to prevent teachers from using it in the classroom.

In 1991, a parent in San Antonio, Texas, objected to *On My Honor,* which was available in a fourth-grade classroom library, because one of the characters chewed gum. The book was reviewed by a school committee, which unanimously recommended that it be retained, but protesters continued to circulate petitions against it.

In October 1992, a group of parents in Alamo Heights, Texas, objected to the words *hell, damn,* and *frigging* in the books *On My Honor* and *The Great Gilly Hopkins.* The school's curriculum director said there had been no complaints about the books in the five years during which they had been used. The parents responded by circulating a petition demanding that all books containing vulgar and profane language be removed from the elementary school. The books were retained.

39. In the Night Kitchen, by Maurice Sendak. Harper, 1970.

Synopsis and Background: In this unusual dream fantasy, a child falls through the night darkness, out of his clothes, and into a bright night kitchen where he is dumped into the cake batter. Just before he is baked, he jumps into the bread dough, which he kneads and forms into an airplane. He then flies the airplane to the Milky Way to get some milk for the bakers. The beautiful illustrations show the bakers assembled in their magical kitchen world set against a starry sky and buildings made of cans, jars, and kitchen utensils. The poetic text, perfect to read aloud, maintains the dreamlike quality throughout.

Selected Challenges in the 1990s: In 1990, parents in Morrisonville, New York, objected to the use of the Caldecott Medal–winning book *In the Night Kitchen* in the elementary school for promoting nudity and child abuse. After a request that the book be removed from the library, the school board accepted the recommendation of a committee of educators that the book be retained.

In 1991, a parent in Jacksonville, Florida, objected to *In the Night Kitchen* because it contained illustrations of a boy without his clothes. The objector called such nudity disgraceful and appalling. A review committee decided to retain the book without restriction.

In Cornish, Maine, a parent objected to the inclusion of *In the Night Kitchen* in the elementary school library because it contained an illustration of a naked boy, allegedly encouraging child molestation. On the complaint form, when asked what harm the book might cause, the objector stated: "Child abuse. Children are taught their private parts are private. This book is contrary to this teaching." A review committee voted to retain the book, calling it "a masterpiece example of the timeless theme of childhood fantasy. . . . The story is certain to entertain readers of all ages."[72]

40. Grendel, by John Champlin Gardner. Knopf, 1971.

Synopsis and Background: In this sophisticated comedy, Gardner presents Grendel, the monster from the classic *Beowulf* saga, as a sympathetic hero who tells us his side of the story. Grendel is an unlikely hero, whose idealized image of man continually brings him disappointment. Grendel's strong conscience is overwhelmed by brute rage, as he attacks the Vikings' mead halls, killing the drunken men and destroying their structures. In the final battle, Grendel is outwitted by a stranger and loses his life. Those who have already read *Beowulf* may particularly appreciate *Grendel,* but there is much here for any reader. Gardner re-creates the rousing Anglo-Saxon sagas with stirring language and authenticity. He tells us much about the nature of monsters as human inventions and the futility of war. This philosophical, witty, and thoroughly contemporary retelling of the *Beowulf* chronical brings new meaning to the classic.

Selected Challenges in the 1990s: In December 1990, a parent in Farmington, Utah, complained that her daughter was asked to read "graphic" passages from *Grendel* in her twelfth-grade English class. Claiming that the book was violent and sexist and had sexual overtones, the parent asked that it be removed from the required reading list. In February 1991, a district review committee made up of six teachers and five parents voted 10 to 1 to retain the book, and School Superintendent Rich Kendell supported that decision. However, Kendell asked teachers to use the book only with twelfth-graders and in connection with the study of *Beowulf,* the medieval epic on which *Grendel* is based. The board reaffirmed its long-standing policy of allowing parents to request alternative assignments for their children. The English faculty noted that while certain passages read out of context may seem shocking, they are in fact effective tools in developing highly moral themes.

In 1991, a settlement was reached in a California lawsuit brought by a teacher against the school district, which had removed *Grendel* and another book from the twelfth-grade English curriculum. The settlement allowed the books to remain in the library or on display in the classroom for outside reading, but teachers were forbidden from assigning the books. The teacher who brought suit commented: "I am sorry that the teacher's right to teach has been limited in this decision, but I am happy that the student's right to read was restored." She added, "I have been attacked on all counts over this. The opposition tried to destroy my credibility. Most teachers don't want to go through what I went through. That's why most censorship happens very quietly."[73]

In October 1992, parents and an elected official in Bass River Township, New Jersey, protested the inclusion of *Grendel* in the curriculum of the high school's English Department. One mother said, "As a parent, I feel violated. I would never give this book to a child." Her husband agreed: "This book is obscene. If someone on the street were to give it to my child I would have them arrested." The town's mayor joined in the criticism, saying, "I don't want to ban the book. If people want to read it, they should be able to get it in the library or buy it. But it shouldn't be given to children at school."[74] The mayor threatened to introduce an ordinance calling for the school board to remove the book, but no action has been taken.

41. **I Have to Go,** by Robert Munsch. Annick Press, 1987.

Synopsis and Background: Before little Andrew's parents take him for a ride in the car, they always ask him, "Andrew, do you have to go pee?" Andrew always tells them no, but as soon as he is fully dressed and in the car seat, he shouts, "I have to go!" His parents are annoyed, but they respond with kindness and flexibility. One night Andrew surprises everyone by getting out of bed to go to the bathroom with Grandpa, breaking a pattern of bed-wetting. The cartoon illustrations and humorous potty-training adventures are intended for preschool children.

Selected Challenges in the 1990s: In 1991, the Genesee–Wyoming School District in New York State received complaints after the book *I Have to Go* was read to a second-grade class. A parent, who had not read the book, objected to the phrase "I have to go pee" and asked that the book be removed from both the class and the library. Because the school district lacked a formal policy concerning challenges, the book was removed from the class and library, pending a decision.

In 1991, a parent in Fort Collins, Colorado, objected to four books on the elementary school reading shelves. Among the challenged books was *I Have to Go,* which was criticized for containing the word *pee.* A review committee voted to retain the books but said that *I Have to Go* should be moved to a more age-appropriate shelf.

In 1992, objections to *I Have to Go* were heard at the Elgin, Texas, elementary school. The book, which was available at a prekindergarten through third-grade library, was called distasteful and unappealing for using the word *pee.* The objector said the author could have used the word *potty* instead of *pee.* A review committee decided to retain the book, and a school official noted that there were children in the school who would find the book helpful.

42. **Annie on My Mind,** by Nancy Garden. Farrar, 1982.

Synopsis and Background: In this tender story of love between two young women, Liza Winthrop, a freshman at MIT, recounts the past year, when she met and fell in love with Annie Kenyon. The narration describes the hesitant development of affection and eventual love between Liza and Annie. They both suffer emotional trauma when their relationship is discovered, but Liza bears the brunt of societal pressure, including her parents' shocked disapproval and the disciplinary action at the private school she was attending. Most difficult for the two girls to accept is the shattering effect their relationship has on the lives of those around them. The author's sensitive characterizations evoke a sympathetic response from the reader.

Selected Challenges in the 1990s: In 1990, a parent in Sedgewick,

Maine, objected to the inclusion of *Annie on My Mind* in the seventh-eighth-grade library because the book portrayed a lesbian relationship. The school did not have a complaint policy in place, so the matter was referred to the school board. The board established a review committee consisting of board members, educators, and community members, who then voted to retain the book in the library.

In September 1991, librarians in San Ramon, California, were angered at the mysterious disappearance of *Annie on My Mind* and another book dealing with homosexuality from two high school libraries. It was subsequently discovered that the vice-principals of the two high schools had taken the two books away shortly after they arrived, claiming that they wanted to examine them. Despite vigorous inquiries by the school librarians, the books were never seen again. The community member who had donated the books said, "This is a clear case of censorship. These vice principals went into the libraries, took the books off the shelves and then lost them. They might as well burn them; clearly the intent is to deny students books having a gay or lesbian theme." The vice-principals denied any censorship, but a spokesperson for the local ACLU said, "One issue here is the sloppiness of the handling that went on. The other issue is that a school district cannot exclude the topic of homosexuality from a school library."[75]

In February and March of 1992, requests were received to remove *Annie on My Mind* from the Colony (Texas) Public Library. After the first complaint, the school board voted unanimously to retain the book. "We run an open library," said the board's vice-chairman. "It's not our job to tell children what they can and cannot read—it is the parents' job." A week later a second complaint asked that the book be removed because its aim was "the recruitment of young girls into a lesbian life style." Once more the board concluded that the book should be retained. The board chairman stated:

> While recognizing that not all material is acceptable to every person who uses the library, the library board or library personnel are not censors of materials made available in the library. . . . [W]e encourage parents to evaluate materials their children are exposed to and decide accordingly for their own children.[76]

43. **The Adventures of Tom Sawyer,** by Mark Twain. American Publishing Company, 1876.

Synopsis and Background: Since its publication in 1876, *Tom Sawyer* has never been out of print. The book has been described as the story of a "bad" boy who triumphs over the hypocritical "good" people of his village. The story takes place during a single summer near the small town of St. Petersburg. The action begins with Tom's pranks at home, in the church, at school, and with his friends. The reader then follows Tom's romance with Becky Thatcher, the adventures of the young "pirates," Tom and Huck's witnessing of the murder of Doc Robinson and Tom's essential testimony in the case, and finally, the hunt for the hidden treasure that ironically leaves Tom and Huck rich and accepted in the community. As he did with Huck Finn, Twain makes the outcast his hero. The reader is given little reason to trust the honesty and judgment of the "good" townspeople, and only Tom, the "bad" boy, shows the courage and conscience necessary to save an innocent man from a false accusation of murder.

Selected Challenges in the 1990s: In 1990, David Perry, the first black city council member in Plano, Texas, asked the school district to remove *Tom Sawyer* and *Huckleberry Finn* from seventh- and eighth-grade reading lists. Perry said his daughter had bought and read *Tom Sawyer* before classes began and was painfully anticipating its use, fearful of how her classmates would react to her after reading the depictions of African-Americans. Perry said he did not want the books removed from the libraries but deleted from the required reading list. The school district's coordinator for secondary education told a review committee that the books were in fact an indictment of slavery and racism. A school district review committee voted to remove the books, but when 500 students signed a petition in support of the books, the school board voted unanimously to retain them.

In January 1992, a parent in O'Fallon, Illinois, objected to the use of *Tom Sawyer* in a sixth-grade classroom, stating that the book's use of the word *nigger* was degrading and offensive to black students. The parent told the school board that it was not always clear to sixth-graders why the book used the word *nigger*. He stated, "I still feel the pain, resentment, rage, fear, inferiority, feelings like apathy toward society, and feelings words don't describe when I recall having to read or hear my classmates read such filth and degradation." He added, "If we want to learn about racism, let's take an hour a day and study racism. Let's not hide behind some fictional book and let Mark Twain explain." A school review committee recommended that the book be retained but also recommended that the novel be used as a "springboard for greater understanding of individual differences and the feelings of others."[77] A program was introduced to increase the awareness, sensitivity, and competence of teachers to address diversity in the classroom. The board decided that *Tom Sawyer* will remain in the curriculum of O'Fallon schools, but parents may request that their children not read the book. The board also endorsed a review committee recommendation that all sixth-grade teachers make a "coordinated effort to treat racial issues in a consistent way."

44. The Pigman, by Paul Zindel. Harper, 1968.

Synopsis and Background: The Pigman is a tale told by two high school sophomores, Lorraine Jensen and John Conlan, who, in alternating chapters, describe their tragic friendship with a lonely old man. These two adolescents, on the edge of adulthood, both come from neurotic and dysfunctional families. We follow their growing friendship and their tentative adolescent love. In their flight from the unreasonable demands of their parents, they form a relationship with the doddering old Mr. Pignoti, who welcomes them into his home and shares with them his simple possessions, including his collection of ceramic pigs. Their tender, humorous, and ultimately heartbreaking relationship with the old man is related in their own words. When the Pigman, as the children call him, has a heart attack and is taken to the hospital, the children selfishly use his house for a party, leaving the house in shambles. The tragic consequences of the children's behavior change their lives, as Lorraine and John are forced to face their own responsibility for Mr. Pignoti's death. In revealing this bitter lesson, the novel tells young people much about youth and senility, cruelty and idealism.

Selected Challenges in the 1990s: On November 19, 1990, a parent told the Harwinton, Connecticut, Board of Education that *The Pigman* and four other books should be removed from use in the Harwinton and Burlington schools because they took God's name in vain and discussed topics like death, dismemberment, witchcraft, torture, and masturbation. The parent said the language and subject matter of the books set bad examples and gave students negative views of life. The parent was told that her sons, who were in the sixth and eighth grades, could be assigned alternative books, but she refused that option, claiming that the children would be ostracized and miss out on class discussions. She subsequently filed a formal challenge to the books, saying that controversial or offensive books should not be taught in class. At a crowded school board meeting, a former student urged the schools to keep the books because of the effective way they deal with real-life situations. He added, "Harwinton is a very small place and it is a big world out there." [78] On February 5, 1991, a curriculum committee for the Burlington, Connecticut, middle school voted unanimously to keep *The Pigman* and the other books on the school's reading list. District Curriculum Director Karen Richards said that one set of parents do not have a right to determine what other children will read.

In 1992, Ralph Brasure, a local PTO president, and Chuck Edwards, a former PTO president, challenged *The Pigman* and another book taught in Lynchburg, Virginia, middle and high school English classes. The complaints charged that the books presented readers with negative role models and values. Edwards told the school board, "It's not that these books are big, gross, bad monster-types of things, but we feel that there are better choices that can be made." Both objectors were allowed to have their children read alternative books, but Edwards chose to challenge the books' presence throughout the city schools. Among other things, Edwards cited twenty-nine instances in *The Pigman* of what he called "destructive, disrespectful, antisocial and illegal behavior . . . placed in a humerous light, making it seem acceptable." Edwards asked the board to take the "unprecedented" step of overruling the review committee that had recommended retaining the books. The school board disagreed. "If I got anything out of public education at all it was a real sense of the power of the ideas behind our own government, and especially the idea of freedom of speech," said board member Julius Sigler. "So I guess I'm inherently opposed to censorship other than the kind where parents can intervene, as these parents have, to move their children to other kinds of books." On June 2, the board voted unanimously to retain *The Pigman* and the other challenged book.[79]

45. **My House,** by Nikki Giovanni. Morrow, 1972.

Synopsis and Background: This collection of thirty-six poems, written in 1971 and 1972, is gentler in tone than much of Giovanni's work but retains enough of her rage and passion to excite the reader. The poems vary in length, subject, and style, but all have an effective economy of language. Her poems show a keen appreciation for the richness of black speech. In "Conversation," she tells an old woman that she's a poet, and the woman responds, "that ain't no reason to be uppity." In "Rituals," Giovanni promises that if she could be a bridesmaid, she "wouldn't say goddam nor even/once no matter what . . . give a power sign." Giovanni paints striking images that convey emotion, and as always, a sense of black pride permeates her work. Her use of lowercase letters only may initially confuse some young readers, but her poems have always been in demand by young adult readers.

Selected Challenges in the 1990s: In 1992, a library in Jacksonville, Florida, received complaints that *My House* contained vulgarity, sex, and racism, including the word *nigger*. The librarian asked either that *My House* be moved from the middle school library to the high school and restricted to students with parental permission or that it be replaced by a more appropriate title. Though admitting that "some of the poems are very good," the librarian objected to the "explicit sexual connotation" and alleged racial bias. A district review committee voted to return the book to the middle school library but required parental permission for student use. One committee member said, "To appreciate her work, one must look at the total, not a word or two. I think we need Ms. Giovanni's work in the junior high world. She is one of the few Black contemporary poets for students to enjoy."[80] This same committee member, however, recommended that the book be placed on a restricted-access shelf.

In 1992, the parents of a Syracuse, New York, high school sophomore asked the school district to ban *My House* because it contained obscenities. The student herself said, "I don't want anything taken out or censored," but her father insisted, "It has pretty bad language. Any book like it should be banned from the shelf." The student's mother added, "If parents want their children to read it, they can take it out in a public library."[81]

46. **Then Again, Maybe I Won't,** by Judy Blume. Bradbury, 1971.

Synopsis and Background: The plot of *Then Again, Maybe I Won't* focuses on a few years in the life of Tony Miglione, an adolescent growing up in a two-family house in New Jersey. Tony's father is an electrician, his mother works in a department store, and Grandma does the housekeeping. Also living in the Miglione house is Tony's brother Ralph and his wife Angie. The book reveals how each generation within the household expresses its needs and concerns, particularly with respect to the family's growing financial burdens. When Tony's father is made the manager of an electronics plant in Queens, they all move to an upper-middle-class suburb on Long Island. But what quickly emerges is an elaborate pattern of "keeping up with the Joneses," which Tony and others in the family find disturbing. Mr. Miglione is convinced by his neighbors that it is inappropriate to own a pickup truck in this neighborhood, so he trades it in for a fancy car. Mrs. Miglione hires a live-in housekeeper, banishing Grandma from the kitchen to her bedroom, where she sits before her color TV, refusing even to join the family at meals. The family's superficial posturing sickens Tony, who develops recurring stomach pains of frightening intensity.

As Tony experiences the sexual awakening of adolescence, he is strongly attracted to Lisa, the sixteen-year-old daughter of the snooty family next door. Though he feels guilty, he watches her regularly from his bedroom window as she undresses at night. The reader follows Tony's growing sexual awareness and the accompanying feelings of anxiety and guilt. When Tony receives a pair of binoculars for Christmas, he uses them to view Lisa more closely, and his guilt feelings increase. At the end of the book, Tony resolves to behave more responsibly toward all around him. He decides he may even stop using his binoculars—then again, maybe he won't.

Selected Challenges in the 1990s: In January 1990, parents in Tyrone, Pennsylvania, objected to the inclusion of *Then Again, Maybe I Won't* in the elementary school libraries. The parents complained that the book's main character is a voyeur and that the book deals with topics like masturbation and alcohol abuse. In April, the school board voted 6 to 2 to retain the book in the library. Parents then objected to the inclusion of the book on the school's reading list. The school board agreed to form a committee, consisting of two community members, two members of the English Department, two administrators, and two school board members, to review policies and guidelines for reading lists, but the parent said the findings of such a committee would be invalid, since the committee included people who had chosen the disputed books in the first place.

In 1991, a parent in Hartford, Wisconsin, requested that *Then Again, Maybe I Won't* be removed from the elementary school library on the grounds that the book contained profanity and promoted shoplifting and voyeurism. A school review committee voted to retain the book.

47. **The Handmaid's Tale,** by Margaret Atwood. Fawcett, 1986.

Synopsis and Background: Like the modern classics *Brave New World* and *1984,* this novel suggests that a very grim future may follow from our present way of life. The author presents a haunting vision of an American society dominated by a highly ritualized, tyrannical religious cult that controls human reproduction throughout the nation. In this society, civilization has been threatened and distorted by the effects of nuclear accidents and toxic wastes: lowered birthrates, birth defects, widespread sterility, diseases, and death. The main character in the story is Offred, who is forced to serve as a "handmaid" in this stark new order, bearing children for infertile couples within society's ruling hierarchy. Offred narrates the story, alternating descriptions of her dreadful life with flashbacks to a time when she was a young working woman with a loving husband and a child. This riveting and believable story of a woman's struggle for personal freedom has implications for the role of women in modern society.

Selected Challenges in the 1990s: In 1990, a religious leader in Rohnert Park, California, criticized the fact that the leading character in *The Handmaid's Tale* was a woman, making it difficult for young men to relate to the character. There were also complaints that the novel, which was being used in a twelfth-grade literature class, was profane, sexually explicit, and anti-Christian. One parent circulated a letter to local residents and school trustees, saying, "If you as parents do not rise up and go to your schools over issues such as these, we will continue to educate our kids for the gutter."[82] The school formed a review committee that subsequently recommended that the book be retained.

In March 1992, *The Handmaid's Tale* and other books were challenged in the Waterloo, Iowa, schools for lack of respect for Christianity, treatment of women as sex objects, use of profanity, and themes of despair. One objector said the books "aren't the caliber of the word of God" and that he opposed any book "that takes the name of my Lord in vain." The protesters requested that the books be removed from optional reading in twelfth-grade English classes and that a new textbook selection process be adopted. Although thirty to forty area churches opposed the books, a local religious coalition released a statement saying these "special interest religious groups" did not speak for them. The coalition pointed out that passages taken out of context may appear objectionable, but those same passages "in context may instead challenge the immoral or unjust in our society." One school board member noted, "The objectors are trying to take away the rights of others to read the books."[83] The board then voted 6 to 1 to approve the books. The protesters appealed, but a spokesman for the Iowa Department of Education said they were not in the business of telling school districts what they should have on their reading lists.

48. **Witches, Pumpkins, and Grinning Ghosts: The Story of the Halloween Symbols,** by Edna Barth. Seabury, 1972.

Synopsis and Background: This book examines the history of Halloween customs and symbols from ancient times to the present. The author discusses the origin of the Halloween holiday and the creatures and activities associated with it, including ghosts, goblins, witches, owls, bats, pumpkins, jack-o-lanterns, the wearing of masks, and bobbing for apples. This entertaining and informative book is illustrated with drawings in black and orange, providing a suitable tone. An annotated list of Halloween stories is also included.

Selected Challenges in the 1990s: In January 1992, a parent in Gilbert, Arizona, objected to the inclusion of *Witches, Pumpkins, and Grinning Ghosts* and other books relating to Halloween in the elementary school library, claiming that the books promoted satanism and the occult. The complaining parent was offered the option of having her child's elementary school library card indicate which books the child could not read, but the parent insisted she wanted these books out of the library so no other children could read them. A parent who supported the books commented, "When that parent begins deciding what my children can or cannot read, I draw the line. This is still a free country, and unless we want to turn it into a dictatorship . . . we must respect the opinions and beliefs of everyone and their right to choose for themselves." Despite an aggressive media campaign to ban the books, a school-level review committee recommended that they be retained. The objector appealed to the superintendent of schools, who upheld the initial decision.[84]

In April 1992, the school board in Salem, Oregon, voted unanimously to retain *Witches, Pumpkins, and Grinning Ghosts* in the elementary school libraries. A parent had requested the removal of the book, claiming that it could lead a child into the practice of witchcraft. The book was alleged to contain references to the occult and suggestions that children born on Halloween can see and talk with ghosts. A review committee had earlier recommended that the book be retained without restriction.

49. One Hundred Years of Solitude, by Gabriel García Márquez. Translated from Spanish by Gregory Rabasia. Harper, 1970.

Synopsis and Background: García Márquez, an Argentinean, describes a small village in Colombia that has been isolated from the outside world for 100 years. The story focuses on the Buendia family, who founded and dominated the little town of Macondo. The history of the town is revealed through the family's love affairs, marriages, and deaths and the cataclysmic events of the town's 100 years of solitude. In a clear parallel to the Old Testament history of mankind, the town suffers through war, pestilence, and disease, but the narrative is so outrageously clever that the reader finds it pure enjoyment. The story contains sex and violence, but it is presented as comic fantasy. *One Hundred Years of Solitude* was a best-seller in Latin America and was well received in the United States as well.

Selected Challenges in the 1990s: In 1990, a lawsuit was brought in Wasco, California, by a teacher who challenged the school district for removing *One Hundred Years of Solitude* and another book from the twelfth-grade English curriculum in response to a parent's complaint. The complaint had asserted that the book was profane, vulgar, and sordid and was negative to the Catholic church. The teacher's suit claimed that the decision to remove the book was not made on educational grounds. The court settlement in 1991 allowed the book to remain in the library or to be put on display in the classroom for outside reading but forbade teachers from assigning the book.

In June 1991, the Darlington, South Carolina, School Board, in violation of its own policy, voted to remove *One Hundred Years of Solitude* from the reading list for twelfth-grade honors English. A single parental complaint had charged that the book was "garbage," that it was profane and anti-Christian. After hearing the complaint, board member Bill Fleming said he could not condone its use by local students. The school's offer to assign an alternative book to the children of the complaining parent was refused. A review committee appointed by the high school principal recommended that the book be retained, stating that it contained strong language but had literary value and was appropriate for mature high school students. Nonetheless, the school board appointed a second review committee, which determined that the book should be removed from the reading list and not assigned as required reading.

50. Scary Stories 3: More Tales to Chill Your Bones, by Alvin Schwartz. HarperCollins, 1991.

Synopsis and Background: Schwartz's third volume of scary tales offers a poltergeist that unscrews bottlecaps, a couple who find that the strange little dog they brought home from Mexico is actually a sewer rat, a Texas girl raised by wolves, and a variety of other creepy characters. These modernized versions of ghost stories and legends are delivered in a matter-of-fact tone that almost makes them seem to be in the realm of possibility. The author tells us that only one story in the anthology is true, but "most may have a little truth, for strange things sometimes happen." As in his two previous volumes, Schwartz provides hints for storytellers, careful source notes, and an extensive bibliography. Stephen Gammell's eerie black and white illustrations add to the spooky effect.

Selected Challenges in the 1990s: In January 1992, parents in Kirkland, Washington, objected to *Scary Stories 3* and two other Alvin Schwartz books available in an elementary school library. A school review committee recommended that the books be retained, and the objectors appealed to the school board. The board appointed another review committee, which again recommended that the books be retained. The school librarian told the committee, "Children have the right to freedom of inquiry and access of information. Attempts to deprive this . . . must be resisted as a threat to learning in a free and democratic society." A sixth-grader said, "I know some people don't like scary stories, but maybe they could help me save those books for people who do like them. Some students would not want to read at all if the books they liked were banned."[85]

In June 1992, a mother in West Hartford, Connecticut, caught her eight-year-old son reading a school library book by Alvin Schwartz in which a woman contemplates serving her husband a human liver for dinner. The mother said her son likes scary stories, but "this was gross. It was just trash. Violence. Goriness." She requested that two Schwartz books, *Scary Stories 3* and *Scary Stories to Tell in the Dark,* be removed from the elementary and middle school libraries. The books were to be reviewed by a committee of principals, teachers, and librarians, but school board chair John Lemega intervened to enforce the removal of the books as specified by the complaining parents. "They are not crazies who say 'burn books,' " explained Lemega. "They are people legitimately concerned with violence and horror for second-graders, and that is reasonable."[86]

NOTES

1. *Fleischfresser v. Directors of School District No. 200,* 805 F. Supp. 584 (1992).

2. "The Controversy over the *Impressions* Reading Series," press release by People for the American Way, Washington, D.C., 1992.

3. John Boe, "Good Impressions in Winters," unpubl. article, 1992 (available from the author).

4. Nicholas J. Karolides and Lee Burress, eds., *Celebrating Censored Books* (Racine, Wisconsin: Council of Teachers of English, 1985), p. 86–87.

5. Ibid.

6. People for the American Way, *Attacks on the Freedom to Learn: 1991–1992 Report* (Washington, D.C.: PAW, 1992), p. 37 (hereafter cited by title).

7. Ibid., p. 83.

8. Reprinted with permission of the American Library Association, Office for Intellectual Freedom, *Newsletter on Intellectual Freedom* (Chicago), January 1992, p. 25 (hereafter, references to this publication are cited by title and date).

9. *Attacks on the Freedom to Learn: 1991–1992 Report,* p. 135.

10. Reprinted with permission of the American Library Association from the *Newsletter on Intellectual Freedom,* January 1993, p. 29.

11. Edward P. J. Corbett, "Raise High the Barriers, Censors," *America,* January 7, 1961, p. 442.

12. People for the American Way, *Attacks on the Freedom to Learn: 1990–1991 Report* (Washington, D.C.: PAW, 1991), p. 49 (hereafter cited by title).

13. *Attacks on the Freedom to Learn: 1991–1992 Report,* p. 61.

14. *Attacks on the Freedom to Learn: 1990–1991 Report,* p. 88.

15. Justin Kaplan, *Born to Trouble: One Hundred Years of Huckleberry Finn* (Washington, D.C.: Library of Congress, 1985), p. 11.

16. Albert Bigelow Paine, *Mark Twain: A Biography,* vol. 3 (New York: Harper, 1912), pp. 1280–81.

17. Kaplan, *Born to Trouble,* pp. 10, 13.

18. Ibid., p. 18.

19. *Attacks on the Freedom to Learn: 1991–1992 Report,* p. 39.

20. Kenneth L. Donelson and Alleen Pace Nilson, *Literature for Today's Young Adults* (Glenview, Ill.: Scott, Foresman, 1989), p. 88.

21. Karolides and Burress, *Celebrating Censored Books,* p. 31.

22. Reprinted with permission of the American Library Association from the *Newsletter on Intellectual Freedom,* May 1990, p. 87.

23. "New Milford Rift over a Book Grows," *Litchfield County Times,* January 26, 1992, pp. 1, 8.

24. " 'Chocolate War' to Remain on New Milford List," *Danbury News-Times,* February 5, 1992, p. A1.

25. *Attacks on the Freedom to Learn: 1990–1991 Report,* p. 83.

26. *Attacks on the Freedom to Learn: 1991–1992 Report*, p. 104.

27. Reprinted with permission of the American Library Association from the *Newsletter on Intellectual Freedom*, March 1991, p. 62.

28. "Scary Books Won't Be Bumped in Night, Committee Decides," *Seattle Post-Intelligencer*, January 30, 1992, p. B1.

29. *Attacks on the Freedom to Learn: 1991–1992 Report*, p. 30.

30. Ibid., p. 41.

31. Ibid., p. 55.

32. Ibid., p. 131.

33. Ibid., pp. 132–33.

34. Ibid., pp. 143–44.

35. " 'Witches': District Puts Kids Books on Restriction," *Los Angeles Times*, February 2, 1992, p. B8.

36. Reprinted with permission of the American Library Association from the *Newsletter on Intellectual Freedom*, September 1992, p. 162.

37. Reprinted with permission of the American Library Association from the *Newsletter on Intellectual Freedom*, September 1992, p. 159.

38. Reprinted with permission of the American Library Association from the *Newsletter on Intellectual Freedom*, January 1993, p. 7.

39. "Removal of Occult Book Urged by Howard Panel," *Baltimore Sun*, October 5, 1990, pp. B1–B2.

40. *Attacks on the Freedom to Learn: 1990–1991 Report*, p. 108.

41. *Attacks on the Freedom to Learn: 1991–.1992 Report*, p. 65.

42. Ibid., p. 86.

43. Reprinted with permission of the American Library Association from the *Newsletter on Intellectual Freedom*, September 1991, p. 153.

44. Reprinted with permission of the American Library Association from the *Newsletter on Intellectual Freedom*, March 1992, p. 41.

45. Reprinted with permission of the American Library Association from the *Newsletter on Intellectual Freedom*, May 1990, p. 106.

46. "Howard Schools to Retain 2 Books Despite Protests," *Baltimore Sun*, June 6, 1991, p. D5.

47. *Attacks on the Freedom to Learn: 1991–1992 Report*, p. 91.

48. Reprinted with permission of the American Library Association from the *Newsletter on Intellectual Freedom*, January 1993, p. 28.

49. *Attacks on the Freedom to Learn: 1990–1991 Report*, p. 56.

50. Reprinted with permission of the American Library Association from the *Newsletter on Intellectual Freedom*, July 1992, p. 106.

51. Reprinted with permission of the American Library Association from the *Newsletter on Intellectual Freedom*, July 1992, p. 109.

52. Reprinted with permission of the American Library Association from the *Newsletter on Intellectual Freedom*, November 1990, p. 211.

53. Reprinted with permission of the American Library Association from the *Newsletter on Intellectual Freedom*, September 1992, p. 142.

54. *Attacks on the Freedom to Learn: 1990–1991 Report*, p. 64.

55. Reprinted with permission of the American Library Association from the *Newsletter on Intellectual Freedom*, March 1991, p. 44.

56. Reprinted with permission of the American Library Association from the *Newsletter on Intellectual Freedom*, September 1991, p. 155.

57. John Knowles, *A Separate Peace* (New York: Dell, 1957), p. 196.

58. Karolides and Burress, *Celebrating Censored Books*, p. 110.

59. *Attacks on the Freedom to Learn: 1991–1992 Report*, pp. 55–56.

60. Karolides and Burress, *Celebrating Censored Books*, p. 113.

61. Reprinted with permission of the American Library Association from the *Newsletter on Intellectual Freedom*, July 1990, p. 128.

62. Reprinted with permission of the American Library Association from the *Newsletter on Intellectual Freedom*, May 1990, p. 108.

63. *Attacks on the Freedom to Learn: 1991–1992 Report*, p. 127.

64. Roald Dahl, *James and the Giant Peach* (New York: Knopf, 1961), pp. 106–7.

65. Reprinted with permission of the American Library Association from the *Newsletter on Intellectual Freedom*, July 1991, p. 108.

66. Reprinted with permission of the American Library Association from the *Newsletter on Intellectual Freedom*, March 1992, p. 65.

67. Reprinted with permission of the American Library Association from the *Newsletter on Intellectual Freedom*, May 1990, p. 106.

68. Reprinted with permission of the American Library Association from the *Newsletter on Intellectual Freedom*, March 1990, p. 48.

69. Reprinted with permission of the American Library Association from the *Newsletter on Intellectual Freedom*, January 1991, p. 15.

70. *Attacks on the Freedom to Learn: 1990–1991 Report*, p. 99.

71. *Attacks on the Freedom to Learn: 1991–1992 Report*, p. 48.

72. Ibid., pp. 93–94.

73. *Attacks on the Freedom to Learn: 1990–1991 Report*, p. 36.

74. Reprinted with permission of the American Library Association from the *Newsletter on Intellectual Freedom*, January 1993, pp. 11–12.

75. Reprinted with permission of the American Library Association from the *Newsletter on Intellectual Freedom*, January 1992, pp. 5–6.

76. Reprinted with permission of the American Library Association from the *Newsletter on Intellectual Freedom*, July 1992, p. 125.

77. *Attacks on the Freedom to Learn: 1991–1992 Report*, pp. 71–72.

78. *Attacks on the Freedom to Learn: 1990–1991 Report*, p. 40.

79. Reprinted with permission of the American Library Association from the *Newsletter on Intellectual Freedom*, September 1992, p. 164.

80. *Attacks on the Freedom to Learn: 1991–1992 Report*, p. 57.

81. Reprinted with permission of the American Library Association from the *Newsletter on Intellectual Freedom*, July 1990, p. 149.

82. Reprinted with permission of the American Library Association from the *Newsletter on Intellectual Freedom*, January 1991, p. 15.

83. "School's Purchase of Four Books Ignites a Furor in Waterloo," *Des Moines Register*, April 15, 1992, p. M2.

84. *Attacks on the Freedom to Learn: 1991–1992 Report*, p. 30.

85. Ibid., p. 175.

86. "Parents Complaint Prompts Review of Two Books," *Hartford Courant*, June 15, 1992, p. C3.

Appendixes

Appendix A: PAW's Most Frequently Challenged Books, 1991–1992

Of Mice and Men, John Steinbeck
More Scary Stories to Tell in the Dark, Alvin Schwartz
Scary Stories to Tell in the Dark, Alvin Schwartz
The Catcher in the Rye, J. D. Salinger
The Chocolate War, Robert Cormier
The Witches, Roald Dahl
Bridge to Terabithia, Katherine Paterson
Blubber, Judy Blume
Revolting Rhymes, Roald Dahl
A Day No Pigs Would Die, Robert Peck
A Wrinkle in Time, Madeleine L'Engle

Appendix B: PAW's Most Frequently Challenged Books, 1982–1992

Of Mice and Men, John Steinbeck
The Catcher in the Rye, J. D. Salinger

Appendixes compiled from People for the American Way.

The Chocolate War, Robert Cormier
The Adventures of Huckleberry Finn, Mark Twain
A Light in the Attic, Shel Silverstein
Go Ask Alice, Anonymous
Blubber, Judy Blume
The Witches, Roald Dahl
Ordinary People, Judith Guest
Forever, Judy Blume
Then Again, Maybe I Won't, Judy Blume
Scary Stories, Alvin Schwartz

Appendix C: PAW's Most Frequently Challenged Materials, 1982–1992

Impressions (textbook series)
Quest (self-esteem program)
Pumsy: In Pursuit of Excellence (self-esteem program)
Developing Understanding of Self and Others (DUSO) (self-esteem program)
Michigan Model for Comprehensive School Health Education
Romeo and Juliet (film)
Tactics for Thinking (thinking skills program)
Sports Illustrated (magazine)
Junior Great Books Series (texts)
Finding My Way (health textbook)

Appendix D: PAW's Most Frequently Challenged Authors, 1982–1992

Judy Blume
Stephen King
John Steinbeck
Robert Cormier
J. D. Salinger
Mark Twain
Roald Dahl
Alvin Schwartz
Shel Silverstein

Anonymous *(Go Ask Alice)*
Katherine Paterson

Appendix E: PAW's States with the Most Challenges, 1982–1992

California

Oregon

Florida

Texas

Washington

New York

Illinois

Michigan

Colorado

Iowa

Ohio

Selected Bibliography

American Library Association, Office for Intellectual Freedom. *Censorship Litigation and the Schools*. Proceedings of a colloquium held January 1981. Chicago: ALA, 1983.

American Library Association, Office for Intellectual Freedom. *Intellectual Freedom Manual*. 4th ed. Chicago: ALA, 1992.

Bryson, Joseph E. *The Legal Aspects of Censorship of Public School Library and Instructional Materials*. Charlottesville: Michie Company, 1982.

Burress, Lee. *Battle of the Books: Literary Censorship in the Public Schools*. Metuchen, N.J.: Scarecrow Press, 1989.

Censorship or Selection: Choosing Books for Public Schools. Transcript of a videotape produced by Media and Society Seminars, Columbia University, 1982.

Craig, Alec. *The Banned Books of England and Other Countries: A Study of the Conception of Literary Obscenity*. 1962. Reprint. Westport, Conn.: Greenwood Press, 1977.

DelFattore, Joan. *What Johnny Shouldn't Read: Textbook Censorship in America*. New Haven: Yale University Press, 1992.

Dellinger, David W. "My Way or the Highway: The Hawkins County Textbook Controversy." Ph.D. dissertation, University of Tennessee, May 1991.

Farrer, James Anson. *Books Condemned to Be Burnt*. Philadelphia: R. West, 1977.

Geller, Evelyn. *Forbidden Books in American Public Libraries, 1876–1939*. Westport, Conn.: Greenwood Press, 1984.

Goff, Robert Oscar. *The Washington County Schoolbook Controversy: The Political Implications of a Social and Religious Conflict*. Ph.D. dissertation, Catholic University, Ann Arbor, University Microfilms, 1976.

Haight, Anne Lyon. *Banned Books, 387 B.C. to 1978 A.D.* 4th ed. New York: R. R. Bowker, 1978.

Hicks, Robert D. *In Pursuit of Satan: The Police and the Occult*. Buffalo: Prometheus Books, 1991.

Hurwitz, Leon. *Historical Dictionary of Censorship in the United States.* Westport, Conn.: Greenwood Press, 1985.

Kaplan, Justin. *Born to Trouble: One Hundred Years of Huckleberry Finn.* Washington, D.C.: Library of Congress, 1985.

Karolides, Nicholas J., and Lee Burress, eds. *Celebrating Censored Books.* Racine, Wisconsin: Council of Teachers of English, 1985.

MacMillan, Peter R. *Censorship and Public Morality.* Aldershot, England: Gower, 1983.

Malley, Ian. *Censorship and Libraries.* London: Library Association, 1990.

Moffett, James. *Storm in the Mountains: A Case Study in Censorship, Conflict, and Consciousness.* Carbondale: Southern Illinois University Press, 1988.

New York Public Library. *Censorship: 500 Years of Conflict.* New York: Oxford University Press, 1984.

Noble, William. *Bookbanning in America: Who Bans Books and Why.* Middlebury, Vt.: Paul S. Erickson, 1990.

Oboler, Eli M. *Defending Intellectual Freedom.* Westport, Conn.: Greenwood Press, 1980.

People for the American Way. *Attacks on the Freedom to Learn.* Annual reports, various years. Washington, D.C.: PAW.

Reichman, Henry. *Censorship and Selection: Issues and Answers for Schools.* Chicago: American Library Association, 1988.

Index

ABOUT THE AUTHOR

HERBERT N. FOERSTEL is the author of *Surveillance in the Stacks: The FBI's Library Awareness Program* (Greenwood Press, 1991), which was a *Choice* Best Academic Book for 1991, and of *Secret Science, Federal Control of American Science and Technology* (Praeger, 1992). He is Head of the Engineering and Physical Sciences Library at the University of Maryland.